THE CHARISMATIC CHALLENGE

– A Biblical Investigation

THE CHARISMATIC CHALLENGE

A Biblical Investigation

John W. de Silva

JOHN RITCHIE LTD
CHRISTIAN PUBLICATIONS

40 Beansburn, Kilmarnock, Scotland

ISBN 0 946351 88 0

Typeset by John Ritchie Ltd., Kilmarnock
Printed by Bell & Bain Ltd., Glasgow

Acknowledgments

I am pleased to express my grateful thanks to -
my wife for her consistent and prayerful support;
Marg Huxtable for her work on the early manuscript;
Dr Bert Cargill for his helpful editing.

Contents

CHAPTER 1

Introduction

If you are a Christian who speaks in tongues and is involved with a charismatic church, you may have been challenged by those who believe tongues and other 'charismatic practices' are unscriptural. If, on the other hand, you are a Christian who does not speak in tongues or one who has rejected tongue-speaking and other charismata (gifts of grace), you may have been told you are missing out on certain blessings of the Holy Spirit. Then again, you may be a believer who has yet to be exposed to the charismatic controversy, and you may be wondering, "Should I be speaking in tongues (whatever their nature) and should I be seeking other 'spiritual experiences' such as a 'second blessing'? "

There are many publications addressing these issues, so why another one? My decision to add to the literature arose after having lengthy discussions concerning spiritual gifts with a professional colleague who 'spoke in tongues', and subsequent Bible studies with a number of Christians who claimed a 'second blessing' and possession of the 'gift of tongues'. They were sincerely interested to know why I, as a Christian, have no desire to seek a 'second blessing' or to speak in tongues, and why I believe that the tongues we read of in Scripture have long ceased, and were never anything other than foreign languages spoken miraculously as enabled by the Holy Spirit.

This book is based on our in-depth discussions over a series of friendly, frank and profitable Bible studies on tongues and related matters. Aspects of the work of the Holy Spirit, His indwelling, sealing, baptism and filling, are also included as a help to believers. Our method was to apply the test of Scripture to questions raised by the study group - the standard of examination so needful today amidst widening conflict of opinion and discord between believers on matters of Christian doctrine! So this study is reproduced with a view to providing help to the beloved of Christ, whether they be within or outside the charismatic camp.

There are three further reasons for this publication. Firstly, to warn individual believers of the danger of seeking or continuing practices that are unscriptural. Present-day tongues for instance closes the door to authentic spiritual experience and fan the flames of strange fire![1] If not quelled, these fires will sear the conscience and consume any conviction for sound doctrine. In Leviticus 10:1-3 we read of Aaron's eldest sons being consumed by fire from God. They were lawfully ordained priests and had the right to serve within the sanctuary. Why then did they incur God's wrath? It was because they offered *'strange fire'* unto God! No doubt the natural mind and heart within each of them conspired to add to what God had set forth plainly concerning His way of worship. It was so with Cain and it is so within the Charismatic fraternity. God's displeasure arose because Aaron's sons engaged in that *"which He commanded them not"*. Their error was not in doing what God had expressly forbidden, but rather in not following that which God had expressly written. This is another complexion of error altogether - adding to the divine order of things (an addition, we observe, involving an imitation of God's provision). Such error is often spuriously denied (as charismatics are wont to do) on the ground of grace. Tongues, as we shall see, were foreign languages and for a sign to the Jews - a truth stamped indelibly in Scripture in word and by example. To support

---

[1] Leviticus 10:1-2; Numbers 3:4

the speaking of some other tongue for some other purpose is to present strange fire before God. This volume considers in some detail, the spiritual damage being fuelled by modern-day tongues.

My second reason for writing is to warn churches of the 'charismatic' invasion! Tongues and the Charismatic Movement have conditioned many congregations into accepting a 'gospel of ecstatic experiences', as seen in the ready acceptance by many of the so-called 'Toronto Blessing' and New Age philosophies! May we be forewarned through God's Word that these are portents of the coming apostate world church, where this other gospel becomes a ground for unification and interpretation of the Bible. The Charismatic Movement and tongues have been particularly invasive among young Christians who, sadly, are rarely encouraged to apply the test of Scripture to their experiences. When speaking with many young believers on the subject of the 'gifts of the Spirit', it is evident that this failure has spawned an accepted superficiality in matters of doctrine, where experience is elevated to a line of truth alongside, or, in many cases, above the Word of God! Finally, having witnessed first-hand the way in which contemporary charismata are charming and claiming many churches within Australia, the UK, and within Europe, it is my hope that this type of study will, even in some small way, embolden, enable and encourage all who are holding fast against the charismatic tide.

How to approach this study

It is critical that we bear in mind that studying the Word of God is a blessed and wonderful privilege! It is a blessing because we do not have to rely on our imagination, our intellect or our experience to know the will of God! However, as Scripture itself teaches us, blessings and privilege go hand-in-hand with responsibility! This means we have an obligation not only to consult, but to rightly divide the Word of God and regard it as the *sole* unerring authority, once-for-all delivered.

'It is written' is the single basis of our Christian doctrine and faith! How can we set about doing this?

There are four things we need to do. Firstly, we must prayerfully commit our way to the Lord and allow His Spirit to be our teacher. Secondly, we must yield to the single authority of Scripture by putting aside 'experiences' - ours or those of others! This may be a very difficult thing to do and we need to pray God's Spirit will grant us the necessary conviction and strength to rely wholly on God's Word! Has He not put His Word into our hands and His Spirit into our hearts? All experiences must be examined in the light of the Scriptures! And, when by the grace of God, we are brought to see the error of our ways, we dare not substitute - *"But I have seen"* or *"But I have experienced"* for *"It is written"*! The difficulty here is not in finding the truth, but having to face it! Are we to place more faith in our experiences or in the clear teaching of the Word of God? Are we not exhorted to walk by faith and not by sight? Thirdly, we must avoid being swayed by 'popular' opinion. Truth is never determined by the popularity of those who profess to proclaim it, or by the number who claim to follow it. Lastly, be prepared for a time of spiritual trial, for we wrestle not against flesh and blood, but against principalities and powers. Remember, greater is He that is in you than he that is in the world.

Now, concerning the material in this study: if you are dissuaded by a large volume of reading, confine your attention to the body of the material. The footnotes (except for the Scripture references), Notes and Commentary on 1 Corinthians 14, can be left until a second reading. Proceed carefully and examine each 'Proposition'. It may be helpful to make notes as you go. Remember, there are no 'short-cuts' to sound study of the Bible. If we are sincere about finding out what it is God says on a matter, we will not shy away from a comprehensive examination of His Word. Our study necessarily will take us to the Old and New Testaments, involve Biblical history and, very importantly, Biblical prophecy. Test all things, especially the Propositions made in this study, in the light of Scripture.

In addition to being daunted by the volume of material, you may consider some of the discussion too 'technical'. The body of the study has been written so you can avoid much of the technical aspects. However, as you begin to read the study, you may (as was the case with many in the study group), become aware of the deep veins of truth exposed by exploring the whole compass of Scripture, benefiting from the findings of grammar and word studies mined by able expositors. The references to grammatical principles and interpretations, are therefore given to assist the reader who desires to profit from digging deeper toward the mother lode of truth! The following texts have been principally cited to this end:

W.E. Vine *"Expository Dictionary of New Testament Words"*; Oliphants, London;

A.T. Robertson, *"Word Pictures in the New Testament"*; Broadman Press".

"Study to shew thyself approved unto God, a workman that needeth not to be ashamed, rightly dividing the word of truth." 2 Timothy 2:15.

"All Scripture is given by inspiration of God, and is profitable for doctrine, for reproof, for correction, for instruction in righteousness: that the man of God may be perfect, throughly furnished unto all good works." 2 Timothy 3:16-17.

What is the Charismatic Movement?

The 'Charismatic or Neo-Pentecostal Movement' (the word 'charismatic' from the Greek *charisma*, gracious gift from God), embraces those who believe all gifts of the Spirit of God are available to Christians today, especially the spectacular gifts - tongues (unintelligible utterances) and healing. They actively seek and promote other supernatural experiences, such as being 'slain by the Spirit' (losing all control and falling backwards), laughing hysterically ('Toronto Blessing'), and a 'second blessing' (a second work of the Spirit of God after personal salvation). Concerning its origins, the movement is a progression of the Pentecostal Movement, which emerged from the Wesleyan Holiness movements in the U.S. around the latter part of the 19th Century. Today it is found within many Protestant denominations - Baptist, Lutheran, Methodist, Episcopalian, Presbyterian, Congregational and evangelical groups. It has also been embraced by Rome!

The Movement is based, bound and built on the primacy of 'supernatural religious experiences' - especially ecstatic tongue-speaking, a major focus of this volume. Doctrinal differences are incidental, they are the product of history, culture and 'understandable' variance in biblical interpretation. This ostensibly inoffensive platform has enabled the Movement to invade virtually every Christian denomination. The Christian is not canvassed to 'join' the Charismatics, for the Movement has no organisational structure. However, as within any Movement, there are conspicuous co-operatives whose aim it is to vigorously promote the basic creed - for example, the 'Assemblies of God', 'Catholic Pentecostals' and the 'Apostolic Church'. The Christian, wherever he or she may be in regard to ecclesiastical position, is coerced to seek some supernatural experience. When this is achieved they then become part of a growing global fellowship comprising all who have had similar 'experiences of grace'.

CHAPTER 2

Tongues –
The Witness of Silence in Scripture

We are informed by present-day tongues-speakers themselves and through their literature, that the principal purpose of tongues is to 'speak to God in prayer'! Now, before we examine specific issues regarding this and related claims, it is essential to review the record of tongue-speaking in the Bible. Let us begin with the Acts of the Apostles, for it especially unfolds the mighty works of the Holy Spirit among believers in the early Church period.

The occasions when tongues were spoken in the early Church period.

Will you acknowledge that a heavenly prayer language given by God to His people would be a most remarkable thing indeed, for nothing like it would have ever existed among them before? I am sure you will agree with me on this. What words could be used to describe it? "Stupendous"! "Monumental"! "Supernal"! Perhaps even "Revolutionary"! Such a thing was not given to the most devout saints of old. Their prayers and praises to Jehovah were made only in their natural tongues - the result of God's judgment at Babel. The coming of a heavenly prayer language, would be the subject of just about every conversation among the sons of Abraham. Who would have thought it, a "prayer language among mortal men, men of Israel"! Would not its arrival, and the occasions of its use among the Jews, consume the very spirits and conscript the pens of the Jewish NT writers?

Now, will you also agree, that where the greater spiritual privileges of the NT saints over the OT saints exist, they are brought to our attention with vitality and clarity by the Spirit of God? We have only to turn to the Epistle to the Hebrews to see how the Holy Spirit speaks at length of all that which was denied to the most devout OT saint, which is now the blessed portion granted to the feeblest believer in Christ![2] If the Holy Spirit intended tongues to be a language for prayer, this would have been a gift of monumental distinction! We would surely see bold evidence of it in Acts, the sacred record of the transition between that which was past, and the wondrously new blessings the ascended Christ was bringing into life through the very breath of His Spirit.

Shall we then consider the four occasions where tongues were spoken during the early days of the Church, recorded for us in Acts 2:4; 2:5-11; 10:44-46 and 19:5-6. It will be beneficial if you read these passages before continuing. Now, observe with me, that on each occasion, Luke refers to 'speaking' and not 'praying' in tongues! He has four Greek words for prayer to draw upon: *euchomai* (to pray - to God); *proseuchomai* (to pray, - which is always used of prayer to God, and is the most frequent word in this respect, especially in the Synoptists and Acts[3]); *erotao* (to ask or to make request); *deomai* (to desire or petition). Yet, this master historian, gifted with a physician's sharp eye and given to clinical discernment, who is renowned for his exacting

---

[2] E.g. Unlike the Jews of the OT, we can, through Christ, enter freely the very presence of God (Heb 10:19-22), inside the veil (but outside the camp). We have been redeemed, not just atoned! (Heb 9). Our greater blessings are seen in Christ as our "*High Priest of good things to come*" (Heb 9:11).

[3] W. E. Vine "Expository Dictionary of New Testament Words"; Oliphants, London. p. 199. Wuest: "...*proseuchomai which speaks of prayer to God...The prefixed preposition pros gives the idea of a definiteness and directness in prayer, with the consciousness on the part of the one praying that he is talking face to face with God.*". K. Wuest: "Word Studies" Vol. 1; Ephesians and Colossians p. 172. Would not this be the most appropriate word to use if they were praying to God in tongues?

account of events and excellent command of the Greek language, ignores all four Greek words for prayer. Instead, he employs the Greek word to speak (out) - *laleo*! So, why does Luke bypass every word for prayer? Do you believe he was careless or guilty of poor observation? I am sure you do not believe so, given the Spirit of God is the One employing his abilities as an historian. Throughout the period of Acts, Luke observes many occasions where prayer is made to God by believers, and he readily uses the word *proseuchomai* to record them.[4] It is strange indeed then, that he consistently discards it when it comes to recording four events that we are told involve a special language for prayer, and entail the use of a gift that would be of such historic distinction! If tongues were given and used for prayer to God on any of these four occasions, Luke would have observed and recorded it, especially if the Spirit of God, who guided his pen, intended tongues to be used as a prayer language![5]

Now, by observing the first tongue-speaking occasion a little further, what more can we learn (Acts 2:1-4)? Many ask, "Have you received your Pentecost - your 'second blessing and gift of tongues'?" Well, what has the Spirit of God to say concerning this? The faithful were in a house (upper room) and it would appear they were waiting, and praying while they waited - waiting times need not be wasted times! Ponder the mighty significance of the event - Pentecost - the coming of the Spirit of God unto men in a manner as never before! The beloved Master had ascended and was

---

[4] The word 'speak' can be used generally to refer to praying, teaching, praising or mere social conversation. In 1 Cor 14:34-35, Paul uses 'speak' in regard to women being precluded from taking audible part in praying and teaching within the church. However, if tongues were given as a special prayer language by God, unprecedented in the history of man, this would be clearly demonstrated through a word which specifically refers to prayer! Further, the record of Acts shows tongues were used to 'speak' to men, not to God! *Parakaleo* in Acts 16:9; 24:4; 27:34 means to beseech or entreat!

[5] The use of '*apophthengomai*' or 'utterance' in Acts 2:4, means 'to say', i.e. 'as the Spirit gave them to say'. W.E. Vine "Expository Dictionary of New Testament Words" p. 179 (Utterance) & p. 323 (Say). '*Parakaleo*' (pray) in Acts 16:9; 24:4; 27:34, means to beseech or entreat! p. 200.

now glorified in heaven. Who was to unite this small faithful band? Who was to keep before them the Person of Christ and empower their prayers to Him and the Father in days to come? Who else but the Holy Spirit, the Comforter, the promised Helper![6] Surely, in such a situation, we would expect to see tongues used in prayer if they were given as a prayer language by the Spirit of God! If tongues were given as a prayer language by the Spirit, we would expect to read concerning this momentous occasion and its unprecedented gift some trumpeting declaration such as, "they began to *'pray'* or *'speak to God'* with other tongues as the Spirit gave them utterance!" But what do we hear - nothing of this at all! No record here at Pentecost of tongues being used to pray! Not a hint of it! Even when they spoke in tongues in public after the crowd had gathered, (vv.5-12), we observe no praying to God at all! The bewildered multitude heard the Galilaeans speaking in tongues and asked, *"What meaneth this?"* Peter's explanation says nothing about tongues being a prayer language! Rather, the record shows the gift of tongues being used to 'speak out', to tell foreign Jews, who had come to Jerusalem to celebrate Pentecost, of the great things of God! Tongues here directed a message to men, and were not used to pray or to praise God! Surely, if prayer was the purpose of the gift, we would expect this to be stated on at least *one*, if not on *all four* tongue-speaking occasions. Would not the Spirit of God demonstrate this purpose to us on at least one occasion in the book that throbs with the breathing of the Spirit of God, a book often referred to as the 'Acts of the Holy Spirit'? We would then have an historical basis for teaching that tongues were given for prayer! The silence of the Spirit in this regard on the four tongue-speaking occasions, raises a resounding voice against claims that tongues were given to speak to God in prayer!

---

[6] The Holy Spirit is referred to by the Lord as our other Helper and Comforter - Paraclete - *allon parakleton*; John 14:16.

But what about the tongues themselves? What record do we have in Acts of them being some unintelligible 'heavenly language'? None whatsoever! Tongues were Gentile (foreign) languages. What better way to signal and persuade Jews, locally, and from foreign parts, that in the Age just dawned, God's grace through Christ is offered to every race and tongue! We will see later how this is clearly demonstrated throughout Acts and taught in the Epistles. The very fact tongues were foreign languages, explains why there is no record of tongues used as a special language to pray to God! (The Corinthians did pray in tongues, but, as we shall see, it was their choice - they wanted to display their miraculous gift of speaking foreign languages on every possible occasion. Tongues were never *given* for praying to God!)

The occasions of prayer in the early Church period - Acts.

Let us now observe the record of the many instances where Christians are found praying and see if on those occasions the Spirit of God associates prayer with tongues. Acts 2:42 - The believers continue in the apostles' doctrine and prayers - no tongues as a prayer language here; 4:31 - we see believers filled with the Holy Ghost, praying and speaking the Word of God in boldness - not in tongues; 6:4 - devotion to prayer - no tongues; 6:6 - again they were full of the Spirit and prayed - no tongues; 8:15 - Peter and John praying after the Samaritan conversion - no tongues; 9:40 - Peter's heavenly petition on behalf of Tabitha - no tongues; 10:9 - Peter praying in private on the house top - no tongues there; 11:5 - Peter's prayer (10:9) - no tongues; 12:12 - many believers were gathered praying - no tongues; 13:3 - the church at Antioch prays - no tongues; 14:23 - the apostles exhort the believers in fasting and prayer - no tongues; 16:25 - Paul and Silas prayed in prison - no tongues; 20:36 - the church at Ephesus prays in sorrow over Paul's departure - no tongues; 21:4-5 - Paul's meeting and praying with Spirit-led believers - no tongues. See also 22:17 & 28:8 etc - which

11

take us to the end of the historical record of Acts. To these we can add the exhortations to pray to God e.g. Acts 8:24, and the absence of tongues!

Search the pages of Acts, spanning some 33 years of Christianity, where Spirit-filled believers are seen in prayer or speaking in tongues, and we will not find a single record of the Holy Spirit associating tongues with praying to God. We see miracles, mighty steps of faith and occasions of elevated praise and prayer. Yet, there is not one instance where we can say, "See, here is a believer praying or being exhorted to pray to God in tongues!"[7] We cannot, for there was never such a purpose given to tongues by God. Therefore, no such instance will be found within this historical record of the early Church which, remember, was written under the omniscient eye of the Spirit of God.

When faced with the resounding silence of the historical record in Acts, the question is asked, as it was by the study group (and it may be your very question), "But what about the Epistles, 1 Corinthians 14 for instance? Were not the tongues spoken there different to those spoken in Acts?" Here present-day tongue-speakers make additional claims in regard to the purpose of tongues - they are to refresh the spirit of the believer, confirm salvation, sanctify against the world etc. The same question must be asked again. If the tongues of the epistles (eg 1 Cor 14) were 'different' to those in Acts and, as we are asked to believe, they were a 'phenomenal' gift of the Spirit of God, then why is there no record of such a noteworthy manifestation in the book that especially emblazons the work of God's Spirit within the early Church? We will see, the Epistles are as mute as Acts when it comes to the claims of present-day tongue-speakers! The silence of the epistles will become plain once we proceed to study what they have to teach us regarding the purpose of tongues!

[7] First Corinthians, wherein Paul raises the issue of tongues to the Corinthian church, was written before the close of the period covered by Acts, a record which never mentions 'ecstatic' tongues!

The underlying argument

When the Jews disbelieved God, they required signs to restore their belief.

God often used signs to judge the Jews because of their unbelief.

Tongues (foreign languages - spoken naturally) was one such sign of judgment to the Jews in the OT

The Jews were in a condition of unbelief in the early Church period.

Tongues (foreign languages miraculously spoken) were used as a sign during the early Church period of God's judgment upon the Jews because of their unbelief.

Tongues (foreign languages miraculously spoken) would cease when their use as a sign to the Jews would no longer be needed!

CHAPTER 3

The Purpose of Tongues

There is absolutely no record in Acts associating tongues with praying to God. What purpose then did tongues serve on those four occasions when they were spoken? We are provided with the answer by the Apostle Paul when he corrects the church at Corinth over their misuse of tongues.

"In the law it is written, With men of other tongues and other lips will I speak unto this people; and yet for all that will they not hear me, saith the Lord. Wherefore tongues are for a sign, not to them that believe, but to them that believe not:" 1 Corinthians 14:21-22.

Now, can we not see immediately why the historical record in Acts is barren when it comes to praying in tongues? Is not this statement made by Paul through the Spirit of God, wholly consistent with what we saw in the historical record also written by the Spirit of God - that tongues were not given or used as some heavenly prayer language? At this point, many present-day tongue-speakers become aware of a grave deficiency in what they have been told concerning tongues! It is not just the silent record of Acts that causes them concern. It is also the plain teaching of the Spirit of God in the Epistles, which is consistent with it, that furthers their doubt. They become aware tongues were not given as a prayer language, but for a sign, and tongues in Acts, being foreign languages, would be an appropriate sign of the character of the new

14

era - the coming of the Spirit of God, God's judgment upon Israel and the bestowing of His grace to people of every race (symbolised by the foreign tongues). How could their pastors and ministers fail to acknowledge such plain evidence? The reasons for this failure will be detailed later. For the present, let it be known that many acquire the 'tongues experience', never having consulted God's Word on the matter! They then use their experience to interpret the historical record of Scripture. In turn, they indoctrinate others to seek a 'tongues experience', - so on goes the cycle of error. We need to remember that Scripture must be compared with Scripture to allow the Word of God to interpret itself. When we conduct our study according to this rule, we will find consistency between biblical history and biblical doctrine. This must be the test by which we examine the truth of this study. Biblical history must agree with biblical doctrine - do not lose sight of this. Beware of any teaching that selects a few verses here and there out of context, supported not by a systematic analysis encompassing the whole Bible, but by a myriad of 'experiences'! Bear in mind, the absolute silence of Scripture concerning praying to God in tongues poses an immense problem to Satan. This is why he must fill the silence by giving people a 'personal experience' which is so real that it speaks louder to them than does the Word of God!

The background to Paul's statement - the tongues error at Corinth!

The reason Paul makes this statement about the purpose of tongues is critical to our investigation. The tongue-speakers at Corinth had lost sight of the purpose of the gift of tongues. They were using it indiscriminately, valuing it above all other gifts of the Spirit and using it to heap glory upon themselves; praying and speaking in unknown tongues (foreign languages) which could not be understood by the church.[8] Confusion and strife followed within the assembly. Paul was not about to withhold stern words, for the situation was bringing the house of God into shame! He was naturally very concerned about this and he needed to remind those believers at Corinth who were given the gift of tongues, indeed impress upon them all, the real reason for that gift. The gift of tongues he says, is firstly not given by the Spirit of God to every one of you (ch.12), so cast aside your petty jealousies. Secondly, the gift of tongues is temporary and is not all-important (ch. 13), therefore do not fix your heart on a fleeting gift, but on a permanent grace - love. Thirdly, some of you are choosing to use tongues, rather than the local language, to pray in the church. Be mindful of the purpose of tongues, they were given to be a sign to unbelievers (not for praying to God). However, if you wish to pray using your gifted foreign language, rather than the local tongue, within the church, let it be in one that is known to the church. If it is not known and no one can interpret what you say, then use it silently when you are in church - let it be kept between you and God - for He understands all tongues (foreign languages)! This will avoid strife within God's house (ch. 14).

Today too, confusion over the purpose of tongues has caused division amongst the saints of God, grieving the Holy Spirit. We are compelled then to give earnest heed to what the Spirit of God has to say to the Corinthians on this very matter. These verses and their context must be our prime consideration when asking, "Why were tongues given?" It is regrettable, though not surprising, to find that some charismatic leaders who seek to persuade us that believers should speak and pray in tongues today, make *no* reference to these verses in their publications. Others, who cannot avoid the clear statement in Scripture that

---

[8] See '1 Corinthians chapter 14 - An Overview' below for a fuller treatment on this Corinthian error.

tongues are for a sign to unbelievers, bury it under a list of 'other' purposes for tongues, which are born of experience and a failure to listen to what the Spirit of God says to a divided, confused and carnal Corinthian church over this very issue!

Essential questions

Paul's statement to the Corinthians that tongues were 'a sign to them that believe not', raises five fundamental questions.

1. What is meant by a SIGN?
2. To WHOM were tongues a sign - who are *"them that believe not"*?
3. OF WHAT were tongues a sign?
4. What was the NATURE of tongues (ecstatic[9] or foreign languages)?
5. How LONG would the sign of tongues be needed?

After examining these questions in the light of Scripture, we will see that:

the tongues of the New Testament were actual Gentile (foreign) languages, spoken miraculously, enabled by the Spirit of God, and given as a sign to the Jews of God's judgment and grace. They would cease once the Scriptures had been completed!

We will examine this assertion through a number of related 'Propositions', considered within the whole sweep of God's Word.[10] Our first task is to identify what is meant by a sign. We need then to determine the identity of *"them that believe not"*, because Paul declares to the Corinthians that it is these people for whom tongues were a sign!

---

[9] By ecstatic languages (tongues), we refer to unintelligible or heavenly languages, in contrast to foreign languages (tongues).
[10] The 'Propositions' have been numbered consecutively to assist reference.

17

The meaning of a Sign

Signs from God are manifestations (signals, tokens) from Him, designed to confirm His presence and His purposes. Generally, divine signs are associated with a particular divine message, related to some past, present or some prospective matter. Specifically, signs may point to a future event; a miraculous phenomenon; the power of God; the glory of God. In 1 Corinthians (as in Mark 16:17), the word *semeion* (sign) is used in connection with tongues, referring to something that is supernatural, a miraculous thing. In the case of tongues then, all will agree, we have a supernatural phenomenon from God, designed to impart a distinctive message. What then was this distinct message and to whom was it directed?

To whom and of what were tongues a sign (and what was their nature)?

These questions must be addressed together. Once we identify the people to whom God directed the sign of tongues, we will discover both why God directed this sign to them, and the nature of these tongues. Further, by considering these questions together, we can watch out for any inconsistency in our findings.

Returning now to the identity of those to whom tongues were a sign. We will have already noticed that Scripture has given us a clear *description* of these people. They were unbelievers - tongues are a sign to them that believe not![11] Who then are these unbelievers Paul has in mind when he corrects the Corinthians on tongues? The historical record of Scripture and the doctrine of Scripture will show they are the Jews! This is so because:

(a) signs were God's special manner of speaking to His earthly people, the Jews;

---

[11] We will see (Propositions 4 & 5) that tongues were a sign to Jews who rejected Christ, as well as to Jewish believers in Christ during the early Church period who, because they regarded all Gentiles as unclean, had to be convinced by a divine sign of the equality of Gentiles in salvation through Christ.

(b) The Jews were in a state of spiritual unbelief during the early Church period.

Our immediate task is to prove *signs* were God's particular custom when speaking to His earthly people, the Jews, and that *tongues* were a sign directed specially to the Jews. One further point before we continue. What we are considering here is not just signs relating to the individual Jew, but to the Jews as a race!

Signs are used by God in speaking to the Jews

Proposition 1 (a): "God used *signs* consistently to speak to the Jews."

When we observe God dealing with Israel, signs are prominent.

1. *God dealing with Israel in the OT:* Joshua speaks of God who *"did those great signs in our sight"*.[12] Jehovah Himself declares, *"How long will this people [Israel] provoke me? and how long will it be ere they believe me, for all the signs which I have shewed among them?"*[13] e.g. the manna from heaven, Aaron's rod that budded, the cloud and pillar of fire. (The foreign languages heard by the Jews whilst in captivity, were also a sign to them, as we shall see later).

2. *God dealing with the Jews during the period of the Gospel:* We have only to read the Gospels to see the signs designed to convince the Jews of the Lord's divine authority, e.g. the Spirit descending as a dove upon Him and His transfiguration. There were also such signs and wonders performed by the Lord as testified by Peter *"Ye men of Israel, hear these words; Jesus of Nazareth, a man approved of God among you by miracles and wonders and signs, which God*

---

[12] Joshua 24:17
[13] Numbers 14:11

did by Him in the midst of you,..."[14]

3. *God dealing with the Jews in the early Church period*[15]: In the NT there is the conclusive testimony of Paul. In writing to the Corinthians he reminds them *"the Jews require a sign"!*[16] We will focus on this later. Many signs are recorded as having taken place during this period.

4. *God's future dealing with the Jewish people:* We see in Joel's prophecy to the nation of Israel that when God reveals Himself in a future day, the *"Great and Terrible Day of the Lord"*, it will be with signs and wonders.[17]

Scripture clearly reveals that signs were used to signal God's purpose to the emerging Hebrew nation. They continued to be used throughout Israel's history, and signs will be used again to herald events relating to Israel in the future.

Proposition 1 (b): "The Jews as a people required *signs* to believe."

What proof do we have of this in Scripture?

1. *The witness of Jews themselves.* Listen to their request of the Lord, *"What sign shewest thou then, that we may see, and believe thee?"*[18] Again, *"Master, we would see a sign from thee"*,[19] show the Jews, as individuals and as a nation, were dependent upon signs.

2. *The witness of the Lord.* *"Except ye [Jews] see signs and wonders, ye will not believe."*[20] When chiding the Pharisees He declared; *"Why doth this generation [of Pharisees] seek after a sign...?"*[21]

---

[14] Acts 2:22. We will not examine them here, but note, when the Lord turned from Israel who rejected Him (Matt 12), He then unfolded the parables of the Church (Matt 13), and these signs and miracles diminished.

[15] Refer to Chart A

[16] 1 Corinthians 1:22

[17] Joel 2:30

[18] John 6:30

[19] Matthew 12:38

[20] John 4:48

[21] Mark 8:12. Generation or *'genea'* - of the same stock (generation) of Pharisees. The

3. *The witness of Paul.* When correcting the Corinthians on tongues, he reminds them *"the Jews require a sign and the Greeks seek after wisdom"*![22] That is, the Jews had a nature that demanded supernatural evidence before they would believe, a nature cultivated by the extensive use of signs by God to speak to them, directly, and indirectly through His prophets. Paul contrasts this with the natural inclination of the Gentiles - they believe only after they are given a reason derived through man's intellect!

Proposition 2: "In the early NT period, the gospel focused on the Jews and *signs* were prominent."

Can there be any doubt of this? The OT informs us this faithless nation required, expected and received signs from a faithful God. The prominence of signs is quite evident in the early days of the NT period too, where the Jews were the principal subjects of the gospel. This was not so with the Gentiles, as Paul clearly states! They did not desire supernatural evidence in order to believe, and they expected no such proofs from God.[23] Now what evidence can we bring to bear on this from the NT?

---

denial of a sign (v.12) is to *these* vindictive Pharisees (vv. 10-11), not to the whole nation. The Pharisees were called a *"generation of vipers"* by the Lord for their animosity towards Him (Matt 3:7; 12:34 etc.). These disputing ritualists, who were out to trap the Lord, caused Him to groan with deep sadness, for they had rejected Him despite the many signs He had already done before them. The sign they were seeking was a further 'miracle' to prove Christ's Messiahship. The only 'sign' they would be given, as recorded by Matthew (12:39-41), was the sign of Jonah, which the Lord used to foreshadow to them, as well as to the whole nation, His death and resurrection.

[22] 1 Corinthians 1:22. The Jews 'ask for' - *aiteo* - a sign when challenged to faith.

[23] This is not to say that Gentiles during this time could not be influenced to *seek* Christ when they observed a sign or miracle performed by the Spirit of God i.e., put the Gentiles on the path of obedience. Paul who declared the Jews require a sign (to believe) but the Greeks wisdom (to believe), acknowledges as much in his Epistle to the Romans (15:18-19). However, the assertion here, and that of Paul in 1 Cor 1:21-22, is that the *initiation* and *intent* of Divine signs are *because of* and *to* the Jew as a means of getting them to *believe!* Why? Because as stated by Paul and proved by Israel's history, the Jews *require* a sign in order to *believe!* A sign or miracle may get the attention of the Gentiles, but at then end of the day, they will require a rational argument to believe. Paul in fact speaks of His work among them as involving '*word*' and deed! Note, when it concerns individual salvation, then it is always by faith in Christ - never by sight (signs) or natural wisdom!

1. *The progress of the gospel during the early Church period.* Have you noted the two divisions of Acts and how they reflect a different order in outreach? It was God's plan that Christianity was to the *"Jew first"*[24], for they must first begin at Jerusalem, then evangelise Judea and Samaria. In the first section (chapters 1-12), the gospel is taken to the Jews, with Jerusalem the geographical centre and Peter the prominent evangelist. In the second section (chapters 13-28), the Gentile city of Antioch is the geographical centre, and now Paul is the prominent apostle. The gospel is taken to the Gentiles throughout Asia and to Rome - *"lo, we turn to the Gentiles"*. Note, Paul also visits the Jews first, those of the dispersion - *"..It was necessary that the word of God should first have been spoken to you* [the Jews]*"*[25]. He becomes the 'apostle to the Gentiles' after these Jews rejected the gospel in disbelief. What does this mean? Well, within the early NT period, where Jews were the main focus of the gospel, signs were used to signal God's purpose. When the gospel is taken to the Gentiles and churches established in Gentile regions, tongues and the other signs became less evident. Why? Because tongues are a sign to the Jews who seek after signs! As the veil descended on Judaism and lifted over Christianity, signs began to diminish.

2. *The prophecy of Joel quoted in Acts 2.*[26] Peter's explanation of Pentecost to the Jews clearly emphasises Israel. Peter was given the keys to the Kingdom of Heaven - the privilege of opening the door of salvation through Christ to the Jews![27] Joel's prophecy is Messianic[28] as confirmed

---

[24] Acts 1:8; Luke 24:47; Rom 1:16. - *proton* (first), means 'first or firstly' in relation to time/order. God must be faithful to His promise of favour to Abraham's natural seed, thus the Jews hear of the gospel and partake of its blessings before the Gentiles (i.e. 'beginning at Jerusalem'). In salvation however, Jew and Gentile must come as penitent sinners. The Jew is equal with the Gentile in Christ.

[25] Acts 13:46. *Proton* as in Rom 1:16.

[26] On the use of the quotation from Joel by Peter, see Note 4.

[27] Matthew 16:19 (never the keys of the Church!)

[28] Messianic means it refers to the coming of the Messiah - Israel's expected King who will rule over the earth with His special people, Israel (Dan 9:25-26 and the various Messianic Psalms).

by the expression *"Day of the Lord"* (2:20).[29] Being Messianic, the prophet's eye focuses upon Israel, in perfect harmony with the purpose of signs (and tongues) being directed to Jews. Peter calls the Jews to attention in Acts 2 with the words, *"men of Judea"* (v.14). He progresses to the point where he identifies them as the *"men of Israel"* (v.22), associating the events of Acts 2 (e.g. tongues) with their national theocratic title and their national guilt for they, the *nation*, in unbelief, with cruel hands crucified Christ - their Messiah, King!

3. *The absence of the completed written Word of God.* During the early years of the NT period when Jews were the focus of the gospel, there were no Scriptures presenting the constitution of the church in Christ, the church's coming and its composition embracing all races. In this situation, what would be the appropriate manner to teach and convince a sign-seeking people of these truths? Signs!

Proposition 3: "*Tongues* were a sign specifically directed to the Jews."

We have proved from the Word of God, that during the early Church period the gospel focused on the Jews. This being the case, signs would be prominent. They required, expected and were given signs from God to enable them to believe what the gospel meant (the setting aside of Israel in judgment and the equality between Jews and Gentiles, as we shall see). We now address the particular case of tongues as a sign to the Jews, individually and nationally. From this point we begin to gather progressive evidence that tongues

---

[29] The *'Day of the Lord'* refers to the Lord's personal involvement with Israel which resumes after the Rapture of the Church, His coming to the earth to defeat Israel's foes (Great and Terrible Day of the Lord), and to reign, and extends to the eternal state. It is first mentioned in the OT (Isa 2:12;11:11 etc., Joel 1:15 etc., Zech 14:1-11). It is therefore *not* a day associated with the Church period! It is always associated with wrath and destruction in association with the Lord's establishment of Himself as King over all on the earth, and Israel's salvation. The *'Day of Christ'* (Lord Jesus Christ, Lord Jesus, Jesus Christ) is wholly a NT subject and refers to Christ's coming for His Church (Rapture) - 1 Cor 1:8, 2 Cor 1:14, Phil 1:6 etc. (Chart B).

were a sign specifically to disbelieving Jews! When we study Propositions 4 and 5 we will see that the *message* signalled by tongues, as well as their very *nature*, offer further proof tongues were a sign exclusively to the Jews!

1. The racial link

When he corrects the Corinthians on tongues, Paul makes an unmistakable association between the purpose of tongues and Israel. Consider the following.

a) We noted earlier, Paul characterised the disposition of the Jews with the statement, *"the Jews require a sign"* in order to believe! In the very same epistle, he stated to the Corinthians, *"tongues are for a sign to them that believe not"*. Now put these two facts together and what are we to conclude? It would be difficult for us (and the Corinthians) to draw any conclusion other than tongues are a sign to the *Jews*! Paul expects the Corinthians to make this association, because it forms the basis of his statement correcting them on their use of tongues.

b) The term *"this people"*. Paul reinforces this association by the use of two racial terms. We can distinguish two races of people in 1 Corinthians 14:21, those identified as "[men of] *other tongues and other lips* [Gentile races]"[30] and those identified as *"this people"*, clearly the Jews. Note, the expression 'men of other tongues' is essentially racial. The contrast in verse 21 is racial - 'other tongues and other lips' with 'this people'. The term *'this people'* in Scripture, refers exclusively to the Jews as a race and is used in this representation extensively throughout the OT and in the NT.[31]

---

[30] OT lexicons give the meaning of stammering (*laeg*) as something that is 'foreign'(strange) or 'mocking'. Isaiah has foreign languages in view, as is certain from the historical and doctrinal context. God would speak to Israel with foreign (i.e. strange) languages. Paul too has foreign (strange) tongues in view, for he renders Isaiah's word 'stammering', as 'other' (*heteros*) - meaning 'strange' (rather than 'mocking'). *Mogilalos* denotes "speaking with difficulty" i.e. a stammering - speech impediment, which is not employed by Paul.

[31] Some examples: OT: Ex 3.21, 5:22-23; Num 11:11; Deut 3:28; Josh 1:2; Jud 2:20; 1

The nation of Israel (this people) declared Isaiah, was spoken to by the Lord during OT times through a 'sign' of tongues, although not supernatural, because of their unbelief! (We take this up again later). Now Paul could have simply said to the Corinthians, "tongues are a sign to them that believe not". However, under the Spirit's guidance, he chose to include in his instruction on the purpose of tongues a term, 'this people'- which identifies and implicates Israel. So Paul, in verse 22, states that 'wherefore' (on account of) what is written in the Jewish law relating to 'this people', (the Jews), tongues are a sign! We note here the use of the present tense. Tongues 'are' for a sign. They continued to be used during those days as a sign, declares Paul, on account of what was stated in the Jewish law.[32]

2. The spiritual link - a sign to 'them that believe not'.

Now, in order to prove further that tongues were a sign specifically to the Jews during the early Church period, what must we do? We must show that Jews during that time were in a condition of unbelief! During OT times, the essential nature of Israel's unbelief was in regard to the life and light God had given them in the promised land. When we come to the period of the early Church, their disbelief was in regard to life and light through the promised Son - the Lord Jesus Christ! In both cases it was spiritual unbelief, but more about this later. There are a few preliminary matters to consider first.

Tongues as a sign to Israel in the Old Testament.- judgment due to unbelief.

In the OT we see Israel spending many years under Gentile

Sam 2:23; 1 Kings 12:6,7,9,10,27; Jer 4:10; Mic 2:11; Zech 8:6. NT: Matt 15:8; Mark 7:6; Luke 21:23; Acts 13:17, 28:26-27.

[32] The meaning of the term 'law' must be determined by its context. Here, as in Psa 1:2 for instance, it embraces all OT precepts and tenets promulgated by the patriarchs and prophets of God.

captivity. God deprived them of the possession and pleasure of their own land. He as it were, 'set them aside' in judgment under Gentile rule! Why? Disbelief! Time after time, Israel wilfully backslid. Isaiah condemns them saying that this people refused the gentle waters of Shiloah and rejoiced in Rezin and Remaliah's son. He then speaks of their coming bondage under the Gentiles - God brings upon them strong (Gentile) waters, even the (Gentile) king of Assyria who filled the breadth of their land.[33] Bondage under the Gentiles, was God's way of chastising His implacable earthly people. Hearing Gentile languages was a sign of God's judgment upon them! Now put yourself in the place of an Israelite under Gentile captivity. Each day you and your brethren would hear foreign tongues spoken by your captors - tongues of men, men of unclean lips - the Gentiles. Day-in and day-out, the sound of these foreign tongues would be a sign that you and the nation were being judged, 'set aside' by God, for you chose to disbelieve Him and His prophets![34] Now these tongues were foreign languages spoken through natural ability. They were not a miraculous sign but, a sign nevertheless. They were used by God to speak to this people! Later on, during the early NT period, God would use miraculously spoken foreign tongues as a sign to the Jews, again because of their unbelief, as we shall see!

Israel's unbelief during the New Testament period.

   As we noted above, Israel's disbelief during the early

---

[33] Isaiah 8:5-8. Gentile tongues would also have been a sign of God's judgment on Israel (Judah) during the time of Babylonian captivity and the dispersion. See also Deut 28:49; *"....The Lord shall bring a nation against thee from far...whose tongue* [foreign language] *thou shalt not understand...."*. In Hebrew *lashon* denotes a foreign "language": as here and in Isa 28:11 (Vine's Complete Expository Dictionary of Old and New Testament Words).

[34] The Lord Himself declared tongues were to be a sign (Mark 16:17). Why then did the Spirit of God direct Paul to Isaiah and not to the words of the Lord to impress upon the Corinthians that tongues were a sign? It is because the words of Isaiah bring to the fore the racial link (this people), and establishes the spiritual link (unbelief), between Israel during the OT period and Israel during the early Church period! In this way, the Corinthians would see foreign tongues were a sign to disbelieving Israel then, as they were in days past! In Mark 16, the Lord's reference to tongues as a sign is prospective, not corrective!

Church period was in general, in regard to life and light through the promised Son, the Lord Jesus Christ. The two underlying aspects of Israel's spiritual unbelief must be noted. Firstly, part of it was in regard to *righteousness*. They rejected Jesus of Nazareth, His claim to be the righteous Son of God, His Messiahship and that only through Him could they become righteous before God. Secondly, their disbelief had a *racial* aspect. They rejected in disbelief any idea that people of other races and tongues, i.e. the Gentiles, could be equally righteous and blessed before God through Christ. This unbelief was directed towards the church, the Body of Christ, within which all races and tongues are one. This was a problem not just for the non-Christian Jews; it was a subject of stumbling disbelief among the Christian Jews as well! Being Jews, they faced great difficulty in accepting spiritual equality between all races - people of different tongues. Their prophets spoke of Jews as the chosen and blessed of God and forbade their mixing with the Gentiles. Indeed, mixing with men of other races was, as Peter declares, 'unlawful'! We can see again why the gifted tongues of the NT had to be foreign languages, it was a most appropriate racial symbol!

The Church - what is it?

At this point in the study it is essential to ensure we have an understanding of what Scripture means by the church! It is a vast subject and we can only touch upon it here.

The word itself, *ekklesia*, means 'to call out from'. In Scripture it is used, in one sense, to identify a group of Christians gathered together at a certain location, such as the 'church of God which is at Corinth', or the 'church of the Thessalonians in God'. There is, however, another important sense in which the word is used in Scripture, not in regard to 'locality' and 'local membership', but in relation to 'totality' and 'total membership'. The word "church" in passages such as Matthew 16:18, Ephesians 1:22; 5:23-25 and Colossians

1:18, refers to all who, through faith, have accepted Christ as Lord and Saviour. All persons, from Pentecost to the Rapture (the close of the Church period), regardless of their nationality, race (Jew or Gentile), gender or Christian denomination, who are born again believers, make up the 'whole' Church.[35] At Pentecost, the 120 individual believers were incorporated as one united whole - the Church - by the Spirit of God. At that point in time, the total Church comprised just 120 believers. As individuals were saved in Jerusalem, Samaria and other parts of the world, they were added to the Church, as they have been since. Thus, the total membership increases over time. The essential truth here is the Church is not an *organization.* It is an *organism,* made up of souls quickened by the Spirit of God![36] What was it that the Lord asked Saul when he was attacking the Christians? "Saul, Saul, why persecutest thou *Me?"* ['Why Saul, are you persecuting My very person - My Body?'] (Acts 9:4). We are all part of His Body - many members yet one body (1 Cor 12:12-13) - of which Christ is the Head. This is why Scripture refers to *the* Church as *the* Body of Christ. Paul, writing to the Ephesians, presents three representations of the Church, the Body of Christ (1:22-23), a holy Temple (2:21-22), and the Bride of Christ (5:25-27). The Church as the Body of Christ indicates *life* - we are all partakers of the life of Christ - a living organism! As the Temple, the Church partakes of the Divine *light* which is of Christ, Him who is Light! As the Bride, the Church is seen as the object of Christ's *love.* Life, light and love, are the three attributes of God!

Now, the Church as a living Body, must have a living Head

---

[35] The local church is also referred to as body of Christ (1 Cor 12:27), because it reflects the character of the Body of Christ! The Body of Christ however, is not made up of all the local churches or denominations, but by individuals! The local church is the visible expression and witness of that which is invisible - the spiritual Body of Christ!

[36] The organizations (institutions) we have in Christendom today e.g. the 'Church of Rome', the 'Church of England', are of man and as such they usurp the truth of God! Their leaders would have us believe their organization is the true 'Church' and they themselves are the head of it. The Church of Christ is a spiritual Body, united to *Christ* whom God gave to be the Head over *all* things to the Church (Eph 1:22).

(that is why it could not come into existence until after Christ arose from the dead). And so the Spirit of God would elevate before us Christ as the Head of the Church, the *risen* Head of the Church which is His Body! His Body came into being at Pentecost, its coming having to wait until He arose and ascended and the sending of His Spirit. The 120 individuals were then, by the Holy Spirit, joined together into one unified Body and individually and collectively inseparably linked to one another and to Christ. Since then, all who are saved, upon their salvation, become part of that Body, united and related to each other in Christ!

We will refer to and amplify this precious truth concerning the Body of Christ, which is His Church, during the study. It lies at the root of the distinctive character of the NT period and at the very heart of God's grace to man. It was also the basis of Israel's unbelief! Let us now resume our discussion on this last matter.

Scriptural evidence of Israel's spiritual unbelief during the early Church period.
1. *Israel's disbelief and rejection of Christ as the Messiah.*
The Lord Himself, at the start of His prophetic sermon, appealed for faith from His brethren, only to lament, *"O Jerusalem, Jerusalem, thou that killest the prophets, and stonest them which are sent unto thee, how often would I have gathered thy children together, even as a hen gathereth her chickens under her wings, and ye would not! Behold, your house is left unto you desolate."*[37] Israel's clear rejection of Christ is further seen through her rebellious declaration, *"Away with this man",*[38] her callous cry of *"Crucify Him......Crucify Him".*[39] Her adulterous heart would have no

---

[37] Matthew 23:37-38
[38] Luke 23:18
[39] Mark 15:12-14

king but Caesar.[40] They delivered the Prince of Life, the Holy and Just One into heathen hands. John, in his Gospel records Israel's unbelief, *"He* [Christ] *came unto His own,* [the Jews] *and His own received Him not".*[41] For three years, He came seeking fruit on this fig tree (Israel) but found it barren![42] The Messiah expected by the Jews was One who would liberate the nation, whose coming would be marked by regal splendour above that of Solomon and whose kingdom would be administered with the strength of one more powerful than David. But He was rejected! He came by way of a lowly manger to usher in a kingdom not of this world, one to be established by personal suffering.

2. *Israel's rejection of Christ and His Church.* Listen to Peter's undaunted prosecution of Israel's unbelief when he declares - *"...Behold, I lay in Sion a chief corner-stone, elect, precious...": "...the stone which the builders disallowed,* [Christ], *the same is made the head of the corner* [of the church], *and a stone of stumbling, and a rock of offence, even to them* [Jews] *which stumble at the word, being disobedient whereunto also they were appointed."*[43] The images employed by Peter speak of Christ, born of Israel and head and foundation of the Church, that Church which embraces both Jew and Gentile. Israel rejected Him in unbelief, they rejected His "spiritual house - the Church", His "Holy Nation", "His peculiar people", "His chosen generation". Note here, Peter like Paul quotes from Isaiah 28: A 'foundation stone', a 'tried stone', a 'precious corner stone', a 'sure foundation' (v.16). Of what? The Church! Peter's first Epistle addresses, in the main, Jewish Christians dispersed over five provinces (1 Peter 1:1). He wants to impress upon them they are part of a new nation and a royal priesthood, one that includes

---

[40] John 19:15
[41] John 1:11
[42] Luke 13:7
[43] 1 Peter 2:6-8. *"I will lay stumblingblocks before 'this people',"* (Jer 6:21), "....For they [Israel] stumbled at that stumblingstone [Christ]" (Rom 9:32), "We preach Christ crucified...unto the Jews a stumblingblock" (1 Cor 1:23).

Gentiles in a new and universal priesthood, to offer spiritual sacrifices to God through Jesus Christ.

3. *The witness of Stephen.* Israel's unbelief and rejection of God's purpose through Christ is also mentioned by Stephen when he set forth the eternal sweep of Christ's work to the new generation of Jews. They rejected Christ, His Church (His Body), His Spirit. Stephen accuses them of denying the Spirit of God. How fitting, given the Spirit's coming and manifestation at Pentecost, His work as the Vicar of Christ, indwelling the Church comprising both Jew and Gentile! *"Ye stiffnecked and uncircumcised in heart and ears, ye do always resist the Holy Ghost as your fathers did, so do ye [present-day Jews].*[44] *Which of the prophets have not your fathers persecuted? and they have slain them which shewed before of the coming of the Just One; of whom ye have been now the betrayers and murderers: who have received the law by the disposition of angels, and have not kept it."*[45]

4. *Israel's blind disbelief - the witness of the Holy Spirit through Paul - Romans 11. "For I would not, brethren, that ye should be ignorant of this mystery, lest ye should be wise in your own conceits; that blindness in part is happened to Israel, until the fulness of the Gentiles be come in"*[46]. It was Moses, the faithful lawgiver, who earlier declared God's judgment upon a faithless nation, *"....I will hide my face from them, I will see what their end shall be. For they are a very froward generation, children in whom is no faith"*[47]. Centuries on, Paul, the faithful champion of Him who fulfilled the law, when writing to the believers in Rome, tells them how God has hidden His face from Israel because of their present wilful blindness and disbelief.

5. *Paul's testimony of Israel's unbelief in Acts 28.* We

---

[44] Their fathers needed a sign of judgment due to unbelief and so did their sons (*so do ye*)!
[45] Acts 7: 51-53
[46] Romans 11:25
[47] Deuteronomy 32:20

should take special note of what Paul has to say and the words he uses in verses 25-28. He again quotes from Isaiah (6:9-10) and we observe he speaks of Israel, linking their past unbelief to their present unbelief. He uses the term 'this people', as he does in 1 Corinthians 14:21 - *"Go unto this people* [Israel] *and say, Hearing ye shall hear, and not understand; and seeing ye shall see, and not perceive: For the heart of this people,*[Israel] *is waxed gross... "*.[48]

There can be no doubt that Israel (the Jews) were in a state of gross unbelief, and therefore they were again deserving of a sign of God's judgment. This is why Paul employs Isaiah's words to the Corinthians. He wants to remind them of this: *"yet for all that* [signs] *will they* [the Jews - this people] *not hear me, saith the Lord. Wherefore tongues are a sign...to them that believe not* [those that will not hear me - the Jews!]*"* (1 Cor 14:21-22).

Preliminary conclusions

Signs were needed because of the particular circumstances at the time. These included the coming of the church, the Body of Christ and the equality of all tongues before God within it; the setting aside of Israel, the people in focus, the Jews and their special disposition in that they required signs to believe. Conditions were ripe and set for a sign to a sign-seeking people! We see this clearly in the racial and spiritual links Paul makes between tongues and Israel's disbelief during the OT, and tongues and spiritual unbelief of Israel in the NT. Signs were used by God to speak to Israel in the OT and foreign languages (tongues) were in those days a sign of His judgment upon Israel because of their unbelief. When we come to the NT, we see conditions exist for God to again use a sign of judgment to the Jews, viz (1) The Jews were a people who required signs. The Jews (not the Gentiles) are

---

[48] This passage from Isaiah is also quoted by the Lord in Matt 13. Interestingly, He uses it there when He begins His parables that relate to the Church, just after He rejects Israel when they have declared their outright rejection of Him (Chapter 12). Israel was, in the Lord's day, as unbelieving as in Paul's day!

identified as those people who look for signs. (2) Christ, God's only begotten Son had come to them. They rejected Him and His church in their unbelief. (We will examine in detail later why this new sign of judgment should be in the form of Gentile languages spoken *miraculously* through the Spirit of God.) Paul reminds the Corinthians of Isaiah's words and draws the connection that *this people*, Israel, unbelieving and rebellious of heart, continue to dismiss the prophets.[49] This is reinforced (as mentioned earlier), by the present tense, tongues '*are* (not were) a sign' (1 Cor 14:22). Paul thus confirms the historical link also between the tongues used in the OT and those spoken by the Corinthians. When the Jews are the focus of God's prophets, ministers and even the Lord Himself, we will find typically, reference to the nation's past, linking the experiences of the forefathers to the particular matter under consideration. This common characteristic further proves the Jewish context of 1 Corinthians 14:21-22, which is also seen in passages such as Acts 7, 15, 28; Romans 11; Galatians 3 and Hebrews 11.

---

[49] Jeremiah 5:23

CHAPTER 4

The Reason for Tongues

Those participating in our study, accepted that foreign tongues heard while under captivity were a sign of God's punishment of Israel during the OT period. They also agreed that Israel was in a state of spiritual unbelief during the early Church period. The discussion now focused on the *miraculous* nature of the tongues of the NT. What was the reason behind God's use of miraculous tongues? What message did they bring to the Jews? Were they only ever foreign tongues or were they some heavenly language used to speak to God? If they were foreign tongues, what was the point of them being spoken miraculously – after all, the foreign tongues used as a sign during the period of the OT were spoken through natural ability?

Remember too, we will discover further evidence proving tongues were specifically to the Jews! Consider carefully the significance of tongues as a miraculously spoken foreign language.

Of what were tongues a sign to the Jews?
The tongues of the NT were to signal three things.

1. *National judgment upon Israel.* Foreign tongues themselves were a sign to Israel that the nation had been set aside in judgment (as they were in past times) because of unbelief - their rejection of Christ and His righteousness. God has therefore postponed national blessings covenanted to them.[50]

---

[50] The blessings promised by God to Israel under the Abrahamic Covenant (Gen 12,

2. *Universal-racial blessing.* Foreign tongues spoken *miraculously* by Jews were a sign to *all* Jews that God was reaching out to the Gentiles - men of all tongues - in blessing and grace. Their miraculous nature meant the Spirit of God had come as promised and was behind this message, giving it divine authenticity.

3. *Spiritual equality between all races.* Foreign languages spoken *miraculously* by Gentile converts to Christ, were a sign to Jewish Christians of spiritual equality in Christ. The fact that Gentiles spoke foreign languages miraculously, was a sign that the Spirit of God had indwelt Gentiles as well as Jews! That is, the Holy Spirit had indeed come upon all flesh (every nation - all tongues). This addressed the problem Jewish Christians had in accepting Gentile Christians as equals in Christ![51]

Our task now is to demonstrate these three purposes being fulfilled during the period of the early Church. In Proposition 4 we will look specifically at tongues as a sign of judgment and grace. In Proposition 5, we examine tongues as a sign of racial and spiritual equality.

Proposition 4: "Tongues of the NT were foreign languages and, as such, were a sign to the Jews of God's judgment on Israel and His grace to people of all races (tongues)."

1. *The witness of the Acts of the Apostles.* Tongues were a sign to the Jews of a kingdom of God, not of this earth, but of heaven; not a kingdom involving an elect earthly nation which had been set aside (God's judgment), but an

---

later developed in the Palestinian, Davidic and New Covenant) are unconditional (compared to the Mosaic covenant). That is, these blessings do not depend on Israel's obedience, only God's promise. These unconditional blessings have only been postponed due to Israel's unbelief and rejection of Christ. They await their literal fulfilment during the Millennial period, when Christ returns to rule the earth.

[51] This ineffable grace must be seen as not only bringing in (engrafting - see below) of the Gentiles into God's blessing, but the positioning of individuals who are saved, Jew or Gentile, as both children and sons of God, through the person and work of the Only Begotten Son of the Father!

elect heavenly people called out from all nations (all flesh - tongues), a Body composed of Jews and Gentiles, sealed together in Christ through the Holy Spirit (God's grace). The Jewish disciples themselves bear witness of this in Acts 11:18: *"When they* [the disbelieving Jews] *heard these things,* [the fact of foreign tongues being miraculously spoken by the Gentiles] *they held their peace, and glorified God, saying, 'Then hath God also to the Gentiles granted repentance unto life.'"* - God's grace! Just what has happened here? There has been a change in the Jewish heart and mind. The foreign tongues showed them that in bringing the Gentiles into blessing (grace), God has set aside His programme for Israel as a nation (judgment). Now the miraculous nature of the foreign tongues authenticated the sign to a sign-seeking people - it was of God! The Holy Spirit had come as promised! They had to be shown there is no immediate earthly kingdom for Israel - it had been postponed. Don't forget, instances of God punishing Israel by blessing the Gentiles are clearly recorded in the history of the nation, as we have already seen in the days of Isaiah. The Lord Himself brings this very lesson to the disbelieving hearts of the Jews in Luke 4:23-29, when He quotes the examples of the widow of Sarepta and Naaman the Syrian leper. During times of Israel's unbelief, God sets His earthly people aside, and His grace extends to the Gentiles, their blessings are used to chastise the nation! You may also recall the penetrating message Paul applies to the present-day Jews in Acts 28 on this very thing, using again the words of Isaiah. *"Go unto this people,* [the Jews] *and say....the heart of this people* [the Jews] *is waxed gross...Be it known therefore* [because of what happened to their fathers through unbelief] *unto you,* [the present-day Jews], *that the salvation of God is sent unto the Gentiles...."* - God's grace! Again, listen to Paul's chiding of the Jews, *"....through their fall* [Israel's unbelief] *salvation is come unto the*

Gentiles, for to provoke them [the Jews] *to jealousy".*[52] Now when we combine this with God's programme for Israel and the Church (Chart B), we see clearly why tongues, as a sign of judgment to the Jews, had to be one of foreign languages. Some 'heavenly language' would never signal God's displeasure and punishment displayed through blessings given to people of other races. It has no racial, spiritual or historical meaning. The sign of foreign tongues spoke of God's judgment *and* His grace. It was in every way a distinct message to the Jews. The wormwood and the water of gall given to *'this people'*[53], of which tongues were a sign, were also a sign of God's grace, full-measure, pressed down and running over. It signalled to the Jews the bringing of the individual Jew *and* Gentile into His salvation, - *"...which at the first began to be spoken by the Lord, and was confirmed unto us* [the Jews] *by them that heard him; God also bearing them witness, both with signs and wonders and ....gifts of the Holy Ghost...".*[54] Within this great salvation there is neither bond nor free, Jew nor Gentile.[55] Can we then see, the unmerited offer of salvation to the Gentiles, of which foreign tongues were a sign, was a salutary signal of God's judgment on Israel - that God is now dealing with the church, not Israel as a nation?

2. *The witness of Romans 11 of God's grace to all and His judgment upon Israel, as seen through the Jews who rejected Christ.* Here, Israel, the natural branches and its national blessings, is symbolised by an olive tree - a cultivated olive tree, with its root in Abraham. Paul writing to the Christians at Rome teaches them the cultivated olive tree (Israel) has had *some* of its branches broken off - referring to the present-day unbelieving Jews. In their place, branches have been

---

[52] Romans 11:11. See also 10:19.
[53] Jeremiah 9:15; 23:15
[54] Hebrews 2:3-4. The word 'gifts' in v.4 is from *'merismos'*, dividing/distributing (gifts), rather than *charismata*' as in Corinthians.
[55] 1 Corinthians 12:13; Galatians 3:28

grafted from another tree - a tree symbolising the Gentiles - a wild olive tree. Because of its present unbelief (v.7), God has set aside Israel and has now in His grace engrafted the Gentiles (vv.11-12) - the wild olive branches (vv.17-24), a people who were *"..aliens from the commonwealth of Israel and strangers from the covenants of promise ..!"* [56] So Paul says to the Gentiles, God's grace has made you partakers of the promises of God.[57] Now note, foreign tongues were not just a sign of the Gentiles being included in divine blessings through divine grace.[58] Gentile tongues signalled something more. They revealed, as seen above and in more detail below, that Gentiles were now *one* with Jews in Christ![59] The Body of Christ comprises *one new man*, not Jew together with Gentile, for new cloth cannot be sewn onto an old garment any more than new wine be put into old bottles.[60] Tongues, foreign (Gentile) languages, were therefore the appropriate sign to them who 'believed not' - the Jews - concerning God's grace, and the admission and equality of all races and tongues in His blessings. Remember, the Jews knew nothing of the church and its spiritual equality encompassing all races and tongues. Their prophets never spoke of this at all. The presentation of the complete truth concerning the one Body, *"which in other ages was not made known unto the sons of men, as it is now revealed unto his holy apostles and prophets by the Spirit; that the Gentiles should be fellowheirs, and of the same body* [the church], *and partakers of His promise in Christ by the gospel"*,[61] had to wait for the call of Paul and

---

[56] Ephesians 2:12

[57] It is not the engrafting into the Body of Christ here (or anywhere else), but engrafting of Gentiles into the place of spiritual blessing of the Abrahamic Covenant (Gal 3: 7-28). The Church is not 'the Seed', in which the covenant is literally fulfilled, but is in a place of promise because of its relationship to the One in whom all covenant blessings will be consummated - Christ! After the 'fulness of the Gentiles', Israel will be taken up again in blessing (Rom 11:25-29)

[58] Isaiah, Zechariah

[59] We see this, the glory of the Church in Eph 2&3.

[60] Mark 2:21-22; Eph 2:19-20

[61] Ephesians 3:5

the completion of the Scriptures. The Scriptures when completed would reveal the whole picture. But what about the period before their completion? How was God to inform the Jews of this great truth? Well, God gave the Jews, a sign-seeking people, a sign of the unity within the Church and His judgment upon Israel; a sign of a miraculous nature, thereby confirming its Divine source - foreign tongues spoken miraculously through the Holy Spirit.

Proposition 5: "When tongues were spoken, they caused Jews to confess the spiritual equality between all races in Christ."

That is, tongues can be seen to be fulfilling their purpose stated above - convincing a sign-seeking people that all men in Christ are equal - again proving tongues were a sign directed to the Jews! Well, do racial and spiritual barriers crumble as a result of tongues? Now let us arrange a test. What would we expect to find if the tongues referred to by Paul in 1 Corinthians 14:21-22 were a sign to the Jews of God's judgment and His equal offer of salvation to the Gentiles? We would expect, on each and every occasion in Scripture where tongues were spoken:

(a) Jews would be in attendance;

(b) we would see a change in the belief of some or all of the Jews who were present. They would accept that God has now offered salvation to the Gentiles and they, with the Gentiles, are one in Christ - His Body!

Have we not already seen convincing evidence of this? And here we note, by accepting the existence of the Body of Christ, the Jews are in reality admitting Israel had been set aside - there cannot be two 'chosen' peoples at the one time! This is what made it so difficult for Jews to accept the existence of the Body of Christ. To accept one is to reject the other.

One further point needs to be made. A sign has to be consistent in its nature to be clear in its purpose - to be effective in changing the hearts and minds of the Jews. Any variance would only cause doubt and scepticism concerning God's purpose. We need to show therefore that tongues were of the same nature throughout Acts. Let us now put these matters to the test.

1. *Acts 2*. The words of Peter offer proof on this first public tongue-speaking occasion. First, foreign tongues spoken miraculously through the Spirit were the sign to the Jews who were present of the Holy Spirit's coming *"Ye men of Judea...This is that which was spoken by the prophet Joel"* (vv.14-16). Then the teaching - note the reference to the Gentiles *"Therefore let all the house of Israel* [the nation] *know assuredly, that God hath made that same Jesus, whom ye* [the nation] *have crucified* [in unbelief], *both Lord and Christ...Repent, and be baptized every one of you in the name of Jesus Christ for the remission of sins, and ye shall receive the gift of the Holy Ghost* [the Spirit Himself]. *For the promise is to you* [the Jews], *and to your children, and to all that are afar off* [the Gentiles]...*even as many as the Lord our God shall call."*(vv.36-39)[62] These disbelieving Jews then accepted Peter's message that salvation was available to them and indeed to all men (those afar off) through Christ. They were converted. Peter's message was confirmed by the miraculous speaking of Gentile languages witnessed at Pentecost: "*Then they* [the Jews] *that gladly received his word were baptized and the same day there were added unto them about three thousand souls"* (v.41).

2. *Acts 8*. There is little doubt that tongues were spoken here. The occasion furnishes us with another example where tongues proved to be a sign to the Jews of the Spirit of God indwelling Gentiles (here the Samaritans, who were their bitter

---

[62] Some interpret "those who are afar off" as Jews in other lands. However, the use of "you and your children" speaks of the totality of Jews, present and future, wherever they be. Also, the term "afar off" used by Luke here, has the same meaning when Paul uses it in Eph 2:17, referring to the great spiritual distance between Jews and Gentiles. This is underscored by the expression "even as many as the Lord our God shall call".

enemies), confirming their equality in Christ (v.17). We will take up this occasion in greater detail later.

3. *Acts 10.* Peter and the Jews with him were in the house of a Gentile, Cornelius. These Jews were believers in Christ, but had yet to believe and accept Gentiles as equals in Christ. What would convince them? There were no Scriptures available. Yet they needed to be brought to believe that God was now moving through the church, and Israel was set aside in judgment. Let us now observe how foreign tongues signal God's judgment and grace to these Jews. Before this encounter Peter, himself a proud and intolerant Jew, had to learn that *"What God hath cleansed, that call not thou common"* (v.15). A special revelation was given to Peter, for he was especially chosen to preach to the Jews - "*God hath shewed me* [personally] *that I* [Peter] *should not call any man common or unclean.*" This was the lesson of Peter's vision of the "*great sheet*" (vv.11-12). God has, as we have seen, brought in the Gentiles to be equal with the Jew in Christ, and set aside Israel as a nation in favour of a new people and a new generation. Listen again to the change in Peter's heart and mind toward the Gentiles, *"Ye know how that it is an unlawful thing for a man that is a Jew to keep company, or come unto one of another nation; but God hath shewed me that I should not call any man common or unclean."* (v.28) This equality had now to be demonstrated by a sign to Peter's Jewish brethren, to move them to belief. And, this is exactly what happens when they witness the events at the house of Cornelius. Hear now what they say: *"And they of the circumcision* [the Jews] *which believed* [in Christ] *were astonished* [i.e. they had not believed it before], *as many as came with Peter, because that on the Gentiles also was poured out the gift of the Holy Ghost. For* [the proof being] *they heard them* [the Gentiles] *speak with tongues* [foreign languages spoken miraculously], *and magnify God"* (vv.45-46). Here is clear evidence that it was tongues - the sign, foreign languages spoken miraculously, that caused

them to acknowledge the Holy Spirit had also come upon the Gentiles, i.e., the Gentiles manifested the same gift of the Spirit (foreign tongues) that Jews had miraculously spoken at Pentecost![63] Now mark Peter's rhetorical question to the Jews after they witnessed the Gentiles speaking in tongues. [Because of the confirming sign] *"Can any man forbid water, that these [Gentiles] should not be baptized, which have received the Holy Ghost, as well as we [Jews]"*(v.47). Note his words carefully here - *"as well as we"* (as well as we Jews - Acts 2)! The evidence (sign) of foreign tongues meant that none could deny the salvation in Christ of these Gentiles, that the Holy Spirit had come upon them also, and that Israel as a nation had been set aside. Fittingly, Paul declares to the Ephesian Gentile believers, *"Now therefore ye are no more strangers and foreigners, but fellowcitizens with the saints, and of the household of God; And are built upon the foundation of the apostles and prophets, Jesus Christ Himself being the chief corner stone".*[64]

4. *Acts 11.* When Peter returned to Jerusalem after the conversion of Cornelius and his household, the disbelieving Jews there rebuked him, for he had associated with unclean Gentiles: *"..they that were of the circumcision contended with him, saying, Thou wentest in to men uncircumcised* [Gentiles at the house of Cornlius] *and didst eat with them."*[65] In his defence Peter declared, *"...the Holy Ghost fell on them* [Gentiles], *as on us* [Jews] *at the beginning* [Pentecost]."[66] The evidence (sign) of the coming of the Holy Spirit was, as we know, the foreign tongues miraculously spoken. When

---

[63] Peter and the other Jews would have no difficulty in identifying the tongues spoken here as foreign languages. Peter himself would have acquired the gift of speaking foreign languages at Pentecost. The words and phrases of foreign languages are readily identifiable, as we ourselves know. Those of unintelligible languages are not. The like gift (Spirit of God) is given upon belief in Christ!

[64] Ephesians 2:19-20. See remarks on the Jerusalem Conference below (Acts 15)

[65] Acts 11:1-3

[66] Acts 11:15

these disbelieving Jews at Jerusalem heard this, we noted earlier, they accepted Gentiles as converts to Christ, confessing, *"Then hath God also to the Gentiles granted repentance unto life."*[67]

5. *Acts 15.* On this occasion the Jews confronted Paul and Barnabas claiming that Gentiles could not be saved unless they were circumcised *"after the manner of Moses"* (v.1). Their claim was raised at the conference at Jerusalem (vv.6-9). Peter, in opposition, declared how the Holy Ghost came upon the Gentiles *"even as he did unto us* [Jews]*"* and there was *"no difference between us* [Jews] *and them* [Gentiles]*"* (v.9). How could Peter draw such a conclusion? He was referring to the miraculously spoken foreign languages by the Gentiles, confirming the Spirit of God had come upon the Gentiles also. The Jews then held their peace and believed the Gentiles were one with them in Christ!

6. *Acts 19.* In this instance Paul meets twelve disciples of John the Baptist. They were Jews. How do we know they were Jews? Because John's baptism was *"to all the people of Israel"*, and concerned with national repentance.[68] The whole nation, the fore-runner declared, had fallen spiritually and must prepare for the Messiah's coming. As in Acts 2 and Acts 10, they received the Holy Ghost upon their belief in Christ and spoke in tongues. Using John's words, Paul preached *"..they should believe on Him* [Christ] *which should come after him* [the Baptist], *that is, on Christ Jesus."* They accepted Paul's message, enabling them to be baptized in the name of the Lord.[69] The foreign tongues spoken miraculously were a sign to these Jews that the followers of John the Baptist ('even as many as the Lord our God shall call') were also included in God's grace and the Body of

---

[67] Acts 11:18

[68] Acts 13:24

[69] Acts 19:4 It was when these disciples of John believed on Christ that they immediately received the Holy Spirit. The laying-on of Paul's hands was mere identification and not the imparting of the Spirit of God! (Refer to the discussion on the work of the Holy Spirit below).

Christ, and a sign to John's disciples, as well, that the Gentiles were no longer aliens.

In Acts 2, [8], 10, 11, 15 and 19 tongues were the sign that the Holy Spirit was now given unto all flesh, which we see testified to directly or indirectly in the presence of Jews. Disbelieving and sceptical Jews were being brought to confess that Gentiles were equally embraced by God's blessing in *redemption* - they were not simply 'proselytes of righteousness' or 'proselytes of the gate'! and, that they were one in the church, which is God's present purpose among men. Confession of the existence of the church and its equality of race meant acknowledgment that Israel, God's earthly race, had been set aside. Mark the deep conviction the tongue-speaking evoked within Peter. *"Forasmuch then as God gave them* [the Gentiles] *the like* [equal] *gift as He did unto us, who believed on the Lord Jesus Christ; What was I, that I could withstand God?"*[70] Peter and his Jewish brethren at Caesarea witnessed a sign of judgment and grace. The middle wall of partition between Jew and Gentile had been broken down. Miraculously spoken foreign tongues were an authentic divine sign that the enmity between Jew and Gentile had been abolished in Christ.[71] The nation of Israel had been set aside because of its rejection of God's Son. The hitherto aliens (the Gentiles) were not only brought in, but incorporated as one with the Jew in Christ. No wonder Peter's Jewish brethren were astonished. They were Christian believers but held racial prejudices against accepting Gentiles as spiritual equals. Mere reasoning would not shatter racial and spiritual barriers! It would make no impression on the Jewish heart concerning God's grace to the Gentiles and the

---

[70] Acts 11:17. 'Like' does not refer to a mere similarity or a resemblance (i.e. *homoios*), but an exactness or 'equality' in nature and substance as given by the word *isos*. "*ISOS (isos), "equal" (the same in size, quality, etc.), is translated "like," of the gift of the Spirit, Acts 11:17*". W. E. Vine "Expository Dictionary of New Testament Words", p. 342. This 'equality' is consistent with and reason for the judgment of Peter in Acts 15:9 that there was 'no difference' between the Jew and Gentile.
[71] Ephesians 2:14-15

setting aside of Israel. An accompanying sign was needed - foreign tongues, witnessed directly or indirectly through reliable Jews. This sign had to be a common one, otherwise where would be the confirmation that the Gentiles were now one in Christ with the Jews? We take this up again later!

The need for a sign of unity

From the above discussion and examination of Scripture, we can identify four dissident groups of people among whom the Spirit of God had to demonstrate the universal grace of God and unity in Christ - the *Jews*, the *Samaritans* (who were Gentiles), all other *Gentiles* and the *Ephesian* disciples. The Jews had no dealings with the Samaritans, and the Ephesian disciples, who were Jews, had little time for the Gentiles, or probably for those Jews who rejected John's baptism. In any event, they were of John![72] How was the Spirit of God to speak to them of the unity that exists in the Body of Christ? Bear in mind, this had to be done in the absence of the completed Scriptures. It had to be demonstrated immediately, so as not to hinder the progress and witness of the Church; and done in such a manner that would convince the Jews it was a message from God! A miraculous sign - supernaturally spoken foreign tongues - was needed for those who disbelieved the unity in Christ, who by their nature required a sign in order to believe. A sign - a consistent sign - was also needed for those who deserved a sign of judgment because of wilful unbelief. A sign of unity of the Body of Christ and the setting aside of Israel was thus given in the coming of the Holy Spirit amongst

---

[72] The Jews hated the Samaritans. *"..thou a Samaritan, and hast a devil"* (Jn 8:48). The Samaritans were Gentiles who adopted Judaism. They erected their Temple on Mt. Gerizim; their religious code was the Pentateuch; they also claimed Jacob as 'our father', and they, too, looked to the coming of the Messiah (Jn 4). John and James wanted fire from heaven to fall upon them (Lk 9:52-54). Note, no outward manifestations of the Holy Spirit took place when the Samaritans were converted (Acts 8:12). This occurred only after the apostles arrived. The explanation is given when dealing with the baptism by the Holy Spirit.

the Jews themselves (Acts 2), [to the Jews before the Samaritans (Acts 8)], to the Jews before the Gentiles (Acts 10) and to the Jews who were present at the conversion of the Ephesian disciples (Acts 19).[73] In addition, we have the indirect testimony to the disbelieving Jews in Acts 11 and 15. On all occasions, miraculously spoken foreign tongues - the sign - caused Jews to alter their spiritual attitude to men of all races and tongues! (We have included the Samaritan experience - Acts 8:17-18, with the addition here of the laying on of hands without which, given the deep rancour and prejudice between Jews and Samaritans, the occasion would signal an uncertain sound, which would cause and raise doubts over the unity and equality in Christ).[74]

Now, as remarked earlier, given the deep distrust between these four groups, imagine what would happen if the tongues spoken in Acts [8], 10 and 19, or within the Corinthian church, were 'heavenly', while those spoken in Acts 2 were foreign languages! The Jews at Jerusalem or anywhere else would

---

[73] We note here the order of the witness of tongues to the Jews is according to the Lord's command in Acts 1:8 - to be witnesses in Jerusalem first, then in Judea, then in Samaria and finally in the uttermost parts of the earth (Gentiles).

[74] In regard to tongues and the Samaritans, we may deduce that tongues were spoken. The presence of confirming signs (undoubtedly tongues), would be evidence that the Holy Ghost had fallen upon them, as noted by Simon the sorcerer and so he coveted the authority possessed by the apostles. Luke, the astute historian, would have noted any significant difference here had one existed. There were also many Jews in Samaria as a result of the dispersion from Jerusalem, to whom tongues would be a sign - as well as to the two Jewish Apostles. Further, Scripture does not always rehearse every detail in like events. There is no need to, if we who have been given the completed Word of God rightly divide it. In the accounts of water baptism of the Samaritans (Acts 8:16), Cornelius (Acts 10:48) and the Ephesian disciples (Acts 19:5), there are marked differences. The Ephesian disciples and the Samaritans were baptized 'in the name of the Lord Jesus', the house of Cornelius, 'in the name of the Lord'. In addition to this distinction, in all cases the Triune representation in Matt 28:19 ("in the name of the Father, and of the Son, and of the Holy Ghost") is not mentioned. Are we to conclude then, that these water baptisms were dissimilar, and, further, not that which was enjoined by the Lord in Matt 28? Indeed not! However, in the events of Acts 8:17 (Samaritans) and Acts 19:6 (Ephesian disciples), the laying on of hands is mentioned, but not so in Acts 10:48 (house of Cornelius). There, the laying on of hands was not required, rather than a case of it being unrecorded. The laying on of hands was a *ceremonial* act of 'religious' identification (Lev 3:2-13; 4:4-33), now employed to reconcile the two bitter rival *religious* camps, Jerusalem and Mt. Gerizim, and also to publicly identify with the converted Ephesian followers of the Baptist (another '*religious*' group requiring ceremonial confirmation).

have had none of it. Confusion would be just one of the problems. We would have seen the divisions and jealousies between these groups persist and deepen, severely undermining unity, hampering the progress of the gospel and marring the Christian witness! There would have been 'Jewish Christians', 'Samaritan Christians', perhaps even 'Christians of the Order of John' and 'Gentile Christians', denying the unity of the Body of Christ'. Any difference in tongues would create dire disunity! The Jews, who were a 'sign-seeking' people, would be very quick to notice any comparative difference in the tongues spoken on any occasion, especially when they are being asked to treat Gentiles and other groups as spiritual equals - a principle and practice decried and described as unclean and unlawful in the OT. They were very swift and persistent in putting differences between themselves and the Gentile believers. Remember their claims in Acts 15? But our God is a God of order. The Spirit's manifestation in all cases, tongues, were the same - foreign languages miraculously spoken. The tongues were the same because the message they signalled was the same. As noted, it was the conformity of the events that caused Peter and the other Jews to acknowledge the Holy Spirit had come on all flesh. The disbelieving and contentious Jews *"...held their peace, and glorified God, saying, 'Then hath God also to the Gentiles granted repentance unto life."* [75] The declaration of acceptance and unity by Peter stands for all these occasions - 'the Holy Ghost fell on them, as on us, as at the beginning'(i.e. Acts 2). Again, we ask how Peter could speak of 'God giving the Gentiles the like gift' (the Holy Spirit), if he heard them speak in tongues which were quite different to those spoken at Pentecost. In passing, we note in Acts 8, 10 and 19, unlike Pentecost, there were no tongues as of fire or sound of a rushing wind. Yet, all occasions were identified

---

[75] Acts 11:18. We are careful to note that now, here in Acts 11, the Jews have witnessed the inclusion of the Samaritans (Acts 8), the unique Gentile case, and the Gentiles per se (Acts 10), which enabled the Jews to make such a yielding declaration.

directly or indirectly with Pentecost. Why? Because tongues were the common sign, and to be the common sign, they must be of the same nature - miraculously spoken foreign languages - on all four occasions!

Some Conclusions

Have we passed the test? In Acts, tongues were consistently shown to be miraculously spoken foreign languages, spoken always in the presence of Jews. They were therefore an effective sign to the Jews of the coming of *one new man*, of the judgment of God upon Israel and the inclusion of the Gentiles in God's salvation. We saw how tongues changed the attitude of many Jews toward the Gentiles. We have seen the Spirit of God's clear witness during the early Church period concerning Israel's unbelief and how tongues were used as a sign to 'this people' because of it. Therefore, when we consider 1 Corinthians 14, we cannot deny that the record of Acts and the Spirit's teaching through Paul to the Corinthians - that tongues were a sign to them that believe not - are in perfectly harmony! We also saw at the start of this study that not one instance of speaking *to God* in tongues has been recorded in Acts by the Holy Spirit. How can there be, when the historical and doctrinal evidence show tongues given and used as a sign? Biblical history agrees with biblical teaching! The spread of the gospel in the early days of the church shows incontrovertibly that foreign tongues, miraculously spoken, were used throughout the early Church period as a sign to them that believe not (the Jews), as Paul declared to the misguided Corinthians. It is also abundantly clear that tongues were never given to assist the preaching of the gospel, as some have suggested. Some benefit may have been derived in the ability to preach to a foreigner in his native tongue, but this was not the purpose of the gift of tongues. *They were a sign!*

CHAPTER 5

The Nature of Tongues

Before examining the nature of tongues in the Epistles, four related questions were raised, their answers critical in identifying the context so necessary in determining the nature of the tongues spoken in the NT.

1. *How does the time of Pentecost relate to what we have studied so far?*[76] The historical and festive background to Acts 2 is important.[77] The Feast of Pentecost was one of three occasions when devout male Jews living in many different countries and districts (*Judea, Cappadocia, Pontus, Asia, Phrygia, Pamphylia, Egypt, Cyrene, Crete, Libya, Rome, Arabia...vv.9-11*), made their pilgrimage to their beloved Jerusalem. There were therefore at that time in Jerusalem, many Jews who were born and bred in many different lands, who spoke the languages of those lands - Gentile languages. It was also a feast and a time when devout Jews would commemorate God's blessing to the nation - the 'in-gathering' of the harvest. They would also remember that the harvest made provision for other peoples, the poor and the stranger - the Gentiles, *"And when ye reap the harvest of your land, thou shalt not make clean riddance of the corners of thy field when thou reapest, neither shalt thou gather any gleaning*

---

[76] The day of Pentecost is considered by many to be the day on which the Law was given by God on Mt. Sinai. If so it marks a grand correspondence with the day on which grace was given to all men!

[77] The significance of the coming of the Holy Spirit and tongues at Jerusalem, the city of the Lord, the embodiment of the pledge and pleasure towards His earthly people, and at Pentecost, is integral to our understanding of the purpose of tongues as a sign, and in identifying to whom it was a sign. This is examined further in Note 2.

of thy harvest: thou shalt leave them unto the poor, and to the stranger: I am the LORD your God." The tongues of strangers spoken at Pentecost in Acts 2 would be wholly consistent in this context.[78]

2. *Do not the exclamations of the observers in Acts 2 suggest ecstatic tongues?* The mocking and reference to drunkenness would have been due to the mingling of various Gentile languages, the general disbelief of the crowd, or a combination of both. (We note a similar situation identified by Paul. He chastises the Corinthian believers because many were speaking in tongues at the same time, giving the impression they were mad.) It could not have been the result of hearing unintelligible utterances, for this is categorically ruled out by Acts 2:5-6. Indeed, ecstatic utterances would fail as an effective sign, and not convince Peter and other Jews throughout Acts of the equality of all races and tongues in Christ. Speaking foreign tongues supernaturally would direct attention to the equal spiritual standing of all races, and the bringing of Gentiles into God's blessing. An incoherent babble would give no such signal. Indeed, anyone can speak 'gibberish' and claim it to be miraculous (and even profess to interpret the same and claim it also as miraculous). But, what is the test? Is it not to observe someone who has never spoken a particular foreign language suddenly acquire such an ability? This verifiable miracle is what arrested the attention of the disbelievers!

3. *Why was there no interpretation of the tongues in Acts 2?* No interpretation of tongues was required, for we read *"...every man heard them speak in his own [native] language."*[79] (Note the correspondence here with the statement by Paul in 1 Corinthians 14:21 concerning *"men of other tongues and other lips".*) Observe that in Acts 2 'tongue', or more precisely

---

[78] Leviticus 23:15-22. A 'stranger' (*ger*), refers to a person of foreign, non-Israelitish extraction who lives within Israel - a sojourner.

[79] Acts 2:6. 'Own' - *"idios, one's own, is translated "their proper" (KJV, "their own")";* W.E. Vine, "Expository Dictionary of New Testament Words", p. 154.

'tongues', - *glossais* (plural), is synonymous with *dialect* - 'languages', that which pertains to a particular geo-ethnic region.[80] The devout Jews had no need for interpretation for they testify *"...we do hear them speak in our tongues* [tongues that belonged to our part of the world - not heaven] *the wonderful works of God. And they were all amazed, and were in doubt, saying one to another, What meaneth this? Others mocking said, These men are full of new wine."*[81] This is not to say that some would not have understood some of the foreign languages spoken, but this was irrelevant on this occasion, because the range of tongues spoken meant that all foreign tongues represented were catered for. The exclamation by the audience, *"are not all these which speak Galilaeans"*, shows that they were amazed that these natives of Galilee were able to speak languages that were not from their own district or region, languages they identified and understood. How can people from Galilee speak languages that are not native to Galilaeans? Before passing, we note again the subject matter of the tongues was, *"the wonderful works of God"*; precisely, the mighty works of God. What these works were we are not told, but we can be assured that they related to divine mysteries concerning the gospel of Christ and the new dispensation.

4. *What about the 'new tongues' mentioned in Mark's*

---

[80] The term 'glossolalia' is often used in reference to speaking in tongues. Observe the interchanging use of *dialect* (language) in verses 6 and 8 with the use of *glossais* (tongues) in verse 11 of chapter 2, both words refer to the same incident. See also Rev 7:9. The whole passage in Acts 2 relates to actual languages proven by the context, historical setting and grammar. Concerning the latter we note: *'heterais glossais'* - the Jews at Pentecost spoke with other tongues - *"Other than their native tongues. Each one began to speak in a language he had not acquired and yet it was a real language and understood by those from various lands familiar with them. It was not jargon, but intelligible language"*. A.T. Robertson, "Word Pictures in the New Testament", Volume III p. 21. See also W.E. Vine, "Expository Dictionary of New Testament Words", - Tongue(s) - *"glossa"* - (b)*"the supernatural gift of speaking in another language without its having been learnt"*; Acts 2:4-13..... p. 142: On Acts 2:6, *"Tei idiai dialektoi"* - In his own language, *"Everyone that came heard somebody speaking in his native tongue"*. A.T. Robertson, "Word Pictures in the New Testament", Volume III, p. 23. On *"Dialektos"* - Language, *"....came to denote the language or dialect of a country or district"*. W.E. Vine "Expository Dictionary of New Testament Words", p. 309.
[81] Acts 2:11-13

gospel? Does this not suggest ecstatic tongues? In 1 Corinthians 12 we have the expression *"kinds of tongues"*. In verse 28 of the same chapter Paul refers to *"diversities of tongues"*. In Acts reference is made to *"other tongues"* and in Mark's gospel, *"new tongues"*. All these are the same. In Acts, *"other tongues"* refers to the fact that the Galilaean disciples spoke in languages other than their own. The *"new tongues"* referred to by the Lord in Mark 16, contrasts new languages with native languages, as often remarked today in the case of foreign immigrants having to learn a 'new language'. His Jewish disciples will speak Gentile languages! The expression *"kinds of tongues"* (or *"diversities of tongues"*) points to the diversity of languages given to the believers as evidenced at Pentecost. The word *"kind"* means 'different', hence the interposition of the word *"divers"* in the text.[82]

The tongues spoken in Acts 2 were then actual foreign languages acquired and spoken through the power of the Spirit of God - through 'supernatural means'! They were, as in Isaiah's day, actual foreign languages, not spoken through *natural* ability, but through *supernatural* ability, by Jews and Gentiles. At Pentecost, the manner was in keeping with the characteristic of the day - the coming of the Spirit of God. We have in Acts 2, accompanying God's judgment upon Israel, the coming of a period of grace characterised by the sending and in-dwelling of the Spirit of God Himself *"...He dwelleth with you, and shall be in you"*.[83]

Proposition 6: "Tongues were Gentile languages in the Epistles."

Despite all this, and accepting tongues throughout Acts

---

[82] *"'The new tongues',' kainos', of Mark 16:17 are the 'other tongues',' heteros', of Acts 2:4. These languages, however, were 'new' and 'different,' not in the sense that they had never been heard before, or that they were new to the hearers, for it is plain from v. 8 that this is not the case; they were new languages to the speakers, different from those in which they were accustomed to speak"*. W.E. Vine <u>"Expository Dictionary of New Testament Words"</u>; p. 109.

[83] John 14:17

were actual Gentile languages, how do you explain the need for interpretation of tongues in 1 Corinthians? After all, the phrase, *"unknown tongue"* in chapter 14, and the need for interpretation, suggest an ecstatic, heavenly language?

The proper method of interpreting Scripture

Paul does not refer to tongues explicitly as foreign or heavenly languages. He does not need to, because the record of the early Church period clearly reveals tongues to be foreign languages, and as we have seen, Paul's teaching about them in this Epistle demands they must be foreign languages! But, some still contend that because of the need for interpretation, the tongues in this Epistle are different, they are heavenly languages. Well, it most certainly does not lead to any such conclusion. Are there not circumstances where a foreign language can be unknown and must be interpreted if any understanding is to be gained? Our only justifiable course is to apply the test of Scripture and let Scripture interpret itself and match biblical history with biblical doctrine. All portions dealing with tongues in 1 Corinthians 14 (indeed within the whole Epistle), can only be interpreted using what Scripture itself has proved regarding the nature and purpose of tongues, viz:

1. Whenever tongues were spoken, as recorded in Acts, they were never used for prayer.

2. Whenever praying is observed in the record of the early Church period, tongues are never mentioned.

3. Tongues, as recorded in Acts, were always foreign languages spoken miraculously through the Spirit of God.

4. Tongues had to be foreign languages because of the need for a consistent message of racial unity in Christ, and to show that Israel has been set aside.

5. Tongues are declared to be a sign to them that believe not - 'this people' - the Jews (1 Cor 14:21-22).The expression 'other tongues' in 1 Corinthians 14:21 is a racial expression and is contrasted with the other racial expression, 'this

people'. The context being racial, tongues in this chapter cannot refer to some 'heavenly' language!

6. On every occasion tongues were spoken, we saw them used as a sign to them that believed not - the Jews (Acts), and as declared by Paul to the Corinthians!

So, for example, when Paul states, *"For he that speaketh in an unknown tongue speaketh not unto men, but unto God"* (1 Cor 14:2), a 'tongue' here, can only refer to a foreign language! What else can we conclude in the face of conclusive scriptural evidence? Our next step is to ask, given Paul is referring to a foreign language, "In what sense can a foreign language be spoken and not be understood by men, only by God?" Obviously it must be in a situation where it is unknown to those in whose presence it is spoken: God is then the only One who can understand it, for He understands all languages![84] The term 'unknown tongue' therefore, was included (quite correctly, although not part of Scripture) as an aid to interpretation, to highlight the fact that Paul was addressing a particular problem associated with tongue-speaking at Corinth. This problem was the speaking of a foreign language that could not be understood by all when the church gathered. Unfortunately, some have incorrectly taken the term 'unknown tongue' to mean 'a tongue or language not known to exist among men anywhere on earth' i.e. some mysterious ecstatic language - not one found among any of the natural languages of men. Such a notion may well fit the experience of tongue-speakers today, but it never finds any example in Scripture neither does it find any legitimacy given Paul's statement that tongues were a sign to them that believe not!

The need for interpretation

So, let us see why a need for interpretation is perfectly consistent with tongues being foreign languages. Refer to 1

---

[84] In Deuteronomy 28:49, 'tongue' (*lashon*) refers to a foreign language and God Himself speaks of it not being understood by the Jews.

Corinthians 12, where the gift of interpretation of tongues is first mentioned in Scripture. Paul makes the point forcibly that tongues were a gift given only to some believers (12:7-11, 30), and that there are diversities in tongues (12:10,28). There is nothing in chapter 12 that defines tongues as ecstatic, heavenly languages. The Greek root is that which is employed in Acts - *glossa*.

Now let us examine the public occasions in Acts again. In Acts 2 the company included a large number of foreign Jews - with at least 16 different languages represented. There was no interpretation here because there was no need for it, each person's language was spoken. We are specifically told this was the case! There was no interpretation (we gather), in Acts 10 or 19, which would mean the Jews who witnessed the miraculous speaking of foreign languages were, as was the case in Acts 2, able to understand what was being said. However, there would have been situations during the early church period where the gift of tongues would have been used, and some present could not understand the particular foreign language(s) spoken. To ensure those people were able to benefit by hearing the wonderful works of God, a gift of interpretation was given by the Holy Spirit.

So this was the situation at Corinth. There were those in the church who did not understand some of the foreign languages spoken through the gift of tongues! The Corinthians *chose* to use their Spirit-gifted ability to speak foreign languages when *praying during church meetings,* and *did so quite irresponsibly,* where the foreign language was unknown! Paul's instructions to the Corinthians on tongues relate particularly to their use within the local church. Note verses 19, 23 & 28 of 1 Corinthians 14- *"..yet in the church..."* *"If therefore the whole church come together into one place..."* and *"..let him keep silence in the church"*! Note also the continual reference to *"edify the church"* (vv.4,5,12...) and *"...except he interpret, that the church may receive edifying"* (v.5)! It is then precisely because the Corinthians decided to use tongues to pray within the church, where some did not understand the particular foreign language(s) spoken, that problems of an 'unknown tongue' arose among them, and Paul had to remind them of the importance of interpretation.

Tongues - the gift of foreign languages, says Paul, is purely a sign to the disbelieving Jews, and not given for edifying the church (cf. the gifts of knowledge and prophecy).[85] In Acts 2, those hearing foreign tongues spoken identified them as such, *"how hear we every man in our own tongue..?"* There was a very broad representation of different nationalities in the multitude. In any event, to be a sign, tongues do not have to be interpreted! All that is required is to witness the speaking of a Gentile language supernaturally, one that was not a native tongue.[86] Besides, here, within the church, the company of believers itself confirms in the most emphatic way the unity of the Body of Christ. The fact that Jews and Gentiles are seated together in prayer and supplication before God, each redeemed by the blood of Christ, is the clearest evidence of their oneness in Him. They do not need the sign of tongues to confirm this at all! Such corporate confirmation did not exist in Acts 2, [8], 10 or 19. Tongues were therefore needed as a sign on such occasions, as Paul points out to the Corinthians.[87]

Although tongues were a sign to those who believe not, and not to the church nor given for prayer, it was not improper, says Paul, to use them when the church came together if so desired - that is, as long as some benefit was derived. What

---

[85] See the exposition on 1 Corinthians 14 below.

[86] We do know the Ephesian disciples spoke in tongues. It is not said they used tongues when they magnified God (Acts 10:46), although this would appear to be so, given this was done in Acts 2. If this was the case, then we assume that the foreign tongues - the phrases used and the words spoken - were not unknown to the Jews from Joppa who travelled with Peter or, there was the gift of interpretation among them. We must remember, the regions around Jerusalem were populated and ruled by foreign nations, and the Jews living among them had to know something of their languages in order to conduct the affairs of life. (Joppa was a commercial port about 35 miles from Jerusalem.)

[87] This broadening witness, plus the coming of the completed NT Scriptures, meant that tongues ceased (see Proposition 10).

was the harm if a person who was gifted by the Spirit of God to speak Latin, for instance, used it in prayer or praise? No harm whatsoever providing Latin was known to all! Where Latin was unknown, it must not be spoken unless one could interpret it - so the substance spoken in the tongue may edify the church! The gift of interpretation was to enable edification where the audience did not know a particular tongue, so that any who did not know the language spoken could hear of the wonderful works of God. The gift of interpretation was not given to provide authentication of the tongues spoken! Scripture never teaches that the gift of interpretation was to prove tongues were of the Spirit of God. Foreign tongues were self-authenticating, in that it was a miraculous gift of the Spirit - someone who could not speak a foreign language suddenly acquired and retained the ability to do so, and moreover, spoke it when and where he willed (subject to Paul's directions in 1 Cor 14)! There could be no duplication of this by Satan! All he can come up with is a counterfeit, incoherent chatter that anyone can claim to be of the Spirit of God.

But why refer to interpretation as a *miraculous* gift of the Spirit when an unknown foreign language can be learned, and there would be no need for any interpretation? There is nothing miraculous in this at all! However, when someone *suddenly* acquires the ability to interpret a foreign language without having learned how, then surely we have a miraculous gift of the Spirit! After all, what is it we see at Pentecost? We witness people suddenly acquire the ability to speak a foreign language![88] Further, where would be the time or opportunity to learn them. We shall see that tongues, and the gift of

---

[88] The root cause of the error concerning tongues, as evidenced in some contemporary Commentaries, lies in their failure to systematically examine tongues in the Epistles in the light of Acts (and indeed the OT). Consequently, erroneous assertions arise, such as - the unknown tongues in 1 Corinthians cannot be foreign languages because we can learn them, they then cease to be unknown. There would then be no need for a gift of interpretation. This assertion is based on the false assumption that everyone at Corinth (any church or any other place) had the ability *and* the opportunity to learn not just one

interpretation, were only temporary gifts which ceased early in the Church period. Why waste time and effort learning languages! There were other more urgent tasks for the early Christians!

Interpretation or translation?

Interpretation is more than speaking and translating! I may speak a language yet not know the full meaning of what I say. I may also translate word-for-word and not understand the translation or be able to convey its meaning. When I am able to extract the full meaning of the speech or translation and impart it in words 'easy to be understood', then I am interpreting.[89] This explains how a person could possess the gift of a tongue which was unknown to him, and why a person

foreign language, but many! A first response here is to ask why could not the sounds of a miraculous/angelic language also be learnt, as one would learn any new language? Surely the tongues of angels - heavenly languages or indeed any language, must have a structure, otherwise it ceases to be a language. And, if it has a structure, then it is capable of being learnt. We do well to mark the work of missionary translators who have interpreted many strange and difficult dialects, each with their 'own sounds'. The gift of interpretation was given so that visitors or those within the church etc., who did not know a particular foreign language, could receive immediate benefit, without having to undertake language studies. What took place at Pentecost? Christians (simple unlearned Galileans), instantly acquired the ability to *speak* foreign languages, i.e. *without* the rigours of academic learning or seasons of expatriate existence. A further example of the confusion that arises when we fail to consult Acts on this matter is found in relation to 1 Cor 14:22-23. Because the prophet's voice of the OT was unheeded, we are told, God punished Israel by having the Jews hear speech that could not be understood. Therefore, during the time of the rejection of Christ and His ministers, it is 'supposed' God again punishes the unbelievers by exposing them to speech that was ecstatic (unintelligible). However, such an argument fails to understand that the punishment meted out to disbelieving Israel was, in fact, the exile and captivity - domination by Gentile nations. Hearing foreign tongues was a mere *sign* of this punishment! Does not Paul say this very thing? Is this not the reason he quotes Isaiah? What can be more obvious? The foreign tongues were not themselves the punishment, only the sign of it! Furthermore, in regard to NT tongues, where does punishment through unintelligible languages arise if those unintelligible languages could be made intelligible through a gift of interpretation? We are then faced with the unsavoury spectre of contradiction in divine dealings in the case of unknown tongues - Paul's command that they must be interpreted so that all may understand and benefit (v.5), as opposed to not interpreting them so that divine punishment upon the unbelievers could be signalled - a contradiction as a consequence of failing to visit the whole of Scripture!

[89] Interpreters who have assisted in the proclamation of the gospel in English to non-English speaking people, have stressed a literal translation does not always give the meaning of what is spoken and can in some cases, convey the wrong sense.

who had such a tongue would benefit himself and the church if he also had the gift of interpretation.

Further, note that a tongue would be 'unknown to the church', if it is unknown to just one member. It would not be expected that everyone in the church, or those unbelievers coming in and observing the church (1 Cor 14:23), knew all Gentile languages as there were some sixteen spoken in Acts 2! The gift of tongues still had a role to play in this early Church period. They were not to cease yet, for there was need of them as a sign until the canon of Scripture was completed. However, to meet occasions where the foreign language was unknown, outside or within the church, the gift of interpretation was given, that all may be edified.[90] We see then, it is the *company* in which a tongue is spoken that causes it to be unknown and in need of interpretation.[91] Clearly, if a tongue (foreign language) was known (understandable) to the church, then there was no need for interpretation!

We need to reassert here and again when looking at chapter 14, that the mere fact that tongues are associated with interpretation in chapters 12 and 14, does not and cannot *by itself*, classify tongues mentioned in these chapters as being different to those spoken in Acts, i.e. something other than actual foreign languages. It can never, through an honest appraisal of the facts, deny the identical nature between tongues in Acts and tongues in 1 Corinthians, especially in the light of a perfectly simple, straightforward, and above all

---

[90] As for the other churches during that time, a few possibilities exist: (1) Tongues may not have been spoken among them. This would be the more likely case, since all tongue-speaking occasions recorded in Acts were outside the church. (2) Tongue-speaking was done with interpretation and order. (3) The company was such that everyone knew the tongues spoken. Paul's reference to the Spirit's bestowals in 1 Cor 12, suggests that the gift of interpretation was not confined to Corinth. It was given to be used during the early NT period, if and when it was needed.

[91] However, this is not to say that the unlearned and unbelievers (the context can only mean that these are Jews, and there were many Jews in Corinth - Acts 18:5) who visit the church cannot be influenced unto belief by the operation of the gift of tongues - a sign - even though tongues were not given for that purpose! The abuse that Paul refers to in 1 Cor 14:23, is not just in regard to tongues being unknown, (this is dealt with by Paul earlier in the chapter and in vv. 26-33), but tongues being spoken at one time!

scripturally validated explanation as to how a foreign language can be 'unknown' to those present. As noted earlier, Scripture itself refers to tongues as foreign languages which are not understood i.e. 'unknown', when Israel was spoken to by God in judgment.[92] Paul in writing to the Corinthians does not present the slightest hint of any difference between the tongues in Acts and those spoken by the Corinthians. Indeed, let us be mindful that nowhere in the narrative of the life of the early church in Acts, which takes us to a period after Paul's correction concerning tongues to the Corinthians, do we find any reference to a gift of 'unknown' tongues.

Proposition 7: "The *tongues of angels* were not the 'unknown' tongues of 1 Corinthians."

We turn now to 1 Corinthians 13, where Paul continues his instruction on the correct use of tongues, and we must note the context given by verse 31 of chapter 12. What exists in chapter 13 then, to suggest tongues are anything other than foreign languages? Facing irrefutable evidence that the gift of tongues in Acts were foreign languages, that tongues were for a sign, and seeing the need for interpretation does not itself mean tongues are ecstatic, some within the studies appealed to this passage to suggest the existence of two *gifts* of tongues: one of foreign languages, the other mysterious heavenly languages that required interpretation. The *'tongues of men'*, they suggested, refers to the gift of speaking foreign languages; the *'tongues of angels'* refers to the gift of speaking ecstatic, 'unknown' languages!

We agreed, the *'tongues of men'* refers to the miraculous gift of speaking foreign languages. The expression, *'of men'*, clearly proves this, as does the context. Paul states, *'if'* I speak with the tongues of men! Therefore these tongues cannot refer to the foreign languages we learn and *'do'* speak through natural ability!

---

[92] Deuteronomy 28:49

There is no doubt Paul identifies two types of tongues, or languages - those of men as gifted by the Spirit, and those of angels. However, the tongues of angels were not the 'unknown' tongues spoken by the Corinthians; the tongues of angels were not a spiritual gift at all! Firstly, if there were two distinctive gifts of tongues, we would expect Scripture to speak of *'gifts'* of tongues and declare their different nature and purpose, especially when tongues were being misused at Corinth. Scripture only speaks of *the 'gift'* of tongues, indicating one type (foreign languages) and one purpose (a sign). Did we not see this on the occasions tongues were spoken in the life of the early church? When Paul corrects the Corinthians in chapter 14, there is never even a hint of two such gifts; 'tongues' he says, 'are for a sign'. If there were two gifts, one of foreign languages and one of ecstatic languages, then there would be two purposes. Where do we find two purposes for tongues in 1 Corinthians 14:21-22, or anywhere else in Scripture? Remember, the record of Scripture is void when it comes to tongues being given for prayer.

It is here that modern-day tongue-speakers call upon 1 Corinthians 14:28! They claim the statement *"Let him speak to...God"*, refers to an instruction to use ecstatic - angelic (heavenly) languages, to speak to God in prayer. We will address this in greater detail later. For the present, assume verse 28 does speak of using an ecstatic angelic tongue in prayer to God. This would mean there would be two gifts of tongues, because we have proved the tongues gifted in Acts related to foreign languages. Now remember the confusion over tongues within the church at Corinth. This ungodly situation calls for utmost clarity from Paul in his teaching on the purpose of tongues. It means he must identify the two gifts of tongues and clearly distinguish their purposes. Verse 28 is part of his corrective ministry to the Corinthians on tongues. If there were two gifts of tongues, Paul has failed miserably in making this clear and has confounded the church at Corinth (and all of us!). Why? In the same chapter, he has just made a clear statement that tongues have only one purpose, they are for a sign to unbelievers (v.22)! Where are his words teaching one gift of tongues, foreign languages as in Acts 2 etc., is a sign, and the gift of tongues - an ecstatic variety, are given as a prayer language? Furthermore, he compounds the confusion in at least five other ways! Firstly, he uses the same word 'tongues', the same Greek root 'glossa', not just in verses 22 and 27, but also in chapters 12, 13 and throughout chapter 14![93] Secondly, he associates the sole purpose of tongues in his correction in this chapter, with a term used exclusively to refer to Jews - 'this people'. He creates a context which is wholly racial. Thirdly, he goes further and establishes a link between this sole purpose of tongues and the spiritual condition of the Jews (unbelief). Fourthly, he states tongues are for a sign and states the Jews are a people who seek signs, provoking the logical association between the two statements, producing the conclusion tongues are for a sign to the Jews. And finally, he seems to have ignored historical evidence to hand showing how tongues, as miraculously spoken foreign languages, were used as a sign to Jews.

When correcting the Corinthians on tongues, was Paul being indiscriminate in using the same Greek root throughout? Is he 'waffling' when he associates the purpose of tongues with the Jews, their history and spiritual condition? Was he in error when he declared tongues are for a sign and the Jews seek signs, drawing us into a misleading connection between tongues as a sign and a people who require signs because of their unbelief? Obviously the answer is a resounding "No" to each question! The faithful Spirit-inspired apostle, who especially cared for the Corinthians, has not failed them (or us). Paul's mindful correction teaches there

---

[93] Apart from 1 Corinthians, Paul uses 'glossa' in Rom 3:13, 14:11 and Phil 2:11. In each case reference is to 'natural', languages. In Rom 14:11 he again quotes the words of Isaiah (45:23).

was only one gift of tongues given by the Spirit of God. Luke's record in the Book of Acts which unfolds the witness of the Spirit during the early Church period, shows us there was only one gift of tongues spoken in that period. If the tongues of chapters 13 and 14 were heavenly, angelic languages, then why does Paul not refer to them as such throughout his correction of the Corinthians?

To press the issue a little further, which gift of tongues was Paul referring to in verse 8 of chapter 13 when he said that tongues will cease? If he is identifying two gifts of miraculous tongues in verse 1, then he must include both when declaring they shall cease! Again we would have Paul being quite confusing, for in verse 8 he makes no distinction between two gifts of tongues! Moreover, we are left with a very interesting question. Modern-day tongue-speakers believe tongues will cease when the Lord returns to take us to heaven. If angelic, heavenly languages are included here, then why would they cease just when they would be most needed? Why does Paul not say that tongues are as abiding, or as great, as love? We take up the cessation of tongues later.

There were a variety of tongues however, which is clearly identified in the 'Acts of the Holy Spirit' chapter 2, where some sixteen foreign languages were spoken.

What then do we make of the statement *"let him speak to God"*? This, as we shall note later, simply refers to the case where a person speaks a tongue not known to the church *and there is no interpreter.* Clearly, if there is an interpreter, he may speak in the unknown tongue and direct his words to the church. However, if there is no interpreter and he wishes to speak within the church using this unknown foreign tongue, let him do so silently. Let him speak to God and to himself only. Do not use it to pray audibly, for the church will not understand. How can they say 'amen' or be edified? The whole matter is clear and unmitigated. Little wonder modern-day tongue-speakers shy away from a thorough study of this portion of God's Word, preferring to interpret it according to their experience and not according to its context which is the OT and the historical record in Acts. There are no instances in Scripture where believers are found speaking or praying in the language of angels! Where do we read words such as "we do hear them speak (pray) with the tongues of angels"? "They magnified God with the tongues of angels"? Do we hear the apostles testifying "these men are speaking (praying) in the tongues of angels"? "They spoke to God in the language of angels"? Consider again why, when solemnly reminding us that our conversation is in heaven and that our conversation must be holy, the apostles are never inspired by the Spirit of God to exhort us to speak in heavenly languages - the tongues of angels![94] If there were two gifts of tongues, with their respective purposes, why is this distinction never seen during the life and circumstances of Christians of biblical times or in Paul's teaching?

What then are these tongues of angels, and where do they fit in?[95] The term 'tongues of angels' is only mentioned once

---

[94] Philippians 3:20; 2 Pet 3:11

[95] The Rabbis have always regarded the Hebrew language as the language of angels. This is not meant here. The term 'tongues of angels' has to have an external source/ origin, otherwise it becomes an invention. If we agree that it has a source external to the mind of Paul, then we can only trace it to Paul's heavenly translation (which predates both Corinthian Epistles - 2 Cor 12:4), or to a special revelation given by the Spirit to Paul - the term is never mentioned anywhere else in Scripture. If it relates to his heavenly translation, speaking these 'heavenly' tongues is prohibited *(not to be quoted - "unspeakable words which it is not lawful for a man to utter"* - in private or in public). If, on the other hand, it is of a special revelation or purely an invention used for illustration, it again extinguishes the claim of modern-day tongue-speakers who say they are speaking a heavenly language! It would appear likely the tongues of angels is associated with Paul's heavenly translation, as he does not claim it to be a direct revelation. (2 Cor 1-3). *Three orders of tongues:* At the highest order, we have tongues of angels (languages that are confined to the heavenlies), followed by the tongues of men spoken through supernatural ability (the gift of tongues) and lastly, the tongues of men spoken through natural ability. This lowest order pertaining to fallen man arises from God's judgment upon man's pride at Babel (Gen 11, before God had chosen for Himself an earthly people), an order of communication which is the result of man's disobedience and rebellion - another instance where tongues are used in judgment. The gift of tongues was the sign of God's grace and judgment (Acts 2), to convict Jews of their disobedience (1 Cor 14:22-23) and to signal the bringing of both individual Jew and Gentile into His family as sons of God. The world is still under the judgment of Babel. Such heavenly languages are not to be evidenced amongst men. There will be, during the Millennium, a unified language (Zeph 3:9).

in Scripture. When it is mentioned, it is to rebuke believers who are carnal and immoral, who had lost sight of the real purpose of tongues. They are merely a device in Paul's argument to correct the Corinthians. We have noted that these carnal believers were using tongues to bring glory to themselves, causing division within the church. The tongue-speakers believed the gift of tongues was a superior gift of the Spirit and therefore they themselves were superior. Paul then sets about stating why this is not so. He begins by identifying the most valuable possession and pursuit in a believer's life - love (*agape*), the love which has God as its primary object and expresses itself in obedience to Him. Paul straightaway brings the Corinthians to compare love with tongues. He speaks hypothetically and in general terms - hypothetical possessions and hypothetical states: "even if 'I' can have the gift of speaking foreign languages (if I speak with the tongues of men), and *even if* I can speak with the tongues of angels, the highest form of communication, and I have not love, I am nothing!" [96] He also places love as greater than the gifts of prophecy and of knowledge, lest the possessors of these gifts believe they are outside his correction. The contrasts continue, the possession and pursuit of love are declared to be superior to other hypothetical states: *even if* I have perfect faith,[97] *even if* I give all my goods to the poor, *even if* I become a martyr - and have not love, I have nothing! He then refers specifically to tongues and declares they are temporary - they will cease. Love is the only perpetuity here.

Chapter 13 offers no support, only detriment to the assertion that the Corinthians were speaking or praying in some ecstatic tongue and that there is a difference between

---

[96] Though - or essentially 'if'. "*...the 'if' introduces a possibility connected with the future*". W.E. Vine "The Collected Writings of W E Vine"., Volume 2 p.146.

[97] *pistis* (faith). The context here renders it as "wonder-working" faith as in 1 Cor 12:9. It is spoken as a special *gift* therefore cannot be the saving faith or everyday faith. See A.T. Robertson. "Word Pictures in the New Testament" Vol. IV p. 177.

the tongues here and those in Acts. The matter before Paul and the Corinthians is the "tongues of men" - foreign languages, supernaturally spoken, and their regulation, never the tongues of angels!

Ecstatic pagan tongues

The pagan religions of the day were noted for ecstatic speech from their appointed prophetesses and priestesses who, it was claimed, were also given a 'gift of prophecy' from various deities: the prophetess at Delphi, Pythia of the god Apollos; the various sibyls, the most infamous being the sibyl at Cumean. Pagan worship was endemic at Corinth. The temple of Aphrodite lay within its precincts with its vestal virgins and prolific sensual rituals.

The existence and prevalence of ecstatic tongues among the pagan religions, and the fact that the city of Corinth was a den of paganism, furnishes circumstantial support that the tongues referred to by Paul in his letter to the Corinthians were not ecstatic languages. If the tongues spoken by the Corinthians were ecstatic, it would be inconceivable that Paul would, in a letter of correction on tongues to them, fail to make a distinction between ecstatic tongues spoken through the Spirit of God and ecstatic tongues spoken though pagan spiritualism. How could he fail to make and dwell on such a distinction given:

(a) the gross misunderstanding and confusion over tongues in the church at Corinth;

(b) the lack of spiritual discernment within the church at Corinth because of their carnality;

(c) the endemic paganism within the city of Corinth;

(d) the serious problem concerning paganism within the church itself (ch.8).

In these circumstances, we would expect Paul to warn and instruct the Corinthians as to how they were to discern between ecstatic tongues spoken through spiritism and ecstatic tongues spoken through the Spirit of God. How were they to authenticate the 'true' ecstatic tongue? What test does he put before them? The gift of interpretation you say! But, this gift was never given to discern the *source* of tongues or to test their *substance*, only to relay their *sense*, and then only in particular circumstances! There is no warning here by Paul to test the spirits as issued by John in his first Epistle. Where in this epistle to the Corinthians does Paul press for the use of the gift of discerning of spirits when tongues are to be spoken? Nowhere! Why? The source of the tongues spoken at Corinth - the Holy Spirit, was evident through the consistency in the nature of the gift of tongues throughout the whole historical period - foreign tongues. The clear fact is that ecstatic tongues are never in Paul's contemplation when he corrects the Corinthian church concerning their tongue-speaking.

Weight of evidence

If my reader covets or speaks in tongues, I would ask him/her to consider earnestly the weight of scriptural evidence against present-day tongues considered to this point. Israel continued on a path of disobedience and unbelief. God in His grace, by *"a new and living way"*, brings His salvation to all men - Jews and Gentiles - both incorporated in the Body of Christ.[98] In His judgment, He sets aside a disbelieving Israel (this people) and brings Gentiles into blessing. How, then, was God to demonstrate these purposes to Israel? They are a people dependent upon signs. In keeping with His past dealings with Israel and their unbelief, at Pentecost and during the transitional early Church period, we see God speaking to them using a sign. Here, as we have noted, the sign of tongues (foreign languages supernaturally spoken), was in keeping with the coming of His Spirit and the need to demonstrate unity between Jew and Gentile within the Church and thus foster the church's witness and growth. Accordingly,

---

[98] Hebrews 10:20

whenever foreign tongues were supernaturally spoken in Acts, they were interpreted as a sign, indicating that Gentiles had been included in 'so great salvation' through Christ (refer to the testimony of Peter, Paul and the many other Jews in Acts). Furthermore, we find Paul confirming all this by his use of Isaiah's words to instruct the Corinthians, identifying the purpose of tongues (a sign), and to whom they were a sign (those that believe not - *this people*, the Jews - those people who require signs). He reminds them that tongues were given only for a sign, unlike the gifts of prophecy and knowledge. He put the ability to speak foreign tongues miraculously in their place, they are lesser than love. Even if they spoke in the tongues of angels, and had not love, they had nothing. Underlying this is of course the historical and spiritual background concerning Pentecost, its meaning and timing - the Church, wherein both Jew and Gentile are one.

But then, if tongues are a sign to the disbelieving Jews, why are they not required today? Is not Israel continuing in disobedience, and therefore are tongues needed as a sign of judgment today? We need to understand, God is not dealing with Israel *nationally* today, despite claims of Zionists and 'regatherings', which are of things to come. God has set the nation aside. The judgment, of which tongues were a sign, has been enacted. God has scattered and sifted the house of Israel *"as corn is sifted in a sieve"* throughout all nations.[99] The *"children of Israel shall abide many days without a king, and without a prince, and without a sacrifice, and without an image, and without an ephod, and without teraphim"*.[100] Why? Because the house of Israel, in unbelief, crucified Him who is both Lord and Christ.[101] This was the essential message of the sign of tongues to the Jews during the transitional early Church period. There is therefore no sign to the house

---

[99] Amos 9:9; Luke 21:24
[100] Hosea 3:4
[101] Acts 2:36

of Israel today, as that house is not constituted. The Jews, indeed everyone, must look to the (completed) Word of God for salvation, and the truth concerning the Body of Christ, not to signs! There will, however, be a regathering of the Jews when the nation is welded together. For, although presently set aside, God's earthly people have not been cast away. He will resume dealing and communing with Israel in the Day of the Lord, accompanied by signs of blessing and wonders (Joel 2).[102]

May we again state that there are no signs given to us today. Are we to look for signs to reach the Jews and proffer wisdom to reach the Gentiles, when it comes to *personal* salvation? *No,* says Paul! Indeed, the Jews ask for a sign and the Gentiles seek wisdom, *"But we preach Christ crucified,...unto them which are called, both Jews and Greeks,.."*. Why? Because God, who spoke in past times through the prophets, has *"in these last days spoken unto us by His Son"*; because the gospel of Christ *"is the power of God unto salvation, to every one that believeth; to the Jew first, and also to the Greek [Gentiles]"*.[103] The just shall live by faith (not signs). Faith cometh by hearing and hearing by the word of God.

---

[102] Romans 11:1 (Chart B)
[103] Rom 1:16-17; 1 Cor 1:22-24; not just Christ, but Christ crucified! Heb 1:1-2.

CHAPTER 6

The Limited Bestowal
and Use of Tongues

It is vital that we understand that the possession and use of the gift of tongues was wholly decided according to the sovereignty of God. We must avoid the error of bringing tongues or any spiritual gift within the realms of human determination.

Proposition 8: "Not all believers in the early church were given the gift of tongues."

Many teach that all believers should speak in tongues. This astounding claim is another example of abandoning sound biblical study. The matter is made so clear in 1 Corinthians 12:30, it hardly needs comment. However, because this error is widely circulated and is of a nature to cause anxiety to many believers, especially those young in the faith who are told they are 'missing out' if they do not speak in tongues, we must address it fully. In verses 7-11 of chapter 12, Paul, under the inspiration of the Holy Spirit, makes it perfectly clear that it is the Spirit of God who distributes the various spiritual gifts according to His will. Take verse 8 as an example - the jealousy over spiritual gifts at Corinth provokes Paul to stress that to *"one* [person] *is given by the Spirit the word of wisdom; to another* [person] *the word of knowledge by the same Spirit"*! This distribution involves all gifts stated in these verses, and includes tongues - *"to another* [person]

prophesy; to another [person] *divers* [different] *tongues"*.[104]
From this passage alone it is plain not all believers were given the gift of tongues. This, of course, does not mean one person could not be given more than one gift. Paul himself possessed the gifts of tongues and healing. The Holy Spirit is here being identified as the one source, the person who has sovereignty in deciding who is given which gift(s). How wrong it is then for anyone to try to usurp this imperial work of the Spirit of God.

Now there are further proofs supporting this proposition. In verse 11 the Spirit of God is again identified as the One who divides (distributes) to each man according to His will. Then in verse 30, we have the final word on the matter *"...have all the gifts of healing? do all speak with tongues? do all interpret?"*[105] These questions are rhetorical, i.e. each demands a negative response: 'have all the gifts of healing?' No! 'Do all speak in tongues?' No! 'Do all interpret?' No![106] The Corinthians are asked to admit to these facts, so that they can benefit from Paul's rebuke, that they should cease their childish envy of the believers amongst them who had the more spectacular and temporary spiritual gifts e.g. tongues. After all, it is the same Spirit who distributes these gifts. If you are going to covet gifts, covet *"earnestly the best gifts"* (v.31).[107] In His sovereignty, the Spirit of God decides who will be given which gift(s), distributing them as He wills

---

[104] The faith spoken of in verse 9 is not the saving faith we all exercise when we are saved, but an extraordinary gift of faith, enabling a believer to enter into the deeper conflicts that they were to experience in their life as a Christian.

[105] 1 Corinthians 12:30. 'Do each and every one of you have the gifts of healing' etc?

[106] *me pantes, "the me expects a negative answer within each group"*. A.T. Robertson. "Word Pictures in the New Testament" Volume IV p.174.

[107] The exhortation by Paul to the Corinthians to desire and covet spiritual gifts is qualified. First, it only applied to the 'best' gifts, which excluded tongues. Second, the motive for coveting/desiring is not for personal exaltation. The context clearly indicates that it is not a case of desiring the better gifts for their own sake. The desire is in regard to their *use*, rather than their acquisition, to build up (edify) the believers, as often expressed in chapter 14. The gifts were *"given to every man to profit withal"*.(1 Cor 12:7). Best *"(meizon)* "greater," is translated "best" in 1 Cor 12:31, "the best gifts," greater, not in quality, but in importance and value". W. E. Vine "Expository Dictionary of New Testament Words"; p. 121.

to each believer, to accomplish His ministry through individuals. Paul's lesson, unity in diversity, is reinforced by his illustration of how different parts of the human body are, in themselves, unique and yet indispensable to each other. It is silly for the eye to seek to become the hand or, can the eye say to the hand, 'I have no need of thee' (v.21)? It is equally vain and silly for an individual believer to want to possess spiritual gifts bestowed by the Spirit of God to another, for the Holy Spirit bestows these gifts according to His knowledge of what is required for the faith and its witness - each gift complementing the other!

The diversity in gifts, a plea for unity and responsibility in the light of it, is also taught in Romans 12:1-6 *"...all members have not the same office* [sphere of responsibility]*:so we, being many, are one body in Christ, and every one members one of another. Having then gifts differing according to the grace that is given to us* [not the degree of faith in us], *whether prophecy,* [prophesy] *according to the proportion of faith; or ministry,* [let us minister] *on* [in our sphere of] *ministering ..."*(vv.4-7). Which particular gift(s) a believer possesses is the result of God's *grace*, not the measure of our *faith*. Therefore there is no ground for self pride. Conditions for responsible exercise of these gifts have also been given in order to recognize diversity, prevent highmindedness and preserve unity. When it came to the gift of prophecy (forthtelling) it had to be *used* according to the measure of faith. This is linked to verse 3, *"according as God hath dealt to every man the measure of faith"*. Do not speak of things beyond the sphere of your God-given faith; for the gift of ministry, *in* the sphere of ministering (not in another sphere of responsibility);[108] for the gift of teaching, *in* teaching (not in another sphere of responsibility); the gift of exhortation,

---

[108] Some have, in desperation taken this line of verse 3 out of its context to support the notion that the receiving of gifts is directly proportional to the measure of our faith. We take this matter up below.

in exhortation (not in another sphere of responsibility); the gift of giving, do it with simplicity (liberality); the gift of ruling, do it with diligence; etc.

Now, we must make two points before passing on. Firstly, Paul's declaration to believers at Corinth in 1 Corinthians 14:5, *"I would that ye all spake with tongues...."*, is, in fact, a rebuke not an exhortation that they should all speak in tongues. For Paul (or anyone else) to suggest all believers should speak in tongues would be a gross presumption of the work of the Spirit of God, who distributes spiritual gifts as *He wills*! What does Paul mean then in verse 5? He speaks hypothetically, and we can paraphrase his teaching as follows, 'If I had my way, you would all speak in tongues which would put an end to your childish rivalry over this more spectacular spiritual gift. But it is not my wish, but the will of the Spirit of God, that you function as members of a body, where there is a diversity of gifts yet unity'.

Secondly, the gift of tongues was not to be coveted (not earnestly desired, individually or collectively). This was not one of the better gifts (they were just a sign, 14:21-22, and a temporary one, ch. 13). Therefore, those believers at Corinth who were not given the gift of tongues by the Spirit of God, should stop coveting tongues and desire to exercise the more profitable gifts of the Spirit within the church.

Despite all this, many insist we all should speak in tongues. They ignore the fact that Scripture never speaks of coveting tongues (only says not to forbid them being spoken, for they had a role to play in the early Church period, v.39). They fail to comprehend that not every believer in the early church had this gift, because the Spirit of God never intended every believer should have it; that tongues were a temporary sign of the Spirit, signalling the unity of the body of Christ, especially required in the early days of the church. In short, they are blind to the very witness of the Spirit of God who they claim has given them their 'gift'.

Proposition 9: "Tongues were never given as a means of communication between a believer and God."

The belief that tongues are a medium for prayer between a believer and God was argued on the basis of 1 Corinthians 14:2,28. It should be clear from our earlier discussion that speaking to God in tongues privately or in public was never the *purpose* of the gift of tongues.

We noted earlier what Paul meant when he said, *"..and let him speak to himself and to God"*. Let us review this statement. Firstly, tongue-speakers had control over when and where they chose to use this gift, otherwise why would Paul issue regulations to this end? Therefore, a person who had the gift of tongues could choose to pray in the local tongue or in the gifted foreign tongue(s); they were never 'out of control'.

Secondly, we note a person can pray audibly or silently during church meetings. Paul's instruction then is this: If a person has the gift of speaking a foreign language, and this foreign language is unknown to the church and there is no interpreter, then if he insists on using that tongue to pray in the church, let his prayer be a silent one - let him keep it to himself and to God. Otherwise he brings confusion into the church. Now, if he offers a silent prayer in church in the local tongue because he wishes to share an intimacy with his God, is he not speaking to himself and to God? Indeed he is, for no one else can hear him. If he wishes to pray in the church and chooses to use his gift of tongues to do so, where the tongue is unknown, he must be content to speak to himself and to God (pray silently), and not share it with the church because they will not profit, being unable to understand what it is he is saying. His 'speaking to God in a tongue', is therefore a *consequence* of the tongue being unknown and the absence of an interpreter (as in verse 2), not a *commission* to do so.[109] The silent use of an unknown foreign language by an

---

[109] It is significant that Paul closes chapter 14 with the words "*forbid not to speak* [lalein] *with tongues*". If prayer was the sum and substance of this gift, then would we not expect him to defend its essence and say "forbid not to *pray* in tongues"?

individual within the church is one of a number of Paul's apostolic regulations concerning tongues, given to ensure order in God's house.[110]

As already noted, if Paul means in verse 28 that tongues are given to speak to God, then we have a contradiction in Scripture because he has just declared without qualification to the Corinthians that tongues are a sign to unbelievers (v.22)! If the Corinthians were not confused over the purpose of tongues before Paul's epistle, then they would certainly be after it, especially if they came to know of the Lord's declaration that tongues were to be a sign - see below. Further, how can tongues be a sign (a public manifestation), if they are to be used, as many assert, in private communion between the speaker and God? In what sense would they be a sign to those that believe not? - clearly, in no shape or form whatsoever. Those who claim tongues are for private use take as their support select phrases in 1 Corinthians 14, yet ignore or fail to see that the entire passage is essentially devoted to tongues *spoken in the church* - in public. (Refer to the commentary given later on 1 Corinthians 14, verse 4).

We must ask here, not just why God would want individuals to speak to Him in a tongue, ecstatic or foreign, but why would he want only *some* of the Corinthians (and only some today) to speak to Him in such tongues? Remember, Paul makes it quite clear that not all Christians had, or should desire the gift of tongues (Proposition 8). Further, the suggestion that only some can speak to God in a tongue is to forge a division within the people of God and foster spiritual elitism, both of which festered in Corinth. A 'special' class who were able to have a unique communion with God would split the saints of God and give rise to a group that assume special status within God's house. How does Paul counter such a situation? By reminding the Corinthians (and us) that

---

[110] Refer to the commentary on 1 Corinthians 14 below.

tongues were merely a sign; they were a lesser spiritual gift compared with prophecy and knowledge; and they would cease. Now, if tongues were a language for communion between God and man, then this would be clearly stated and *all* of us would be commanded to follow it. Where in Scripture are we all exhorted to greater spiritual heights by offering our praises and prayers to God in some heavenly tongue, either as a church or as individuals? We find nothing of it at all.

Observe again the silence of Scripture. We saw the clear record of the Word of God in Acts. Time and time again prayers were made and there were no tongues, and where there were tongues spoken, they were not used for prayer. Instead, the Holy Spirit has recorded the many occasions when tongues were used as a sign to unbelievers - the Jews. And did not the Spirit of God move Paul to declare the doctrine on this very thing to the Corinthians - 'tongues are a sign ....to them that believe not - *'this people'*? We have here the demonstrated consistency between the practice (Acts) and the purpose (1 Cor 14) - perfect accord between biblical history and biblical doctrine. The only occasion where tongues and praying are associated, is where a person *chose* to use his gifted foreign tongue to pray audibly in public. It was only because of the misuse of tongues by the Corinthians, that Paul is moved to raise the matter of tongues at all. Let not the silence of Scripture be overtaken by the roar of deception from Satan.

Praying in the Spirit

"But," say some, "What about the exhortation to pray in the Spirit? Does not this mean we are to pray in tongues?" Now, Paul's teaching to the Corinthians in chapter 12 is that the Spirit of God did not bestow the gift of tongues on all believers. It must follow that an exhortation which is given to all believers (to pray in the Spirit), cannot therefore mean praying in a tongue. Where in Scripture are tongues associated with praying in the Spirit? Remember the occasions of prayer recorded in Acts noted earlier. There were no tongues there. Are we prepared to say then that these prayers were not in the Spirit? Take for instance Acts 4:31 and 6:6. There were no tongues when they prayed. Yet we are told they were Spirit-filled when praying. When Paul talks to the Corinthians of speaking and preaching in demonstration of the Spirit and power, he makes no mention of tongues or prayer. Paul refers to himself being in fear and trembling due to the ordeal confronted at Corinth (1 Cor 2:3), but the Spirit of God enabled him to overcome the weakness of the flesh, to speak and preach with strength.[111] The exhortation to the Ephesians to "pray in the Spirit" is to all, and no tongues are mentioned. Note what it is that Paul exhorts - *"praying always with all prayer and supplication in Spirit"* (not with tongues).[112] A contrast is made here between praying in the Spirit - being led by the Spirit of God where the subject matter of prayer is governed by the Spirit, and praying in the flesh, where the subject of prayer is governed by the will of the natural man.[113] Young Timothy is instructed by Paul that (all) men should pray everywhere, not with tongues but without wrath and doubting.[114] Jude

---

[111] 1 Corinthians 2:4. Also a brief comment on speaking *"the wisdom of God in a mystery"* (v.7); this does not refer to tongues! The mystery here refers to the gospel of God's grace, salvation through Christ, to our glory (the blessings from it v.9). It is a mystery here because it was kept secret from before the foundation of the world, but is now revealed. Mystery does not refer to that which is spoken unintelligibly! The Holy Spirit has revealed and taught us concerning this mystery (v.13). There are many 'mystery' doctrines in the NT. Paul speaks of preaching the *'mystery of the Gospel'* to the Ephesians (Rom 16:25; Eph 6:19); The 'mystery' of Israel's blindness (Rom 11:25); The 'mystery' of godliness (1 Tim 3:16); See also 1 Cor 15:51 (Rapture); Col 1:24-26 etc.

[112] Ephesians 6:18

[113] In Romans 8:26-27 we have the intercession of the Spirit of God within us as our Helper, cultivating within us the correct attitude and direction of our prayers. He educates our spirit with His deep sympathy (groanings) because He understands our inability in these matters. The way in which the Spirit of God therefore moves our spirit to effective prayer cannot be put into words - cannot be uttered. The outcome of the Spirit's help and sympathy, is then effective prayer, prayer that is *'according to the will of God'*. This passage is also directed to all believers. In no manner can it refer to praying in tongues as some, in desperation, suggest.

[114] 1 Timothy 2:8

encourages all believers to build each other up in their most holy faith by praying in the Holy Ghost, no tongues are mentioned.[115] In 1 Thessalonians 5:17, Paul exhorts to *"pray without ceasing"* - not, *"with* tongues*"*.

In Scripture, tongues are subordinated, they are not to be sought after, they will cease, they are inferior to other spiritual gifts. They were not given to (possessed by) all believers. It is a tactic of Satan to take the lesser and elevate it into that which is of the greater, creating a pernicious distortion which leads many into error, dividing the saints of God.[116]

In conclusion, let us be instructed by our Lord, who always prayed in the Spirit. Do we hear any unintelligible heavenly languages from Him? In His private ministry to His disciples, He spoke in detail of the coming of the Holy Spirit, instructing them of the time of His coming, His work and the effect of His advent upon them. What does he say about tongues? Nothing at all except that they will be a *sign*.[117] How could He, when He Himself declared they are a sign, when one of His apostles through His Spirit was to teach that they were a mere sign, and His Spirit was to demonstrate and record their use as a mere sign during the early Church period? How Satan has managed to deceive so that the clear statement of the Lord Himself is obscured by personal experience.[118] Moreover, we have recorded for our learning, comfort and spiritual elevation, the Lord's prayer from the Son to the Father in John 17. There is no mysterious language there. I ask my reader to listen to the conversation between the Father and His Beloved Son during the dark hours of

---

[115] Jude 20

[116] Some charismatics declare that tongues open the way to receive the other spiritual gifts. This would make it *the* most important spiritual gift. Scripture ranks it as an inferior gift, never states we are to covet it, shows clearly it is was never given to all believers in the early Church period and, declares it to be temporary! Such a belief also denies that the Spirit of God determines the distribution of gifts.

[117] Mark 16 (refer below on this passage).

[118] In the 'disciples' prayer of Luke 11 and Matt 6 there is no instruction by the Lord to pray in tongues. However reference here is to the coming kingdom (of the Father) rather than to the Church.

Calvary. Do we hear unintelligible utterances ascending to the Throne of God from the lips of the suffering Son? No! And what of those who suffered in the footsteps of the Saviour? We need only observe the prayers of the martyrs of whom Stephen was the first (Acts 7), to see the utter irrelevance of some ecstatic, heavenly prayer language during the deepest of faith's trials. It was the filling of the Spirit of God that emboldened his and the hearts of others after him as the stones, flames and rack of the infidel tormented their bodies. Do we hear of a heavenly prayer language being employed by such worthies in their final and finest hours, as they commit their suffering and spirit to God? No!

Praying in the Spirit refers to praying in accordance with the mind and will of God (as opposed to praying in the flesh), allowing His Spirit to determine in us the correct attitude (Jude, 1 Timothy) and so direct our petitions and praise relevantly and reverently, so that we ask not amiss.[119] Now, what better example can we have of 'praying in the Spirit' than that shown by the Son of God, who through the eternal Spirit, offered Himself without spot to God. Listen to His prayer in the Spirit in that garden of suffering: *"O my Father, if it be possible, let this cup pass from me nevertheless not as I will, but as thou wilt".* [120]

"O ye of little faith"!

But what about the promise given to faith? There is the frequent claim by many that we do not possess these gifts simply because our faith is lacking. We are told, that no limit is set to the effects of prayer in faith. A selection of verses is then cited to support such a contention, viz Matt 17:19-20; 21:21-22; Mark 11:22-24; John 14:13-14. Have we not heard the unbridled promises from charismatic pulpits offering

---

[119] Refer to Note 3 - Fruit of the Spirit, the gifts of the Spirit and the gift of the Spirit.
[120] Matthew 26:39; Heb 9:13

untold health, wealth and 'spiritual gifts' if only we have faith? Are we to believe, that we can petition without limit the distribution of gifts from the Father of lights, with whom is no variableness, neither shadow of turning;[121] that we know what is best for us, rather than our Heavenly Father, and that we can expect everything and anything to be granted, to consume it on our lusts, if only we have faith?[122] Where is selflessness and holiness in prayer? Where is divine prerogative and sovereignty in all this? What of the declaration by Paul that the selfsame Spirit bestows gifts to each man severally as He will?[123]

But then, what of the Lord's promise in Mark 11:24, *"I say unto you, What things soever ye desire, when ye pray, believe that ye receive them, and ye shall have them"*? The essential error in using such words to advertise unlimited gifts from God, is the failure to understand what it is we are to ask for. It is the Spirit of God who must determine within us what it is we are to desire. And so, if the subjects of our requests to God are determined by the Spirit of God, we will indeed receive all that we ask, for then all we ask will be according to the mind and will of God - according to His name. Here again we see the essence of 'praying in the Spirit'. When the Lord speaks of 'whatsoever things ye desire' (ask), He is speaking of those things which are legitimately in accordance with God's plan and purpose. So, we read, *"And this is the confidence that we have in Him, that, if we ask anything according to His will, He heareth us and if we know that He hear us, whatsoever we ask, we know that we have the petitions that we desired of Him"*.[124] To request tongues today is not according to God's will! How do we know His will on this? From the pages of Holy Writ! They tell us that tongues were a sign for a particular people during a particular period

---

[121] James 1:17
[122] James 4:3
[123] I Corinthians 12:11
[124] 1 John 5:14-15

of time, which has ceased! It has been well said, 'Prayer cannot alter God's will, but it will alter our will to be in keeping with His'!

Finally, to argue as some do that tongues or any spiritual gift is dependent on the measure of our faith is to deny, or be ignorant of, the meaning of grace - as touched upon earlier! In Romans 12:6, Paul clearly identifies the grace of God (in harmony with His Spirit, 1 Cor 12:11 etc.) as determining which gift(s) we possess as believers! Grace is defined as unmerited favour - God giving us something we do not deserve! Therefore, to assert that gifts are given according to the degree of our faith is to rail against the very meaning of grace and Paul's plain teaching in verse 6. Satan and his ministers will try to worry us by suggesting we are deficient in faith because we do not speak in tongues. This can cause profound anxiety among sincere Christians. If we do not ground our faith on God's sure word, this is where Satan will have his way with us. Anxiety is a spiritually destructive emotion and Satan will seek to relieve it by substituting another emotion - 'soulish euphoria'. This is his domain; 'emotional experiences' appeal to the body and the soul. If he succeeds here, he will move us away from the biblical principle of assurance, "it is written", to an uncertain life relying on "I have experienced". His techniques are varied and powerful but never spiritual (see below and also Note 6). We must see the divine principle of grace in every aspect of our Christian life. Let us be comforted and assured by the truth that it was by grace (unmerited favour) that we were saved through faith. Not by the merit of our faith, but by the all-sufficient merit of the person and redemptive work upon whom it rested - Christ. Blessed be His name!

A Warning

The sober lesson from Scripture is that if we persist in asking God for that which is not according to His revealed purpose, He will grant or allow that very thing, and it will work upon us as an instrument of judgment! May we mark the salutary lessons from the history of Israel: they clamoured for meat when God had given them manna from heaven, they lusted exceedingly and tempted God, *"..He gave them their request; but sent leanness into their soul"*; their persistent demands for a king against the will of God and they were given Saul - *"I gave thee a king in my anger, and took him away in my wrath"*.[125] Are we not convinced, and it must be asked in love, that on the strength of God's Word concerning that which is called 'fullness' within the Charismatic Movement, is this in fact God's judgment of leanness? The whole programme is sadly characterised by a leanness in doctrine, through a preoccupation with spiritual gifts and associations bound by the fragile thread of emotion!

---

[125] Psalm 106:13-15; Hosea 13:9-11

CHAPTER 7

The Duration of Tongues

All agree that tongues will cease, but not all agree on when they will cease. Typically, modern-day tongue-speakers believe that tongues will cease with the return of the Lord. They take Paul's reference to *'when that which is perfect is come'* in 1 Corinthians 13 as the return of Christ for His church.[126] Therefore tongues, they claim, last over the *whole* Church period.

Proposition 10: "Tongues will cease when they are no longer relevant as a sign of God's judgment and grace."

The Big Picture

Before we consult God's Word on this matter, we must highlight the changes that challenged the Jewish people when the Church period began. We have noted these already, but not referred to them in this context.

· Israel had been set aside by God in judgment because of its unbelief.

· God's offer of salvation now was to individuals of all races, through Christ.

· All who accepted this offer became part of the church - His Body.

· All within the Body were equal in Christ - 'One New Man'.

---

[126] Scripture teaches there are two stages involved in the 'second coming of Christ': Stage 1, His coming *for* His Church (His Body), to the 'air'; (John 14; 1 Cor 15; 1 Thess 4). Stage 2, His coming to the earth, (Dan 7; Zech 14; 1Thess 3:13; and *with* His Church; Jude 14; Rev 5:10). (Chart B)

· The church, not Israel, was then the centre of God's programme for man.

· The Spirit of God had come as never before - to indwell the Body and each believer in Christ (Refer to the Spirit's indwelling below)

Now there are some important questions here. How were the Jews (and others) to know:

what these changes were?

what these changes meant?

how they should respond to such changes (their responsibility)?

They could have referred to the OT, but they would not see the church there, for it was hidden - 'in mystery'. They could not have consulted the NT for it had not been written. How then was God to address this situation? A written testament would have been appropriate. But this had to contain the history of the early church - its commencement, course and constitution for the benefit of those down through the ages. It could not, therefore, have been given immediately such as the giving of the Law on Mt. Sinai. So, until such a testament came into being which progressively unfolded the complete revelation, God introduced, through His Spirit, a transitional, or temporary programme that would inform of the changes and teach their meaning. This program involved equipping individuals with special gifts, gifts of the Spirit -

· the gift of prophecy - telling forth - revealing the changes;

· the gift of knowledge - explaining what the changes meant.

These gifts enabled the believers during this transition period to be informed of these changes. There was, however, a pressing need which required special attention, a necessity in regard to God's chosen earthly people, the Jews. They faced an extraordinary challenge, a real revolution in their religious and secular lives, i.e. having to accept as equals those of whom their prophets spoke as spiritually unclean. They had to know, too, of God's judgment upon them as a nation and that His Spirit had come upon men of all races. This required a special gift, one in the form of a sign, for these people required signs to believe and, after all, God had spoken to them in signs so often. So, in addition to the gifts of prophecy and of knowledge, He gave some, through His Spirit, the gift of tongues, to be a sign to the Jews of the coming of the Spirit of God upon all races, the judgment of Israel and of the equality of Jew and Gentile within the church. God was not indiscriminate when He chose such a sign, because He had used foreign tongues before to judge Israel when they disbelieved and He placed them under Gentile dominion. What is more, their prophet, Isaiah, spoke God's mind on this to their fathers. And God's apostle, Paul, raises it again in connection with the present generation and their unbelief when he corrects the Corinthians over their misunderstanding of tongues.

This transitional and temporary nature of the period and its requirements, must be kept in view when studying the duration not only of tongues, but the other two gifts as well.

Let us consider then the relevant passage, again bringing Scripture to bear upon it.

"Charity never faileth: but whether there be prophecies, they shall fail; whether there be tongues, they shall cease; whether there be knowledge, it shall vanish away. For we know in part, and we prophesy in part. But when that which is perfect is come, then that which is in part shall be done away. When I was a child, I spake as a child, I understood as a child, I thought as a child but when I became a man, I put away childish things. For now we see through a glass darkly; but then face to face: now I know in part; but then I shall know even as also I am known." 1 Corinthians 13:8-12.

Paul's concern was to put the gifts of tongues, knowledge

and prophecy in their proper place. The church at Corinth, as we have noted often before, had elevated tongue-speaking in particular far above its value. Paul begins with a general statement (v.8) comparing these three spiritual gifts with love. Love, declares Paul, is spiritually superior, it will last forever. The spiritual gifts of tongues, knowledge and prophecy will not last forever, they are temporary.

Now in verses 9 and 10, he turns his attention specifically to the gifts of knowledge and prophecy, reinforcing their temporary nature. After all, they provide only a 'partial' or 'incomplete' understanding of the purposes of God - 'for now I know in part'.[127] He compares this to looking 'through a glass darkly'. These gifts were to impart knowledge concerning the events of the day - the coming of the Spirit of God, the formation and progress of the church, the One New Man in Christ, the setting aside of Israel etc.[128] Knowledge concerning these matters among Christians at that time was obscure, because the only means they had of receiving it was through these gifts. Truth revealed by the Spirit of God would be proclaimed - the gift of prophecy i.e. forthtelling not foretelling. These truths were taken and explained by those having the gift of knowledge. So, we can see how the knowledge gained through these gifts would be 'piecemeal' and 'obscure' - a bit here and a bit there.

However, when 'that which is perfect (complete) is come', we shall know fully (then I shall know as I am fully known, v.12) not a piece here and there, but through a complete revelation - that which is perfect, or more correctly, that which

---

[127] Verse 12. A. T. Robertson "Word Pictures in the New Testament" ; Volume IV p. 179, *ek merous* - in part, *"as opposed to a whole"* - a piece. The context would be 'piecemeal' - 'in part".

[128] We must distinguish between the gift of knowledge and the possession of knowledge. The latter will not pass away, but endures as the Word of God endures (Matt 24:35). The gift of prophecy refers to the speaking of truths directly revealed by the Holy Spirit during the early Church period. This was necessary in the absence of the completed Scriptures. The gift of knowledge refers to the explanation of those truths which were prophesied, the Holy Spirit empowering. This is in contrast to the acquisition of knowledge today through our reading Scripture and being enabled in our understanding by the Holy Spirit.

is full-grown.[129] Paul is referring to the completed inspired written Word of God. The finished Scriptures unfold the complete revelation of those things the spiritual gifts revealed in part: with this completed revelation, the gifts of knowledge and of prophecy were not required - they would become inoperative.[130]

Moreover, Paul speaks of an object - '*that* which is perfect' and its associated state - maturity. This is contrasted with the two gifts and their associated environment - childhood (immaturity). When the time of maturity, (adulthood) arrives, these gifts which belong to the days of childhood must be 'put away'. They only serve the needs of a child - a time of immaturity. What then is able to meet the needs of adulthood when it comes to a matter of understanding the purposes of God? It can only be the completed volume of Scripture. What exhortation does Paul give to Timothy concerning spiritual life and knowledge? *"All Scripture is given by inspiration of God, and is profitable for doctrine, for reproof, for correction, for instruction in righteousness....."* Why? *"..That the man* [adult] *of God may be perfect* [complete], *throughly furnished unto all good works."*[131] And further, with the coming of the completed canon all people, Jews and Gentiles, must live by faith not by sight (signs). These two spiritual gifts and the signs were for a season, for the early days of the church! Today, the clear rule for any individual is *'faith cometh by hearing and hearing by the word of God'*[132] If the sign gifts were to coexist with the completed Scriptures, what confusion would result. We would be continually looking to men and

---

[129] That which is perfect: *"The perfect, the full-grown..."*. A. T. Robertson "Word Pictures in the New Testament" Volume IV p. 179.

[130] The gifts of knowledge and prophecy shall be done away with - made idle or inoperative. A. T. Robertson "Word Pictures in the New Testament" Volume IV p. 179.

[131] 2 Timothy 3:16-17

[132] The 'gift of discerning spirits' would likewise cease with the coming of the completed canon. We must distinguish between 'discernment' as gifted by this supernatural endowment, and discernment by 'testing the spirits' exhorted in 1 John 4:1. The latter is acquired and exercised in the light of the full revelation of Scripture, the former was gifted until the completed revelation was come.

for signs rather than to God's Word for our spiritual exercise and growth. What confidence would we have in the Bible as God's final statement to man? How can you and I detect false prophets? By the signs and wonders they perform? Absolutely not! Only by testing what they profess against the Bible (that which is written)!

Here, too, we find the subtle undermining hand of Satan at work. He will have us believe that there are amongst us today people who still have the gifts of knowledge and of prophecy. But more, he will have us believe it right up to the return of Christ. Why? Because he desires ever to worry the saints by adding to and subtracting from the completed Word of God. Christendom abounds with people professing to have 'additional revelations of truth' - the result, they claim, of possessing the gifts of knowledge and of prophecy. It is all of the Adversary, designed to undermine our confidence in the Bible. Divine revelation stopped with the completed Scriptures. Let us be wary and heed the exhortation of Jude, I *"exhort you that ye should earnestly contend for the faith which was once* [once for all] *delivered unto the saints"*.[133] These two gifts were made unnecessary when the Scriptures were completed.

But what about the gift of tongues? They have not been specifically dealt with by Paul so far. We are simply told they will cease (*pausontai*) - make themselves cease, automatically cease of themselves, stop.[134] The context demands that we place the gift of tongues in the same 'temporary' and 'partial' category as the gifts of knowledge and prophecy. The gift of tongues was very much a part of

---

[133] Jude 3, '*hapax paradotheisei*' - *"once for all delivered"* A. T. Robertson "Word Pictures in the New Testament" Volume VI p. 186.

[134] A. T. Robertson "Word Pictures in the New Testament" Volume IV p. 179: See also W. E. Vine, "Expository Dictionary of New Testament Words", p. 176: Cease - "*to stop, to make an end, is used chiefly in the Middle Voice in the NT, signifying to come to an end......a willing cessation (in contrast to the Passive Voice which denotes a forced cessation)...... 1 Cor 13:8, of tongues"*.

the 'incomplete' revelation a unique part, for it was in the form of a sign, unlike the other two gifts which were to build up the church. It was included as part of the transitionary program to speak directly to the Jews, for they seek after signs. Without such a 'spectacular' sign, they would not be convinced that 'God also to the Gentiles (has) granted repentance unto life', that the 'Holy Ghost fell on them as on us', that 'God gave them the like gift'! Mere knowledge and prophecy would not convince those 'who kill the prophets and stone them that are sent unto them'.

As part of this partial revelation, the gift of tongues ceased with the coming of the completed Scriptures. There would be no further need of them. Why? Those things which were confirmed by tongues are now seen in their full measure in the Scriptures. We see fully unfolded in the NT both the setting aside of Israel and the oneness in grace between Jew and Gentile [135]; the dawn, nature and course of the Church period; the coming of the Holy Spirit (Acts) and the adoption of both Jew and Gentile as sons of God and fellow heirs (Romans, Ephesians, Galatians). Mark how the Epistles to the Romans and Galatians elevate grace above law, how the Epistle to the Hebrews elevates the abundance in Christ over the barren wilderness that is Judaism. Above all, the completed Scriptures present fully the work and person of Christ, upon whom all this rests.[136]

It does appear (from the later lists of spiritual gifts), that the gifts of knowledge and of prophecy outlasted the gift of tongues.[137] This should not surprise us, since they were superior to tongues, in that they were designed to build up

---

[135] 1 Corinthians 12:12-13

[136] We need to bear in mind that 1 Corinthians was an early Epistle written about 57 AD by Paul while in Ephesus (1 Cor 16:8). Of the NT Scriptures, it was preceded only by the Epistle of James and the Epistles to the Thessalonians.

[137] What is peculiar and confined to the (early) Church age, is the particular manifestation and use of prophecy and knowledge - as gifts of the Holy Spirit. Their purpose was to reveal that which pertains to the truth of the Body of Christ, as incorporated and united by the Holy Spirit, (which was not the subject of OT prophecy, nor will it be of that which is to come), until the arrival of the completed canon.

the church with truth during the early apostolic period (until the arrival of the canon of Scripture).[138] The epistles written after 1 Corinthians that refer to gifts make no mention of tongues.[139] In the list of gifts given in Ephesians 4 tongues are not mentioned; *these* gifts are given by the risen Christ and refer to the 'persons' gifted to the church - apostles, teachers etc. In Romans, a (slightly) later epistle to 1 Corinthians but predating the Epistle to the Ephesians (circa 63 AD), the list of spiritual gifts make no mention of tongues.[140] Would not this be consistent with the teaching of Scripture that they would die out, fall into disuse as the NT came into being? Therefore, we see that even before the completion of the canon of Scripture, tongues were becoming less relevant. There are significant reasons explaining why they are never mentioned in the later epistles:

1.　The use of tongues as a sign to the Jews that all nations were subjects of the grace of God had been well demonstrated. By the time we arrive at the period corresponding to the end of Acts 19 (circa AD 59), tongues have borne this witness before the Jews from Gentile lands at Jerusalem (Acts 2), the Jews within Samaria (Acts 8), the Jews in the house of a Gentile, Cornelius (Acts 10), before the Jews meeting the disciples of John the Baptist (Acts 19), the Jews in Jerusalem (Acts 11) and the Jews at the Jerusalem conference (Acts 15).

2.　The rejection of the gospel of God's grace by the Jews, represented by the leaders of Judaism - (Acts 18 & 28) *"....when they opposed themselves, and blasphemed, he* [Paul] *shook his raiment, and said unto them, Your blood be*

---

[138] See Note 1.

[139] Romans 12:4-8; Eph 4:8-12

[140] In his instruction to the church at Rome concerning spiritual gifts (Rom 12:4-8), Paul is not inspired to repeat the correction on tongues given to the Corinthians. We may reasonably suppose, here, further proof that tongues were gradually being superseded as a sign to the Jews with the unfolding of truth within Holy Writ! See "An overview of the gifts in the New Testament" below.

upon your own heads; I am clean from henceforth I [Paul] *will go unto the Gentiles.* "[141]

3. The progressive, widespread dispersion and fragmentation of the Jews as an independent nation, a nation which all but ceased when Titus claimed and sacked Jerusalem in 70 AD[142]. Israel had been set aside and sifted among the nations through divine judgment!

4. The growing evangelization, apostolic missions, conversions and churches within Gentile lands, as seen in Acts, all bore witness to the unity of the Body of Christ. Is it not instructive that the Lord granted signs to the Jews, for they are a sign-seeking people but, to the Church (comprising Jew and Gentile cast as one new man), no such provision is made? *"Faith cometh by hearing, and hearing by the word of God".*[143]

5. At the time of Titus and especially during the rule of the Domitian, circa 95 AD, Christianity, as the historians relate it, was seen as a distinct religion, without its past Jewish 'national' or 'racial' links. The Christian church was singled out for special repression and persecution. Her denial of idolatry and religious symbols led to a charge of atheism. Her separation from the world led to a charge of social subversion. The church of God had now become truly distinctive and owned no political centre, select priesthood, territory, race or culture. There was little need for distinguishing signs to the Jews of the unity of all flesh in

---

[141] Acts 18:6; 28:28

[142] As observed above, the formation of the State of Israel in 1948 and subsequent in-gatherings of Jews to that realm is not according to God's design for the national restoration of Israel. This, we know, will only occur during the Millennial period when the two sticks of Ezekiel, Ephraim and Judah, come together (Ezek.37:15-24). It will be then unity in the 'Land' - 'ONE STICK'; now, we have in the Church, the unity of the 'ONE NEW MAN' (Eph 2:15), in heavenly places in Christ - unity in the 'LORD'!

[143] Romans 10:17. A passing remark may lend added force here. We note a certain parallel between the early period of the Gospels and the early period of Acts. In the former, the signs and miracles of the Lord used to confirm His divine presence on earth, diminished in number as the Jews increased their hostility to Him. During the period of Acts, the signs and wonders given to confirm the divine presence of the Holy Spirit on earth, likewise diminished as the gospel was rejected by the Jews - eventually ceasing!

Christ and the Holy Spirit's coming on Jew and Gentile. The numerous local churches, from Jerusalem to Rome, bore increasing witness to such oneness!

However, with the coming of the completed Word of God, all tongue-speaking, like the other two gifts, would end. It is the completed, inspired Word of God then that Paul refers to as 'that which is perfect'. Tongues were no longer needed. The completed Scriptures once for all delivered to the saints, contained the complete revelation of God's judgment and grace.

But what about the statement in verse 12, I shall see then *"face to face"*? Does this not refer to the coming of Christ and the end of the Church period? This statement is an illustration and does not speak of an event. It is one of the metaphors Paul uses to contrast a partial with a complete revelation. The partial revelation, given by the gifts prophecy and knowledge, is like looking into a polished metal plate which were the mirrors of the day. The city of Corinth was well noted for such mirrors![144] No matter how finely polished, they still gave an imperfect and 'darkened' revelation.[145] When the believers 'looked into' the information revealed by

---

[144] The expression *"through a glass, darkly"* was in common usage. Plato states *"there is no light in the earthly copies of justice or temperance....they are seen through a glass dimly"* (Phaedrus, 250). There is a finer rendering to be noted here - the word 'darkly' expresses the obscure *form* in which the revelation appears. This corresponds to the partial nature (form) of the gifts mentioned. Compare this, says Paul, with the lucid, full view one gets when looking at someone face to face. Scripture, the completed canon, is the form in which the complete revelation is manifested - it presents the entire panorama of the perfect will of God as revealed to man. Corinth was noted for its brass mirrors.

Now we see darkly - 'now' (*arti*) signifies *"up to the immediate present"*; *"blepo"* - '*we see*', *"indicates the manner of seeing"* rather than the object seen! 'Now' does not refer to the whole Dispensation! See W. E. Vine: "The Collected Writings of W. E. Vine", Volume 2 p. 150.

[145] An additional view was advanced by a member of the study group. Could not the coming of perfection refer to the spiritual state of a believer? Definitely not! We are sealed by the Spirit of God unto the day of redemption: we are already perfect - complete in Christ, *"To the praise of the glory of His grace, wherein He hath made us accepted in the Beloved."* (Eph 1:6). On this, the testimony of Scripture is full and explicit. If the argument is in respect of personal spiritual growth, it must follow that mature believers have no use of tongues. The first order in the progress to spiritual maturity would be to discard tongues would it not? The possession of the gifts themselves is not a measure of spirituality, for we are told by Paul of the rule of carnality in Corinth.

these temporary gifts they would, at best, see an incomplete picture of the changes that had come about. Compare this, Paul says, with the perfect revelation we get when we look into the completed Word of God. Compared to the information from these temporary gifts, it is as clear as looking at someone 'face to face'!

The silence of the epistles

Before passing we must, in the light of the above, dwell again on the insistence by some that all Christians should speak in tongues and that tongues are angelic or heavenly languages. We have already seen the all-consuming silence of God's Word in regard to praying to God in tongues. However, it will be gainful to refute some specific claims of the 'heavenly-tongue universalists' in view of the silence of the epistles concerning this aspect. We saw earlier how the sign of tongues profoundly changed the Jewish heart and mind of Peter, and those of other Jewish penmen at Pentecost. Yet, within their epistles, and those of Paul, written after 1 Corinthians, which focus on the practical life of the children of God, not one reference to tongues is made, whether it be as a guide for obedient walk, as a means for effective witness, as a medium for holy prayer, as an exhortation for Spirit-filled praise or, indeed, as a sign to them that believe not.[146] Despite such clear opposition, the tongues-universalists insist we should all speak in tongues because tongue-speaking stimulates faith, keeps us apart from worldly evil and refreshes and builds us up spiritually. (Again, we have already refuted these claims when examining the purpose of tongues, but let us add further argument against them.) Now if these claims were true, then we would expect tongues to be an *essential* ingredient and boldly advocated in every epistle which addresses spiritual refreshment, faith, sanctification

---

[146] Peter's Epistles - AD 65-67; Jude - AD.65-67; John's Epistles - AD 85-90. Refer to note on 1 Corinthians 14 verse 4 below in the section '1 Corinthians 14 - An Overview'.

from worldliness and fellowship with God. But what do we find? Tongues are never in view at all.

Let us return to Paul's correction on tongues in 1 Corinthians, which is an early epistle. The church there had overvalued the gift of tongues. Paul's purpose is to put before them the proper worth of this gift. In doing this, he finds no place for tongues as a medium for holy communion with God, a stimulus to faith, or a safeguard from worldly influences. Now, we know, he does refer in 1 Corinthians 14 to a tongue speaker being built up spiritually when he speaks in tongues. However, when any spiritual gift is used there is a building up of the person using it. For this reason Paul declares to the Corinthians, speaking in tongues - the exercise of the gift - should not be forbidden! Moreover, do you not regard it as very strange that on the one hand the Corinthians were prolific tongue-speakers, yet on the other hand they were spiritual babes and in a condition of carnality? If the claims of the modern-day tongue universalists were true, then with all their fervent tongue-speaking, the Corinthians should have been paragons of virtue and the epitome of corporate spiritual maturity! There is an obvious corollary to the claims of the tongues universalists. If tongues were given for spiritual health, then would we not see acknowledgment of this somewhere in those who were spiritually hale?

Consider the Ephesians who, because of their robust spirituality, Paul was able to speak of spiritual blessings in heavenly places. Where is the recognition that their healthy condition was in any way attributed to tongue-speaking? There is none here or anywhere else in Scripture! We must understand that tongues were never given *in order* that believers should be built up![147] After all, they were just a sign, directed to unbelievers, not given for edification; they were temporary; they were not of the 'best' gifts - e.g. the gift of

---

[147] See the note on verse 4 in '1 Corinthians 14 - An Overview' below, regarding the tongue-speaker 'building himself up'!

prophecy, which was given for edification, exhortation and comfort. The 'bewitched' Galatians had lost their way, falling back into bondage through the weak and beggarly elements of Judaism, forgetting that they received the Spirit of God through faith. So Paul reminds them to stand fast in the liberty in which Christ has made us free. Their walk in the liberty wrought by faith would then yield the fruit of the Spirit, not tongues. Paul was very familiar with the gift of tongues, having this gift himself and he was inspired by the Spirit of God to teach the Corinthians about its proper use. If anyone knew of the value and purpose of speaking in tongues it certainly would be Paul, who spoke in tongues more than most.[148] Why then does he not prescribe tongues to the Galatians so they can refresh their faith? Where are the tongues when he exhorts them to walk in the Spirit (Gal 5:25)? The Colossians, on the other hand, lost sight of Christ as the Head of the Body and were in danger of succumbing to evil worldly philosophies, weakening their faith. No tongues are prescribed here to shore up their faith and refresh their shallow spirituality. Paul exhorts them to 'put on the new man' and 'put off the old man' but never anything about speaking in tongues. Rather, it is by the word of Christ dwelling in them that they are to sanctify themselves.[149]

Within the noble pastoral epistles, we are exhorted to flee youthful lusts and follow righteousness; we are instructed on how to behave in the local church and taught how to recognise those who are spiritual leaders amongst us; we are warned against worldly social and doctrinal evils and furnished with a multitude of practical principles that are to refresh and quicken our Christian testimony and faith. Yet, tongues are never mentioned! When John pens his first Epistle, he speaks principally of the character of God: God is light, love and

---

[148] This would refer to variety rather than frequency. Because of his special role during the early Church period and his extensive journeys, Paul would have been gifted with a great diversity of foreign languages!
[149] Colossians 3:16

life. As children of God, he seeks to cultivate our fellowship and communion with our heavenly Father. Tongues are not mentioned here. Neither do we find any role for tongues in John's second Epistle which urges steadfastness in faith and warns against spiritual loss. James pens his epistle (pre 50 AD) to build the faith and revive the spirituality of dispersed Jewish Christians who were being oppressed by the world and its temptations. No comfort or strength from speaking tongues is mentioned here. So too Peter. In his first Epistle, he seeks to strengthen the believers amidst their trials. He reminds them of their constitution as a spiritual house and calls upon them to make spiritual sacrifices unto God. Tongue-speaking is not mentioned as a means of strengthening their faith or communing with God.

Then we come to the Epistle to the Hebrews, essentially Jewish in its direction and heavenly in its theme, presenting Christ enthroned and our unfettered communion with Him before the throne of Grace. In this blessed Epistle, earthly Judaic privileges and rites are contrasted with the *'new and living'* way of communing with God.[150] *"By Him* [Christ] *...let us offer the sacrifice of praise to God continually, that is, the fruit of our lips".*[151] The forty verses of chapter 11 are given to impress upon us that without faith it is impossible to please God. The very fact that these examples of faith are from the OT tells us that miraculous tongues in any shape or form were not given for the building up of our faith. In 10:19-22, we are informed by the Spirit of God of the blessed privilege we now have, which was never the portion of the saints of old. We can with boldness (with freedom and in confidence), *"enter into the holiest by the blood of Jesus"* (v.19). The way

---

[150] Hebrews 10:20
[151] Hebrews 13:15. The sacrifice of praise, the fruit of *our* lips is the product of our *own* thoughts and meditations on the Person and work of Christ! Praise is mentioned here as a sacrifice, since it is seen as our offering as priests unto God. And, it is through Christ these offerings are made, because it is Him who has made us all kings and priests unto God, He being our High Priest (Heb 8:1; 10:21 etc.).

is open for us, in spirit, to enter the very presence of God in prayer and praise. In this epistle then, we would surely expect to find some reference to tongues as a heavenly medium to commune with God, and as a stimulus to our faith, if they were ever so intended by the Spirit of God. But, tongues are not there. What do we see? We are to draw near not *through tongues*, but through the blood of Christ. Not *with* some *heavenly tongue*, but with a *"true heart with a full assurance of faith"* [which comes from the Word of God]. Not possessing some *heavenly prayer language*, but *"having our hearts sprinkled from an evil conscience"* and our bodies washed with *"pure water"*, not the cleansing power of a special prayer language. Paul exhorts the Ephesians, whom he addresses as crucified and risen in Christ, sitting in heavenly places in Him, to avoid worldly evils, to be filled with the Spirit and give thanks unto God always for all things. His focus is on the believer's positional sanctification (ch.1-3) and progressive sanctification (ch.4-6). The Spirit-inspired apostle who knew what it was to speak in tongues, has no place for them here. Paul reminds the Philippians, who were living in a Roman colony, that their citizenship is in heaven. Therefore, they were to conduct themselves, i.e. their speech and manner, as befitting citizens of heaven not earth. He makes no reference to heavenly languages in this exhortation.

The One who holds the seven stars,[152] has nothing to say concerning the benefit of tongues to Ephesus, the church that has lost its first love; nor to Smyrna, the church that is under suffering; nor to Permagos, the church holding the doctrine of Balaam; nor to Thyatira, the church committing spiritual fornication. To the lukewarm and indifferent Christians at Laodicea, tongue-speaking is not commended as a means of refreshing their faith.

Why the deafening silence on tongues? As the Word of

---

[152] Revelation 3 & 4

God unfolded, signs (tongues) became unnecessary.[153] More importantly, tongues were only a *sign - to the Jews*, a fact that Scripture voices loud and clear through history and doctrine. Contrary to what Satan would have us believe, tongues were not given for spiritual refreshment, communion with God, protection against worldly lusts or strengthening of faith. There is now, with the coming of the completed Scriptures, an exhortation as stated above, that we in this age should fully grasp, - *'faith cometh by hearing and hearing by the word of God'.*[154] Satan would have us seek strength anywhere except from the Word of God, in direct opposition to the Holy Spirit. *"All Scripture* [not tongues] *is given by inspiration of God, and is profitable for doctrine, for reproof, for correction, for instruction in righteousness: that the man of God may be perfect, throughly furnished unto all good works."*[155]

One final remark here. If God intended all Christians to speak in tongues and tongues were a vital universal requirement for spiritual refreshment, faith, communion with God and as a safeguard from the world, then failure to speak in tongues would be grievous to the Spirit of God. Yet, failure to speak in tongues is never mentioned when Paul raises the subject of grieving the Holy Spirit (Eph 4:30). Nor is it mentioned in regard to the possibility of quenching the Spirit (1 Thess 5:19).

---

[153] Some hold that tongues ceased when the Jews rejected Paul's ministry and he took the gospel to the Gentiles (Acts 13:42-51). However, Paul's first letter to the Corinthians, wherein he instructs concerning tongues, is subsequent to the events of Acts 13. For those looking for a date, a more plausible case may set the cessation at the time of Acts 28:28.

[154] As noted earlier, the 'gift of discerning spirits' would likewise cease with the coming of the completed canon. We must distinguish between 'discernment' as *gifted* by this supernatural endowment, and the 'discernment' by *'testing the spirits'* exhorted in 1 John 4:1. The latter is acquired through our study of the full revelation of Scripture. The former was gifted to certain believers only (1 Cor 12:7-11), and ceased when the completed revelation was come. John does not mention it when he pleads with the believers to 'try (test) the spirits' (1 John 4:1).

[155] 2 Timothy 3:16

Proposition 11: "Church history supports the cessation of tongues after the early Church period."

Tongues, which were spoken in the early post-Apostolic period, did not agree with the scriptural pattern of the Church period. Montanus was a 'tongue-speaker'. The early Church historian Eusebius (circa 130-180 AD) noted his ravings and ecstatic behaviour.[156] Montanus and his followers were discredited through their heresies, chief of which was their belief that Montanus was the incarnate Spirit of God. Origen (circa 85-254) makes no reference to biblical tongues existing during his day. Chrysostom (circa 347-407) observed that the Spirit manifestations spoken of 1 Corinthians 12-14 no longer occur.[157]

Further, let us acknowledge the shining Christian evangelical revivals of recent centuries centred upon men mightily moved by the Spirit of God, who never sought or claimed possession of tongues or second blessings and who taught that tongues and the other sign gifts of the Spirit have long ceased.

However, while these and other historical accounts do support the case against modern-day tongues, our concern must always be to interpret history in the light of Scripture.

Proposition 12: "The Gospels witness that tongues were a sign."

Mark is the only Gospel that refers to tongues - 'new tongues' - *glossais lalesousin kainais* - not some 'new prayer language'. The word for prayer is not used here.[158] The reference in Mark 16 is to a period within Acts. The Lord Himself declares that tongues were a sign - *"and these signs shall follow them"*. In verses 17 & 18 the Lord speaks of the early Church period, not the whole course of the Church age that follows His ascension (v.19). In verses 19 & 20, Mark records that which took place in Acts and the early Church

---

[156] Eusebius, *"Ecclesiastical History V"*.
[157] Chrysostom, *"Homilies on First Corinthians"*, *XXIX*
[158] Mark 16:17

period after our Lord's ascension.[159] Signs and wonders indeed followed them that believed, as they bore witness (confirming, v.20) the 'spoken' word of God to them that *did not believe* - the specific sign of tongues remember, was to those that believed not![160] We noted earlier that the Lord speaks of tongues in a prospective sense, whereas Paul deals with them in a corrective sense in 1 Corinthians. The gospels (Mark) present the *promise* of tongues as a sign, Acts their *practice* as a sign, and the epistles (1 Corinthians) their *perversion, purpose* and *provisionality as a sign*. In passing, we note the sign gifts include: tongues, Acts 2, (8), 10, 19; immunity, taking up serpents - Paul being bitten by the viper, Acts 28:5; healings, Acts 3:7, Paul healing in Acts 28:8.[161]

Proposition 13: "The fact that people speak in tongues today, does not prove the case for modern-day tongues."

We come now to the question most raised in defence of tongues today. *"If all this is true, how do you explain the fact that I and others speak in tongues?"*

The test of Scripture

We should never interpret the Word of God by our experience (or by our emotions). Rather, we must judge our experience by the unerring Word of God. This is true for experiences that are individual or corporate. Experience is validated only when proven in the light of Scripture. Let the mind be in us that was in Christ Jesus, who when He was tempted, answered thrice, *"it is written"*.[162] If I, and the many other Christians who have

---

[159] Some doubt that the latter verses in Mark's gospel are genuine. Such a notion, which is based essentially on 'style', is irrelevant in the light of the inherent consistency of events stated in the passage with the whole NT. The reason why some manuscripts omit the said section, it has been fairly suggested, is because Mark's gospel it would appear was written between 68 - 70 AD, at a time when the miraculous gifts stated in these verses were no longer evidenced. This would cause some to regard their place in Scripture as doubtful (see below and refer again to Proposition 13).

[160] The consistent, clear witness of Acts in regard to the use of tongues.

[161] See the section on 'Healings' below.

[162] Matthew 4:4-10

not spoken in tongues, claim on the basis of this experience that tongues today are unscriptural, we present a dishonest witness before God and man. Likewise, those who discard the test of Scripture, just because they speak in tongues, also present an untrue witness. I was assured by those in our study who spoke in tongues that they would not agree with practices based upon experiences such as visions of the apostles or weeping statues of the virgin Mary. Such experiences, they rightly agreed, are not supported by Scripture (even though Scripture declares young men will see visions and old men will have dreams).[163] Though this confession was reassuring, we must beware of being selective when applying the test of Scripture.

The supposed "supernatural" phenomena such as those stated above may appear very real to those experiencing them, but they contain not a shred of authenticity! Cultism is founded on the experiences of individuals.[164] I would urge readers who speak in tongues to prove their experience in the light of the Word of God. Just because they and others have experienced tongues and the euphoria that often accompanies them does not, of itself, give tongues scriptural legitimacy.

"But", you say, "look at the converts!" Can such a thing that is associated with bright, bubbling and "successful" energies be unscriptural? Be warned! Safety or truth measured on the basis of large numbers professing salvation is a false assurance which Satan is ever ready to exploit. Let God be true but every man a liar![165] Further, we need to examine the fruits of those who claim to be converts, so that we do not embrace them too quickly! Popularity is a trick of Satan, who would never use that which was "unpopular" to achieve his ends. We noted earlier a mark of Satan was to elevate the lesser to the greater. Well, there is another subtle stamp of his guile. It is to contradict God's purpose by appealing to the flesh. Tongue-speakers

---

[163] Acts 2:17. Reference is to the Day of the Lord here, not the Church period!
[164] See Note 5
[165] Romans 3:4

declare their tongues are a special blessing which is a denial of the real purpose of tongues as a sign of God's judgment, judgment as we have seen, against Israel (and therefore His grace to Gentile races)! Remember how the adversary tempted Eve, *"Ye shall not surely die"*, when God had clearly warned *"in the day that thou eatest thereof thou shalt surely die"!* Satan's deception and contradiction was successful because it appealed to that which looked good, pleasant and desirable.[166]

The Table below presents three illustrations of how Satan has reversed the truth. Note the role of modern-day tongues in confirming the deception in the last two examples. (The 'baptism by the Spirit' is taken up later).

	God's word	Satan's words and reversal
Statement	"Thou shalt surely die" (Gen 2:17)	"Ye shall not surely die" (Gen 3:4)
Basis	*Divine judgment*	*Promise of personal blessing - "ye shall be as gods." (Gen 3:5)*
Statement	"...Tongues are for a sign ...to them that believe not" - unbelievers (1 Cor 14:21-22)	Tongues are to speak to God and a sign to the believer of a second blessing.
Basis	*Tongues were a sign of divine judgment on Israel and grace to the Gentiles. (1 Cor 14:21-22; Isaiah etc.)*	*Tongues have nothing to do with divine judgment. They are evidence of a 'second blessing' of the Spirit.*
Statement	The baptism by the Holy Spirit was the *putting* of believers *into the Body of Christ* - "...by one Spirit are we all baptized into one body, whether we be Jews or Gentiles..." (1 Cor 12:13) - regardless of strength of faith!	The baptism by the Holy Spirit is the receiving of the Holy Spirit *into the body of the believer* - promise of a second (personal) blessing to those who ask and have the 'necessary faith'!
Basis	*Unity and peace among believers within the Body of Christ* - (Eph 4:1-6)	*Disunity among believers within the body of Christ due to a promise of a second blessing - division between those who have had and who have not had such a 'second blessing'.*

---

[166] Genesis 2:15-3:7

What, then, are we to make of reports today from 'apparently' reliable and reputable people, who have themselves witnessed miracles, wonders (in some cases, the alleged miraculous speaking of a 'foreign language'), and, further, witnessed the ensuing 'salvation of souls'?[167]

Some who do not agree with tongue-speaking today seek to explain such 'credible' reports as being 'special instances' that have been permitted through the sovereign grace and wisdom of God; that in certain supernatural environments and primitive cultures, where people look for miraculous signs before believing, God will allow signs as an exception so they can be saved! The uncompromising apostle has this to say to them, *"the Jews require a sign, and the Greeks seek after* [worldly] *wisdom: but we preach Christ crucified"*.[168] Claims of such 'divine exceptions' are often accompanied by the statement, that 'God, because He is Sovereign, can do anything'! We ask, can God lie? No, because of His immutable righteousness and holiness! Can God cut across His divine plan? No, for He is a God of eternal order, not chaos! If God has shown us in His Word, that tongues were appointed for a season and a special purpose, and that season and purpose has ended, then any tongue-speaking after that season can never be of God! No matter how plausible or successful the results appear, we are duty-bound to reject all such energies as counterfeit! The Word of God documents for our learning, occasions where satanic powers copy that which is done by God.[169] And, as the day

---

[167] If miraculous speaking of foreign tongues is taking place, then they appear to be taking place in great obscurity. They are certainly not making headline news, which is quite strange given we are supposed to be in a Pentecostal revival. Where is the parading of people on national and international circuits who have this 'gift'? Why are we not being urged to make a pilgrimage to the corners of the earth where this supposedly is happening? Was this not the programme in the case of the "Toronto blessing"?

[168] 1 Corinthians 1:22-23

[169] Exodus 7:12 *"For they* [the Magicians & Sorcerers] *cast down every man his rod, and they became serpents.."* So it was with the river and the frogs - they did in 'like manner". However, the magicians were not able to counterfeit all the miracles done by Moses and Aaron. God authenticates His works, so that we can say *"this is the finger of God"* (Ex 8:19). Let us then heed that which is the work of the finger of God which He has given to us - the Scriptures.

lengthens and the Lord's return draws nigh, are we not to expect such satanic activity to increase and invade the very churches? Is not the Neo-Pentecostal-Charismatic Movement, a fraternity held together by 'common experiences', one of the fastest growing religious movements? Harvests of souls based on 'miraculous gifts' are the result of sowing of another gospel under the influence of other spirits! We must never grant one iota of credence to the witness of any person, no matter how unblemished their character or how devout their life, if what they claim is contrary to the Word of God. Satan's subtle efforts can deceive anyone of us if we fail to look to God's Word for instruction, prayerfully and legitimately.[170]

Let us heed the warning given by Paul, which cannot be quoted too often in these times. *"And no marvel; for Satan himself is transformed into an angel of light. Therefore it is no great thing if his ministers also be transformed as the ministers of righteousness; whose end shall be according to their works'.*[171] The test of our experience must be Scripture. We are not called upon by God's Word to make expedient exceptions, even if we personally witness such instances. We cannot replace *'it is written'* with *'but I have seen or experienced'*. We would say to readers who speak in tongues, *"Beloved, believe not every spirit* [that part of man that speaks of spiritual things], *but try* [test] *the spirits* [the spirits of the

---

[170] A discerning review of many articles supporting modern-day tongues and other charismata, reveals a common failing. Typically, the writers focus on their own experience, and then select one or two verses from Scripture to support it. These verses are not examined with any depth with regard to the passage, the particular book, historical or grammatical context. They then proceed to give further support to their experience, not by testing it against a systematic study of Scripture, but by quoting experiences of others, completing a full turn. This method of persuasion - experience -> selected verses -> experience is, in some instances, hidden by emotive language and the quotation (not examination) of a mass of other verses. We see it fully used in public charismatic rallies, where the time and depth given to serious and reverent expounding of the Word of God is devoured by the parade of personal experiences, concerts and other activities designed to capture emotional commitment! This root of the contemporary charismatic methodology is evident in the writings of the progenitors of Pentecostalism, e.g. R. A. Torry "The Holy Spirit". Revell.

[171] 2 Corinthians 11:14-15

prophets] *whether they are of God because many false prophets are gone out into the world."* [172] John warns that the words and deeds of these false prophets appear very credible. Their attractive mimicry of the truth is capable of beguiling the unwary child of God. John does not mention seduction and delusion through false signs and wonders here. He does not have to. This is the hallmark of the spirit of antichrist (v.3), as evident in the strategy of the Anti-Christ, who is none other than the false prophet who works miracles (Rev 16:13-14) and comes with signs and lying wonders (2 Thess 2:9). How are we to try the spirits and *"prove all things?"* [173] - by the Word of God. If tongues of today do not have Scriptural validity, they cannot be of the Holy Spirit. All it takes to succumb is a mind surrendered to experience. As confessed by a member of our study (who had been a tongue-speaker for some ten years), if what has been shown above is true, as it seemed, then Satan has cast a masterful deception upon all who seek and speak in tongues. The Holy Spirit requires our minds to be in a state of reason, guided by the knowledge of Scripture, in order that we manifest intelligent and sober faith. In contrast, what Satan's ministers require is a mind which has yielded self control, unable to reason and apply the articles of faith from the Word of God. *"Gird up* [do not let loose] *the loins of your mind, be sober,"* says Peter. [174] The whole charismatic programme is designed

---

[172] 1 John 4:1 'Spirits' here do not refer to the spirits of the spirit world, but the spirit within each human being - that part of us which governs our spiritual beliefs and spiritual character. John exhorts us to test the spirits of the prophets to see if they speak words of truth: whether their spirits are taught by the Holy Spirit or by another spirit which is of the Anti-Christ! Paul declares the 'spirits of the prophets are subject to the prophets' in 1 Cor 14:32. Great care must be taken here, for 'New-Age/ Charismatic Christianity' uses this verse to justify contacting the spirit world (spiritualism) and communing with 'spirit-helpers' - spirits that have been contacted and found to be 'good'. The Bible prohibits any contact with the spirit world (Lev 19:31; 20:6,27; Deut 18:10-12; 1 Chron 10:13 (case of Saul); Isa 8:19-20; Gal 5:20-21; Rev 21:8; 22:14-15). It would appear that the gift of discerning of spirits has ceased (circa 90 AD) in view of the unfolding of God's written word. John would have made reference to this gift if it was to play a role here.
[173] 1 Thessalonians 5:21
[174] 1 Peter 1:13

to 'free-up', 'let go' and 'empty'; relinquish the mind, giving potential access to demonic influences of varying degrees. The essential emphasis in charismatic meetings is upon 'receiving' some energy, power, influence or experience.

Some conservative Pentecostals rightly denounce the 'excesses' seen today, and hastily declare that their tongue-speaking is controlled.[175] Indeed, controlled by whom? Modern-day tongue-speaking itself means the speaker has succumbed to another 'power'. The degree of emotion is immaterial. Satan can speak in whispers or roar like a lion, seeking whom he may devour. Therefore, *"Be sober"*, says Peter, and *"gird the loins of your mind"*.[176]

There is a further consideration against tongue-speaking of great significance, and indeed, against the so-called 'Toronto blessing' that we have been told is of the Spirit of God.[177] Can people, while 'slain in the spirit', speaking in tongues or while cackling hysterically under the 'Toronto phenomenon', obey the command of God that we be *always* ready to answer every one who requests a reason of the hope that is in us? And, further, do so in meekness and fear?[178]

---

[175] It is of interest to ask how some of these 'conservatives', who speak in ecstatic, mysterious tongues themselves, deny that the 'Toronto Blessing' is of the Spirit of God! After all, do not those who claim the 'Toronto Blessing' also speak in ecstatic, mysterious tongues, which we are told, is of the Holy Spirit? (See below).

[176] 1 Peter 5:8 & 1:13. See also Phil 1:9-11; Col 1:9

[177] This is the supposed blessing of the Holy Spirit, evidenced by a person laughing uncontrollably while often rolling about on the floor. It is 'infectious' in that one person starts to laugh and others 'follow'. Soon the whole congregation or group are laughing hysterically, falling down and writhing in 'ecstatic' joy! It is called the Toronto Blessing because it is said to have first occurred in a church in Toronto. This 'spiritual laughing' however is not new. The noted Bible scholar Sir Robert Anderson K.C.B., LL.D., in an article he wrote entitled "Spirit Manifestations and The Gift of Tongues", referred to the self-confessed experience of a leader of the tongues movement, which was quoted in "The Dawn": Volume VIII No.3 June 1932. *"The power began to seize me, and I laughed all through the following Communion service."* At an evening prayer meeting, *"...after some waiting, I began to laugh, or rather my body was used to laugh with increasing power until I was flat on my back, laughing at the top of my voice for over half an hour."* During the Reformation (16th and 17th Centuries) sects arose (e.g. the 'French Prophets') speaking in tongues, claiming miraculous healing and 'holy laughter'. Such groups were characterised by gross immorality and biblical error.

[178] 1 Peter 3:15

Instead of anxious souls being informed of the sober truths concerning the inevitable judgment of God and their need of salvation, they are confronted with confusing utterances and immodest bodily contortions. Take the case of a sinner who is in deep concern of soul, or one who is in need of divine counsel due to some fret or folly in life. What message of hope can possibly come from a mouth speaking words of bafflement? What comfort flows to a heart enquiring, *"Sirs, what must I do to be saved?"* [179] from a bosom heaving not with sober Christian sympathy, but with indifferent laughter or confused tongue? Let us, in kindness and with a deep sense of love for the fraternity of Christ, speak as plainly as Scripture, which warns of the multitude that will be ensnared. 'False teachers *shall* come among us, who *shall* bring in damnable heresies. *Many shall* follow their pernicious ways. Through covetousness *shall* they with feigned words make merchandise of *many*', as evidenced by the outward appeal of such erroneous doctrines. Let us beware, for there are many Absaloms, who would through things superficially beautiful and seemingly plausible steal our hearts. [180]

> *Tell me the Story softly,*
> *With earnest tones and grave;*
> *Remember! I'm the sinner*
> *Whom Jesus came to save.*
> *Tell me that Story always,*
> *If you would really be,*
> *In any time of trouble,*
> *A comforter to me.*

(Miss Hankey)

Satan's counterfeit - ensnaring believers

Is it possible for believers in Christ to succumb to demonic

---

[179] Acts 16:30
[180] 2 Sam 15:5-6; 2 Peter 2:1-3.

influence? Sadly, it is indeed so.[181] Scripture warns that counterfeit activity by Satan is not a respecter of persons.[182] Our Lord was attacked, but could never succumb. Observe Satan's handiwork in the new versions (perversions) of the Bible which deny salient truths, yet are readily accepted by many believers. Revelation speaks of the counterfeit prophet and deception on a grand scale in a day to come.[183] Paul, as noted earlier, warns the Corinthians of Satan's transformation into an *"angel of light"*[184] and to the youthful Timothy, he mentions the capture of many by *"seducing spirits"*.[185] Paul exhorts believers to *"put on the whole armour of God"*. Why, if there is no danger of being assailed and wounded? It is to ensure *"we may be able to stand against the wiles of the devil"*. For we *"wrestle not with flesh and blood, but against principalities, against powers, against the rulers of the darkness of this world, against spiritual wickedness in high places..."*[186] Sadly, *many* sincere believers have succumbed to the wiles of the devil as a result of subtle counterfeit, and are following the errors of another gospel (the so-called 'Full gospel').[187]

Satan's assault on evangelical Christians

Satan is little concerned with those who hold and propagate outright error, such as the Jehovah's Witnesses, Mormons, and Christadelphians. The battle there has been won. He has those cults firmly in his grasp. His greatest threat comes from evangelical Christians who reverence doctrines such

---

[181] Such demonic 'influence' may be direct. It may also be indirect, where Satan uses psychological conditioning to evoke tongue-speaking (and other contemporary charismata). See Note 7
[182] See Note 6
[183] Revelation 16:13-14
[184] 2 Corinthians 11:14-15
[185] 1 Timothy 4:1
[186] Ephesians 6:10-17. The word 'wiles', *(methodias)* means a *plan* for deception. Through the Charismatic Movement, Satan has brought together a masterful strategy of truth mingled with error so he can deceive many.
[187] See Notes 4&5, also Gen 3:1; 2 Cor 11:3-4

as the Trinity, the Deity of Christ, the personality of the Holy Spirit and salvation exclusively by faith through the blood of Christ. Some 'evangelicals' may be swayed by bold-face error, for we know of apostates who deny the very incarnation, whose end shall be according to their works. But what strategy will reap a bountiful harvest among the faithful? Clearly, it must be a strategy which enables error to creep in unawares, error that closely resembles the truth, which is not only accepted but promoted! This is the art of counterfeiting, at which Satan is a consummate master. But mere counterfeit will not garner the extensive harvest he desires. Those who accept his counterfeit must be Bible-believing, fervent Christians. Satan is prepared to give ground to gain the land. "Let them have their doctrine", he would say, "let them even preach it, for in so doing they advance the error that I sow with it." Is there no truth within charismatic circles? What we see is an admixture of truth and error, Satan's most dangerous potion. Total error can be readily identified, but error mixed with truth is insidiously deceptive. This is Satan's way of sugar-coating the poison. Satan has made concessions in order to gain greater ground, a strategy nowhere more evident than in his failed temptation of our blessed Lord!

Eight reasons why Satan has chosen modern-day tongues as a device for deception.

In our discussions, many have asked "Why has Satan chosen tongues for deception?" He is a master of guile. He has chosen tongues, ecstatic unintelligible languages, to 'validate' the Charismatic Movement, because tongues are uniquely suited to deceiving Bible-orientated evangelical Christians.

1. Tongue-speaking is mentioned and exampled in Scripture, giving Satan something to counterfeit, creating seeming *'credibility'* amongst professing Christians.

2. Tongues in the early church were intimately associated with the programme and person of the Godhead - the Spirit

109

of God. Ascribing contemporary tongues to the work of the Holy Spirit promotes an appearance of *'authenticity'*.

3. Because tongues are audible, Satan's counterfeit is observable, thus giving it *'reality'*.

4. Tongue-speaking is 'spectacular', enhancing its *'acceptability'*.

5. Unintelligible tongue-speaking is not self-authenticating, its phrases cannot be tested (as with foreign languages) - promoting *'duplicity'*.

6. Tongues provide immediate reinforcement of false teaching and emotion, giving them *'dependability'* in deception.

7. They are an ideal medium through which demons can voice their doctrine, as seen in occult communication - here we see their *'adaptability'*.

8. Because tongue-speaking is seen as a supernatural religious experience, it promotes *'transferability'* between ecclesiastical boundaries.

Tongues are indeed an ideal device in Satan's deceptive strategy. We may not find 'spiritual breathing' or 'spiritual coat flinging' in every charismatic gathering, but you will certainly find tongues.

The damage being inflicted by modern-day tongues and the Charismatics

May those who speak in tongues, who seek to further the honour of the Lord, consider prayerfully the gravity of the error of tongues as noted in what follows. A sinister purpose lies behind Satan's counterfeit activity. And, may all who say it really does not matter that some Christians speak in tongues, take heed. It has been and continues to be Satan's principal objective to detract from the honour and glory of the Son of God as Lord and Saviour. He pursues this in many ways: the superstition and error of Rome, the blasphemy of the Cults, and in recent times, his seduction of many evangelical Christians through their blinding preoccupation with tongues and other charismata, viz:

1. *Denial of the power and all-sufficiency of the blood of Christ - our Great High Priest!* In Hebrews 10 we have heralded our greater blessings in Christ over the saints of the OT. No Jew (save the High Priest on the Day of Atonement) under the OT economy, could conceive of entering let alone actually enter the holiest - the very presence of God without impunity. But now, *every* child of God through the efficacy of the blood of Christ is not just permitted to enter the holiest, but is *invited* to enter in - to *"draw near"* (v.22)! 'Come, for all things are ready!' To what end? That we may as *priests* offer our praise and supplications to God. No priest of the Mosaic economy could enter the holiest. But we who have been made kings and priests unto God by the blood of Christ (Rev 1:5-6) can enter that inner sanctum of God and render priestly service to Him.

But, what are we told with fervent importunity by the charismatics? We need a special language to gain some special hearing and audience with God - a denial of the truth that every saved person, no matter how feeble their faith, has been invited and can with boldness "enter into the holiest of all by the blood of Jesus"! The way *is* opened! It is through His precious shed blood - all sufficient and ever present before God, not some 'tongue', that we have boldness to enter. What a tragic stumbling block is cast here by Satan before the dear saints of God, who have been brought near by the precious blood of Christ, yet are told they need a special prayer language (or a 'second blessing') to have 'privileged' communion with God! Further, what a slight on the person and work of Christ, our Great High Priest of "good things to come"; through whom our prayers ascend to God![188] To hear such a charge may cause a tongue-speaker distress for many are sincere in their beliefs! But let all take heed, for it is a

---

[188] Hebrews 9:11; 13:15

subtle attack by Satan on the person of Christ and a cunning deprivation upon the believer. What Satan has sought to deny to believers through priests, religious institutions and solemn statutes, the virgin Mary and patron saints as mediators, he seeks in pernicious subtlety to deny many through some notion of a special prayer language. Multiply this deception by the millions who today believe they have access to God through their tongues and we see something of the monstrous magnitude of Satan's attack on the Son of God.

> *"Boldly our heart and voice we raise,*
> *His Name, His blood, our plea;*
> *Assured our prayers and songs of praise*
> *Ascend by Him to Thee".*
>
> (James G. Deck)

2. *Depreciation of Christ's Lordship and Divine order.* All things are His in praise, worship and service. *"All things that the Father hath are mine: therefore said I, that he* [the Holy Spirit] *shall take of mine, and shall shew it unto you."* [189] The Charismatic Movement and the so-called tongues experience exhort us to praise and pray to the Holy Spirit, when our praise and prayers should be directed to the Son through the Holy Spirit - again a reversal of truth! Our focus must be upon the Son as Lord, as led and exhorted by the Spirit. Tongues and other modern-day charismata run contrary to the intention of Christ, *"Howbeit when He, the Spirit of truth, is come, He will guide you into all truth: for He shall not speak of [from] Himself......He shall glorify Me.."* And again, *"But when the Comforter* [the Holy Spirit] *is come, whom I will send unto you from the Father, even the Spirit of truth, which proceedeth from the Father, He shall testify of Me"* [190] The Spirit of God is to keep before us and amplify the

---

[189] John 16:15. '*anaggello*', to announce or make known.
[190] John 16:13-14; John 15:26.

words and work of the Son, who is to occupy that divinely ordained place as Lord "in our midst"! While the Lord dwelt among men they could behold *"His glory, the glory as of the only Begotten of the Father, full of grace and truth"*.[191] His saving work accomplished, the Firstborn from among the dead ascended to the Father. Who then testifies of His glory among men? Who but the Spirit of God! The Lord further declares in John 14:25-26: *"These things have I spoken unto you, being yet present with you. But the Comforter, which is the Holy Ghost, whom the Father will send in My name, He shall teach you all things, and bring all things to your remembrance, whatsoever I have said unto you."* Now dear reader, let us ask ourselves this question! Do we wish a divine test to determine if our prayers and praises are led by the Holy Spirit? Then let us examine them by the measure they centre and confess,(see below) the Lord and His glory.[192] The Spirit of God will always draw us to the person of Christ, for it is He, the Son (not the Spirit), who died for us and who occupies that ordained position "in the midst".

3. *Denial of the Holy Spirit.* "How is that?" you may ask. "Surely this cannot be so, for charismatics are noted for their focus on the Spirit of God?" Deceptively, there may be no outright denial of His deity or personality. Rather, denial 'validated' by tongues, is in regard to His distinctive works, e.g., the charismatic doctrine that the baptism by the Holy Spirit involves the Spirit being received by individuals, and the teaching of a 'second blessing'. These notions are not authenticated by Scripture, but by tongues, which they say is the sign of the reception of the Holy Spirit. We take this up further when studying the work of the Spirit of God. For the present, let us observe a particular denial of the Spirit of God in regard to believers as priests unto God (as noted above). It reveals another subtle manoeuvre by Satan to deprive believers

---

[191] John 1:14
[192] How grieved the Holy Spirit must be to hear songs of praise and prayer to Him rather than to the Son. It is, assuredly, the subtle work of Satan.

of that which they possess inalienably in Christ. Satan has lured modern-day tongue-speakers into relying upon and teaching with great fervour, that their tongues not only enable them to have access to God, but 'condition' them for it. We hear claims that the quality of communion with God is positively dependent on the frequency of speaking in tongues - citing personal experience as proof! Such claims are in direct opposition to the work of the Spirit of God. It is the Spirit of God who moves us to draw near into the holiest of all. He does this not only by inspiring the writer to the Hebrews to pen words of invitation, which seems to be clouded by the tongues experience, but lines that inform us of the spiritual propriety required to approach and enter the holiest - a true heart and full assurance of faith. These are not conditions to be met for the way to be opened. The veil is rent, the way into the holiest has been made clear by Christ as we noted earlier. Drawing near with a true heart and in full assurance of faith refers to necessary conditions *within* us which, if not realised, will inhibit *our* response to the invitation - denying ourselves that boldness (confidence) to enter. We are to keep in mind too, as enabled by the Spirit of God, that the preparation for us as priests has been done, effected by the Lord (the sprinkling of the blood and the washing at the laver that was so necessary before the Levitical priests could render service to God). As with any beneficent provision from God, there is always our responsibility in regard to it. Now, it is the Spirit of God (not tongue-speaking) who fits us to meet such responsibility. That is why He has been given to dwell within us. To rely on 'heavenly language' in order to commune with God and 'condition' us to come before His throne of grace, is to deflect our focus from the true spiritual propriety in responding to the invitation to enter the holiest, and to deny the Spirit of God His work in us. This is why so much of charismatic 'worship' is not according to the Spirit of God.

4. *Denial of the doctrine of Divine Headship.* Women are observed unashamedly speaking in tongues alongside men during church meetings (frequently with uncovered heads, 1

Cor 11). This is in direct opposition to the injunction given by the Spirit through Paul in 1 Corinthians 14:34, and to Timothy, regarding the proper behaviour within the house of God, which is the pillar and ground of truth (1 Tim 2:11). Again, liberty is sought and found in the false belief that tongues are of the Spirit, and as long as we can speak in tongues, no error exists.

5. *The assault on the Word of God.* Often, the so-called interpretation of tongues is said to voice new revelations from God. Tongue-speakers are thus elevated as modern-day prophets and their 'revelations' vie with Biblical truth, perpetrating another error.[193] We need to remember that many cults owe their origin to such people and their tongues.[194] Because tongues supposedly indicate the sanction of the Spirit, the Bible is devalued as a source of assurance. 'Faith' and 'spirituality' are cultivated outside the fertile expanse of truth provided in the inspired Word of God, and repose on a wasteland of counterfeit signs and lying wonders.

6. *Perversion of the prophetic Scriptures.* Modern-day tongue-speaking is used to misinterpret Biblical prophecy, clearly apparent in the appalling mistake of ascribing (spiritualising) prophecies which relate exclusively to Israel as referring to the church of God, e.g. Ezek 11:19; Joel 2:28-32; 3. Amillennialism is a product of such error.[195] And, it is worth noting, that amillennialism (particularly the liberal

---

[193] John (Rev 1:10) and Peter (Acts 10:10) were both given new revelations while completely under the control of the Spirit of God - i.e. they were transfixed by the Spirit in order to impart the revelation through a vision. With the completed Scriptures - 'once for all delivered', this operation of the Holy Spirit no longer occurs! All modern-day instances are Satan's counterfeit!

[194] The shelves of many Christian bookshops confuse many believers, gladden the heart of all sceptics and delight Satan. We are faced with a plethora of 'versions' of the Bible appealing to gender, age and denominational bias. Of the latter is the charismatic 'Spirit Filled Life' Bible, the very basis of which is predicated on a wrongful interpretation of Joel's prophecy (see Note 4).

[195] Amillennialism (the 'A' represents the negative view) teaches that there will be no literal millennium (1000 year reign by Christ) on earth following His second coming. It holds that the blessings God made to Israel are not literal and are being fulfilled today in the church. Therefore amillennialists confound the distinction between the Body of Christ and Israel. We can see then why many charismatics believe we are in the end-time of great spiritual blessing - latter rain, tongues and other charismata.

115

form) has become increasingly popular because it allows many denominations within Christianity - Protestant and Roman Catholic, to find common ground, enhancing ecumenicalism. Many tongue-speaking believers are unaware that when they defend modern-day tongues as the fulfilment of Joel's prophecy, they are promoting amillennialism.

7. *The use of tongues to minimise doctrine.* The prevailing rule of biblical interpretation within the Charismatic Movement is 'validation by tongues'. This explains how charismatics are comfortable in many denominations and why many denominations are comfortable with charismatics - even Rome, tongues being the trademark of tolerance. Growing numbers of practising Roman Catholics have received the gift of tongues through a 'second blessing' - the 'baptism by the Holy Spirit'. We are told that the gift of tongues received by charismatic Catholics renews their faith in their holy sacraments. One such sacrament is holy communion, based on the grave error of transubstantiation: upon consecration during Mass, the bread and wine disappear in substance and become totally converted into the body and blood of Christ. Now remember, the Spirit of God is also the Spirit of truth. If you are a Protestant present-day tongue speaker, ask yourself how the Spirit of truth can be party to, or enrich, a practice which is wholly pagan and blasphemous?" How can the Spirit of truth bestow a 'heavenly prayer language' to those who pray to the virgin Mary and various so-called saints, in flagrant denial of the truth of one mediator between God and man, the Man Christ Jesus?[196] Doctrine, it appears, matters little. Our common tongues experience unites us!

8. *False assurance of salvation.* There is the fearful

---

[196] 1 Timothy 2:5. This total conversion is (erroneously) said to be taught by Christ when He declared - "this is my Body"; "this is my Blood"! Conversely, we would ask Roman Catholics who speak in tongues and support transubstantiation, how can the Spirit of Truth be party to enriching those who speak in tongues and who disagree with their holy doctrine?

prospect that many who speak in tongues may not be saved at all, falsely regarding their tongue-speaking as evidence of salvation and indwelling of the Holy Spirit; much to do about charismata and experiences, but never actually confessed Christ as redeemer. Satan is ever seeking to beguile the unwary, and this terrible prospect, in many cases, has become a grim reality. Charismatic meetings are more to do with cultivating feelings than with conviction of sin before a righteous God. Let us mark well the principle contained in the solemn warning of our Lord concerning the counterfeit work of other spirits. "Not everyone that saith unto Me, Lord, Lord, shall enter into the kingdom of heaven;....Many [not a few] will say unto Me in that day, Lord, Lord, have we not prophesied in Thy name? and in Thy name have cast out devils? and in Thy name done many wonderful works? And then will I profess unto them, I never knew you depart from Me, ye that work iniquity."[197] I trust, my reader, you are not such a case. Are you saved? Your tongues do not mean that you are. Rest on the Scriptures, not on your experiences, your emotions, or those of religious teachers who cry "Lord, Lord" while performing counterfeit works. Our salvation is based solely on the precious shed blood of Christ. Our faith must rest on this and this only, not on some unintelligible language. Permit me to dwell on this warning, as it occupies the heart of John in his tender concern for the children of God. He warns (with particular reference to the Gnostic heresy), "every spirit that confesseth not that Jesus Christ is come in the flesh is not of God".[198] It is not just a case of speaking the correct words, but of the words reflecting deep conviction and a submissive heart. A mere profession of the name of Christ does not mark a true confession. Is Jesus the Christ, the Son of God? 'Yes', says Simon son of Jona; 'Yes' say also the sons of Beelzebub.[199] The commended words of

---

[197] Matthew 7:21-23
[198] 1 John 4:3
[199] Matthew 16:16; Luke 4:41

Peter, "Thou art the Christ, the Son of the living God" compose the blueprint and foundation of the church. However, when the demons cried, "Thou art Christ the Son of God", they were rebuked by Christ. The words of Peter were a confession born of divine revelation and Peter's subjection to the Lord.[200] The cries of the demons were a mere profession, not a confession, born of knowledge, but void of honour and obedience unto Him. Have you made that all-important confession of Romans 10:9?

9. *False assurance of sanctification.* Many tongue-speakers feel quite at liberty to frequent places of worldly entertainment and indulge in worldly pursuits, because their tongues are a sign of wholesome spirituality. As long as they can speak in tongues they live under the allusion of the Spirit's sanction of such ways.

10. *Feigned worship.* We noted earlier that Satan seduced Eve by appealing to her physical senses (the flesh): the fruit was good, desirable and pleasant. What was Satan doing here? He was using the lure of a "sensational experience" - that which delights the body (physical senses) to ensnare Adam and Eve into error! His methods have not changed. Paul, in his closing words to the Thessalonians, reminds them of the tripartite nature of man - spirit, soul and body.[201] The order reflects the priority and supremacy of the spirit in the spiritual life of the believer. The body, the basest level, is our window to the world - sight, smell, taste and hearing. The soul is the seat of our emotions, our feelings. The spirit represents that inner realm which is capable of knowing God and possessing a conscience toward Him. Therefore, it is the spirit of man that is appealed to when worshipping God. True worship can only be on a spiritual level - the body and soul are subordinated. Why? Because God Himself is a Spirit and we must, therefore, worship Him "in spirit [according to

---

[200] Paul in 1 Cor 12:3 is speaking of a confession, and not a mere declaration, of which the Lord speaks in Matt 7:21-23.
[201] 2 Corinthians 11:3; 1 Thess 5:23

His nature] and in truth [according to His word]". After all, it is His Spirit that bears witness with our spirit that we are the children of God.[202] We see the practical outworking of this in Paul's teaching to the Corinthians - "I will pray with the spirit [the inner highest level of man] ... I will sing with the spirit" [and with the understanding when I pray and sing - understanding as from the Word of God].[203] Within the charismatic-tongues fraternity, we see another order in worship - body, soul and spirit, yet another reversal of God's order. The body is the principal vehicle in worship - body swaying, hand-clapping, trembling, rolling, dancing etc. Bodily senses are also ignited through tongue-speaking sessions, seeing 'healings' and other 'miracles'! Then there is appeal to the soul where feelings are fanned by perpetual bodily motion, music and sensational sermons promoting happiness through promises of wealth and health - the so-called 'full gospel'! This is taken to be the 'joy or fullness of the Spirit', 'refreshing faith'. It is nothing but a recycling of emotions, with no opportunity to hear the still small voice of God! There is little or nothing of the Spirit, for it does not engage the human spirit! There is little desire for the cool, fathomless, still waters that flow from the Good Shepherd of Psalm 23. Only there can we drink deeply to refresh the spirit and render reverent praise and worship! Instead, there is a lust for the shallow turbid tide of fevered emotion from which to gulp!

11. *Retardation of spiritual growth.* Paul refers to the believers at Corinth in his first Epistle as 'babes' (ch. 3) and 'children' (ch. 13 & 14). They had made little spiritual progress because their attitudes and desires were as babes in the natural world. That is (a) they were swayed by personal appearances (2:1-4); (b) they were more interested in having 'experiences' than coming to grips with doctrinal truth -

---

[202] John 4:24; Rom 8:16
[203] 1 Corinthians 14:15

chapters 12,13 and 14; (c) they were, like infants, preoccupied with 'gifts' rather than with 'graces'! There is much of this Corinthian condition amongst believers today. A lack of spiritual advancement is evident in immature worship, the need to be constantly entertained and occupied, i.e. senses - sight, hearing, continually fanned and fed. Worship is not forgetting self and wholly focusing on the Lord, His person and work, but what we must do to make ourselves feel good - pleasant sights, sounds and activities - we must not become bored! Sadly, many have yet to appreciate the all-sufficiency of 'Christ in the midst', the spiritual fullness He imparts in this ordained place and the reverence He demands, such that our "hearts burn within us". How can the Lord's presence ever make us bored? If the Lord is present, what else do we need? Immature worship also reckons that making a 'joyful noise unto the Lord' is to 'entertain' Him, supposing He can 'be worshipped with men's hands'.[204] Let us ask, "What does God want from our worship of Him?"

12. *Ecumenicalism.* We have typified in Genesis 11 for our learning the seeds of ecumenicalism in the building of the tower of Babel (Babylon). The Charismatic Movement will help pave the way for the love-child of ecumenicalism, the Great Whore - the apostate world church, ecclesiastical Babylon (Rev 17). How? There is today the growing desire for ecclesiastical unity and it will be furthered in part by the one tongue - the common 'heavenly tongue' espoused by charismatics within many denominations (and non-Christian religions) - a tongue which will unite a spiritual edifice designed to reach into the very 'heavens'. (An attempt to mitigate the judgment of God meted out in Genesis 11). The part Rome will play is, of course, central and she must fully embrace the Charismatic Movement, and all within Protestant denominations who espouse it! She already cradles the

---

[204] Acts 17:22-25

charismata. In 1995, the Pope gave charismatic Catholics ("Catholic Fraternity of Covenant Communities and Fellowships") his blessing and has since then officially encouraged their active role in local churches. The official Papal line is that tongues, 'second blessings' etc, renew faith in the sacraments and the liturgy and enhance understanding of the greater mission of the (Roman Catholic) Church as it moves into the next millennium.

13. *Rebellion not revival.* We often hear of a 'charismatic' or 'tongues' led revival. How do we identify a true revival? Professions of salvation? Numerical increases in congregations? Increasing mission and evangelical activity? These may well accompany a revival. But the essence of a true revival is marked by a return to God's holy order. A true revival cannot be effected in disobedience. The people of Israel with much "singing, and with harps, and with psalteries, and with timbrels, and with cymbals, and with trumpets", sought to restore the presence of the ark of the covenant among them. But, alas, their zeal was not according to understanding - for they placed it on a cart and earned God's displeasure and wrought confusion.[205] Before the faithful second remnant from Babylon entered Jerusalem, Ezra halted the journey to bring the "ministers for the house of our God" among them.[206] The tongue-speaking movement however, is a total reversal of God's order, as we have seen. Further, true revival is marked by self judgment, not on a calling for 'power'. Look to that mighty servant of God once again. Ezra prepared his heart to seek the law of the Lord, and to do it, and to teach in Israel the statutes and judgments of God. This is where true revival begins, with self judgment and the expounding of the Word of God, entrance of which 'giveth light'.[207]

14. *Spiritual casualties.* Apart from the personal spiritual

---

[205] 1 Chronicles 13
[206] Ezra 8:17
[207] Ezra 7:10; Psa 119:130

damage being done to those who speak in tongues, there is a trail of spiritual and emotional wreckage in the wake of many believers who have failed to speak in tongues or experience some 'second blessing'. Many who have failed, even after months or years of trying, are informed their failure is due to a lack of personal faith or some besetting sin. Because of a 'unsuccessful experience', they fail to come into the blessing that there is now no more conscience of sins (Heb 10:2). This leaves them vulnerable to Satan. They regard themselves as inferior Christians and far worse, many begin to doubt their salvation.

Flee the 'charismatics'

Beloved in Christ, be warned! If you speak in tongues today, you are being deceived. You are also being used by Satan. You may hold dear the truths of the Deity of Christ, redemption through His precious blood, the Trinity etc, but you are unwittingly being used by Satan to further his kingdom. You may genuinely believe you are enriched in your spiritual life, but consider this to be the lure that has led you into error. Now be encouraged. We have come to know many believers over the years who have forsaken tongues and now show greater spiritual stability in their lives, and an authentic enrichment in their walk with the Lord. There has been that inner joy and assurance derived from rightly dividing the Word of God. They were liberated from the bondage of having to seek signs and emotional experiences in order to live joyful and productive Christian lives. Indeed, their yielding to the truth concerning tongues has unlocked the Scriptures, revealing the error of the doctrine of the "charismatics". This, too, can be the portion of all those who speak in tongues, who are willing to deny their experience in favour of the scriptural position on this matter. To deny personal experience and the prospect of altered personal relationships is daunting. Yet, be assured, *"Greater is He that is in you, than he that is in the world.*"[208] Let us be warned, to deny Scripture in favour of personal experience is not only a programme for spiritual instability, it will earn condemnation from the One who thrice declared, *"It is written"*. Remember too, the Lord's reply to Thomas when he wanted to see in order to believe: *"blessed are they that have not seen, and yet believed."*[209]

There is a solemn warning here, too, for believers who, themselves, neither seek nor speak in tongues, but are prepared to be indifferent to present-day tongue-speaking; who tolerate tongues within their gathering under some (misguided) notion of brotherly love. Present-day tongues are either scriptural or they are not. Brotherly love should be exercised through a gracious explanation of the error involved and a sanctifying separation from it.[210] Finally, we should ensure we conduct ourselves in a manner that gives no liberty to the charismatic error by guarding against the hollowness of formalism as well as the frivolity of super-emotionalism.

---

[208] 1 John 4:4
[209] John 20:29
[210] 1 John 5:2

CHAPTER 8

The Holy Spirit

There is a good deal of confusion concerning the ministry of the Spirit of God, much of it due to the 'tongues experience'. Are the four works of the Holy Spirit - indwelling (anointing), sealing, filling, and baptism - distinctive operations of the Spirit, or are they one and the same? There are many who proclaim and practise little distinction between them. Let us again apply the test of Scripture with care and consideration for each other, always seeking to gain one's brother and sister in Christ. The following study will, with the help of the Spirit of Truth, show what the Word of God has revealed regarding His distinctive and varied ministry in this Church age.

Indwelling

1. *This refers to the Spirit of God Himself indwelling the believer.* Scripture teaches an indwelling (or anointing) of the Spirit of God. The anointing emphasizes a particular truth concerning the Spirit's indwelling, which we take up below. For the present, we note the distinction between the *gift* of the Spirit and the *gifts* of the Spirit.[211] The former speaks of the 'person' - the Holy Spirit, who is the actual Gift; the latter, of the gifts He distributes. The Lord promised before He ascended that He would pray the Father to send *His Spirit*, "who dwelleth [at present] *with* you and *shall be in* you [future]".[212] The Spirit of

---

[211] See Note 3
[212] John 14:17: "He abides", not just *"with you"*, but *"at home with you"*; *"By your side"* (timeless present tense). A. T. Robertson "<u>Word Pictures in the New Testament</u>" Volume V p. 253.

God Himself is promised here, that He may dwell (reside or live) in us. He was already with them, from Pentecost onwards. He will also be *in* them.

Firstly, this a dispensational matter, that is, it speaks of a new period of God's dealing with man. The Holy Spirit *Himself* is to be sent and shall be in you. Remember, this is one of the 'changes' that we spoke of earlier that had to be signalled by a sign - tongues. The Lord's promise points to a future period - the Church age, from Pentecost to the Rapture - characterised by a new, personal ministry of the Spirit of God. The Lord's words are clear - the Holy Spirit at that time had not come into the world as He is today - He had to be *sent!* We have here the difference between the ministry of the Holy Spirit before Pentecost and after Pentecost, within the church period - which is characterised by His personal dwelling in each believer. Consequently, He enters into a new relationship with us as individuals. Scripture teaches us that He also indwells the church.

Further, we note it is the Lord's right - His prayer, not ours, that sends the Holy Spirit, *"I will pray the Father"*. It is His sovereign right to petition the Father concerning this, because it is upon His glorification, based on His redeeming work at Calvary, that the Spirit of God was sent *"..if I go not away, the Comforter will not come unto you; but if I depart, I will send Him unto you"*.[213] Sorrow filled the hearts of the Lord's disciples when the reality of His leaving dawned on them. However, He assured them that divine fellowship with the person of God's only Begotten Son on earth, will give way to divine fellowship with the person of His Spirit on earth. And, through the fellowship of the Spirit, they will be brought into blessed communion with the ascended Christ. So He personally pledges to send the person of the Holy Spirit to indwell them (and us). See also John 15:26, *"the Comforter...whom I will send"*. We cannot, dare not, assume any part in this - shall a man rob God?

2. *The promise of the gift of the Spirit and His indwelling*

---

[213] John 16:7

is unconditional. Next, we note the blessed certainty of the Lord's promise - He *shall* be in you. This is an unconditional promise to us because it is based on the all-sufficient redeeming work of Christ. It is founded upon, and hence is as secure as, the promise of salvation itself, *"believe on the Lord Jesus Christ and thou shalt be saved."* For us to pray to receive the Spirit of God is a denial of the perfect work of redemption by Christ and to try to usurp His Sovereignty. It is also a folly to pray for the Holy Spirit to be with us and in us. He has been sent. He is here. As believers, we have Him with us and dwelling in us because of the Lord's reconciling work and His prayer.

3. *The indwelling of God's Spirit occurs at conversion for each and every believer.* Scripture clearly teaches the blessed companion truth, the moment a sinner accepts Christ as Lord and Saviour, without exception, he/she is indwelt by the Holy Spirit, i.e. receives the gift of the Spirit: *"Now if any man hath not the Spirit of Christ, he is none of His"*.[214] It is impossible to be 'born again' i.e., to become a child of God, without the regenerating and renewing work of the Holy Spirit - "that which is born of flesh is flesh, *that which is born of Spirit is Spirit"*; "except an man be born of water (the washing of the Word of God) and *of the Spirit,* he cannot enter the kingdom of God".[215] *"...not by works of righteousness which we have done, but according to his mercy he saved us, by the washing of regeneration* [to be born again by the Word of God as imparted by the Spirit of God - the cleansing from sin at conversion], *and renewing of the Holy Ghost* [the Spirit's

---

[214] Romans 8:9. The whole portion here (vv. 9-16) is wonderfully instructive. Paul refers to the 'Spirit of Christ' in verse 9 as well as the 'Spirit of God' in order to: (1) convey the thought that the gift of the Spirit rests on the risen and glorified Jesus of Nazareth, the Christ; (2) present the co-equality between God, His Spirit and Christ, and practical instruction in the light of it. The Spirit of God is also a 'quickening' Spirit. In verse 11, Paul speaks argumentatively - if the Spirit dwells in you (as He in fact does), then He will quicken your mortal bodies.

[215] John 3:3-8. The Holy Spirit reveals the Word of God to our heart and mind, convicting us unto salvation.

on-going work in remaking or renovating the new life in the believer gained at conversion]."[216] Paul reminds the Ephesians that salvation is through faith not of works lest any should boast. Now hear his question to the Galatians: *"Received ye the Spirit by the works of the law, or by the hearing of faith? Are ye so foolish? having begun in the Spirit......?"*[217] It is by faith they were saved - by faith they began, having received the Holy Spirit.

Note again, we do not have to pray to receive the Spirit of God. Paul reminds *each* Corinthian believer, even though they were carnal, their body is a temple of the Holy Spirit, *"which is in you, which ye have of God"*[218], confirming the unconditional promise of the Lord to very believer, that the Holy Spirit 'shall be in you'. Do you remember the case of the Ephesian (John's) disciples (Acts 19)? They were not saved until they heard the gospel of Christ from Paul (v.4). Paul asks, *"have ye received the Holy Ghost when ye believed?"* The receiving, here the

---

[216] Titus 3:5. *'paliggenesia'* - 'to be born again';*'anakainosis'* - 'to renovate'. Washing does not mean baptism, but the cleansing application of the Word of God to our heart and mind by the Spirit of God unto conversion (Eph 5:26). Baptism (whatever form) is never a requirement for salvation. But what about Acts 2:38, *"Repent and be baptized......for the remission of sins, and ye shall receive the gift of the Holy Ghost"*? There is no formula or sequence for salvation (the remission of sins) here. It is simply a general statement of the elements of the new Order. The grammar is of little help here and we need to compare Scripture with itself. Let the clear words of Peter and the Lord Himself decide the matter. Remission of sins is only ever on the basis of the shedding of blood, not ritual. Baptism is only an external expression of it! Peter declares, *"....that through His name whosoever believeth in Him shall receive remission of sins"* (Acts 10:43). In 1 Peter 3:21 we have: *"The like figure whereunto even baptism doth also now save us (not the putting away of the filth of the flesh, but the answer of a good conscience toward God,) by the resurrection of Jesus Christ."* The Lord declares in Mark 16:16, *"He that believeth and is baptized shall be saved: but he that believeth not shall be dammed"*. This latter statement and that of the Lord's in John 3:16, *"..whosoever believeth in Him should have everlasting life"* refutes any notion of baptism being required for salvation. When the imperilled jailer cries. *"Sirs, what must I do to be saved"*, Paul and Silas reply, *"Believe on the Lord Jesus Christ, and thou shalt be saved...."* (Acts 16:29-31). See Eph 5:26 on the washing of water by the Word of God. Ceremonies and water cannot wash away sins. Also, to use Acts 22:16 in support of salvation through baptism, is to make water rival the precious blood of Christ (1 Peter 1:18-19). In Acts 22:16, baptism is presented as symbolically washing away sin and the start of the new life in Christ.
[217] Galatians 3:1-3
[218] 1 Corinthians 6:19

indwelling of the Holy Spirit, is that which determined whether or not they were converted in Christ and not just some of John's converts. Their answer was that they had not even heard of the Holy Spirit.[219] Their faith was in the message of John the Baptist, the need for national repentance for the Jews. Before Christ's coming, John preached the 'baptism of repentance to Israel'.[220] So they had not received the Spirit of God for they had not heard the gospel of Christ. Paul was asking these Jews to recall a sign to prove they were really saved - born again by the Spirit of God, for he knew that they were John's disciples and may not have truly believed on 'the One who was to follow John'. Remember, Paul and the others, being Jews, required a sign that the Spirit of God had come upon these converts of John. Paul then preached Christ to them and they believed. At that moment they received the Spirit of God and were baptized according to the Lord's command in Matthew 28:19 (water baptism). Each received the 'gift of the Holy Spirit' at that moment of belief, which was acknowledged by the ceremonial laying on of hands and evidenced by the sign of tongues (required as we saw earlier for the witness to the Jews - the Holy Spirit fell on them and they received the Spirit of God). The 'gift of the Spirit' in Acts 2:38, is to everyone who repents - the *individual* receives the Holy Spirit upon repentance - *"ye shall receive the gift of the Holy Ghost"*; not gifts but *gift*, upon belief in Christ.[221] To them and all afar off (Gentiles), is the promise, the promise of the indwelling of God's Spirit.[222]

---

[219] Acts 19:1-7. The correct grammatical meaning is *when* ye believed, not 'since' (A. T. Robertson "Word Pictures in the New Testament" Volume III p. 311). 'Since' implies the receiving of the Spirit can be some time after believing, which is doctrinally incorrect. Also, 'not heard' is in the sense of not hearing of the Spirit's new work: being Jews and John's disciples they would have heard of the existence of the Holy Spirit.

[220] Acts 13:24

[221] Repentance here is forsaking self because of sin and turning to Christ as Saviour.

[222] Acts 2:39. *"The promise refers to the gift of the Holy Spirit and not the supernatural manifestations"*. W. E. Vine "The Collected Writings of W. E. Vine", Volume 5 p. 83.

All this may be summarised as follows:
- We are saved the moment we place our faith in Christ as Lord and Saviour (i.e. Acts 16:31 - our obedience to the call - "Believe on the Lord Jesus Christ, and thou shalt be saved").
- The moment we are saved we become a child of God (John 1:12).
- Every child of God has the Spirit of God (Christ)(Romans 8:9).
- Therefore, we have the indwelling of the Spirit of God - the gift of the Spirit - the moment we believe in Christ as Saviour.

4. *The indwelling of God's Spirit is permanent (therefore not repeatable).*The indwelling of the Spirit of God in each believer, in marked contrast to the OT, is permanent by virtue of the unconditional promise and the regenerating work of the Holy Spirit, required for salvation. In addition to the Scriptures cited above, this is forcibly presented to us in James 4:5, *"Do ye think that the Scripture saith in vain, The Spirit that dwelleth in us lusteth to envy?"* The words 'dwelleth in us', actually means 'made/caused to take up permanent residence'. The Spirit does not do this of Himself, He acts in accordance with the will of the Father and Son.[223] In this short statement, we have the indwelling of the Spirit of God, the permanence of it and the delegation of it, in that the Holy Spirit is 'made/caused' by the Father to dwell in us because of the Son. The permanence of the indwelling (anointing) is also seen in 1 John 2:27 (refer below). Further, as we noted in the case of the carnal Corinthians, the indwelling is not dependent on our spiritual condition as believers. The prayer of David in Psalm 51:11,*"take not thy Holy Spirit from me",* is wholly irrelevant today, as also the

---

[223] *"katoikisen"* - *"Made to dwell"*. A. T. Robertson "Word Pictures in the New Testament" Volume VI p. 51.

Spirit's leaving Saul in 1 Samuel 16:14 is blessedly impossible!

Anointing with the Spirit
We often read of the Spirit's ministry as an anointing in both the OT and the NT For saints in the NT, (compared with the patriarchs of the OT), the anointing of the Spirit is, in fact, the *permanent* indwelling of the Spirit - it takes place at the time of conversion to Christ and it is never repeated. The indwelling is called an anointing in various instances because it emphasizes a particular purpose of the Spirit's indwelling, which is to set apart (sanctify) the believer for life and service in Christ. It has an essential ceremonial connotation as indicated by the word itself.[224] In 1 John 2:27, we are reminded of the *"anointing which ye have received of him abideth in you"* - the permanent indwelling; and we note it is not in the plural, 'anointings', but a once-for-all (the) anointing, and this once-for-all anointing in the past is permanent - abides. The words *"abideth in you"*, means 'to live and remain' in you (every believer). Then we have the sanctifying work of the indwelling Spirit: *"and ye need not that any man teach you but as the same anointing teacheth you of all things..."* We have here the unlimited resources of the Spirit of God to draw upon in our life of sanctification. The once-for-all nature of the anointing is again seen in that it is the *same* anointing. The anointing of the Holy Spirit does not mean repeated fillings or 'receivings'. Finally, we have in 1 John 4:4, *"Greater is He* [the Holy Spirit] *that is in you, than he* [Satan - the prince of this world] *that is in the world"*, which

---

[224] The word 'chrio' is used for the anointing of the Holy Spirit in the NT. The Levitical priests were anointed - set apart for their sanctified service - the oil symbolic of the Spirit of God. *"It* [chrio] *is more limited in its use than No. 1* [aleipho]*; it is confined to "sacred and symbolical anointings"*; W. E. Vine "Expository Dictionary of New Testament Words", p. 58. Saul was 'anointed', indwelt by the Spirit of God, for a purpose. We see the setting apart of the Lord for service in Luke 4:18; *"The Spirit of the Lord is upon me, because he hath anointed* [chrisen] *me* (set me apart or sanctified me) *to preach the gospel to the poor...."*. It was in respect of His (perfect) manhood that the Lord was anointed with the Spirit. In His perfect manhood he was typified as the meal offering which contained oil within and was also anointed with oil (sanctified - set apart)!

again speaks of the sanctifying work of the Spirit of God as He dwells 'in' us. Note here (and elsewhere in Scripture) the reference is to the Spirit of God as a Person -*He* that is in you. The Holy Spirit is not a 'force' but a person of the Godhead!

Sealing

Apart from indwelling at the moment of salvation, the Spirit of God, at that same time, seals the believer. It is, like the indwelling, a work of the Spirit of God in regard to the *individual* and is inextricably linked with the permanency of the indwelling. Scripture never even hints at a 'probationary period', after which we are sealed. The Holy Spirit Himself is the seal of divine ownership, the guarantee of God taking possession of us who have been purchased by His Son at Calvary.[225] The believer is thus sealed by the Spirit of God unto the day of redemption (Christ's coming to the air; the Rapture of the church).[226] Again, *"In whom ye also trusted* [Christ]*...in whom also after that ye believed* [having done], *ye were sealed with that holy Spirit of promise,* [the Holy Spirit].[227] This sealing is spoken of as an event in the past, as the result of having believed in the past. We were sealed *in Christ* when we believed.

There is permanence and eternal security here too. Believers cannot be 'unsealed'. Our ways may grieve and/or quench the Holy Spirit, but it is never said the Holy Spirit will leave or His seal be broken.[228] *"My Father, which gave them me, is greater than all; and no man is able to pluck them out of my Father's hand".*[229] Ephesians 4:25-29 speaks of our responsibility in the light of our security. We learn from

---

[225] A seal is used to prove: ownership, security, and a completed and legally binding transaction.

[226] Ephesians 4:30

[227] Ephesians 1:13. The AV has 'after' ye believed. *"There is no interval as is suggested by the AV rendering 'after'. The tense of the original indicates that the sealing takes place upon believing".* W.E. Vine. "The Collected Writings of W.E. Vine"; Volume 5 p. 87.

[228] Ephesians 4:30; 1 Thess 5:19-21

[229] John 10:28-29

Ephesians 1:14 that the Holy Spirit is the pledge (security or earnest down-payment) of the consummation of our salvation, i.e. the time when our earthly bodies are transformed into incorruptible bodies - our glorification at the Rapture.

One final remark before we pass on. For us to lose the indwelling Spirit of God, would be to lose our membership in Christ's Body. This raises the possibility of the Body of Christ, which is the church, being assailed and dismembered by Satan and sin. No comment is needed here, save to quote the wondrously emphatic assurance of the Head of the Body, *"...I will build my church; and the gates of hell shall not prevail against it".*[230]

The Filling of the Spirit

Sometimes spoken of as the 'fullness of the Spirit', the filling of the Spirit refers to the Spirit of God governing the life of the believer. It is scripturally incorrect to illustrate the filling, as many do and as some have even demonstrated from the pulpit, as the filling of a glass with water. The glass unlike the believer, is empty before the filling. Blessed truth, the Spirit of God, as Scripture teaches, permanently indwells all believers at the moment of conversion. Therefore, being filled by the Spirit of God cannot in any way refer to receiving the Holy Spirit. The filling means allowing the Spirit of God, who is in us, to take *control* of us. This is made very clear in Ephesians 5:18, where believers were exhorted not to be filled with wine but to be filled with the Spirit. The contrast is between actions controlled by wine and those controlled by the Spirit. How do we know when a person is filled with wine? It is when that person is under the 'influence' or control of the wine. The wine which is in him takes over (fills) and governs his senses. Similarly, how do we know when a person is filled by the Spirit of God? It is when that person's life is

---

[230] Matthew 16:18

under the control of the Spirit that is within - the Spirit of God is allowed to govern all aspects of (fill) that person's life. Further, the tense used in the exhortation *"..be filled with the Spirit.."*, refers to a constant filling with the Spirit, moment by moment. Paul is exhorting us to be continually under the *control* of the Spirit of God who indwells us -who is 'in' us. It is not a case of us receiving more of the Spirit, but one of the Holy Spirit receiving more of us!

Now there is a vital difference between the filling, the indwelling and sealing of the Spirit. We receive the latter two upon conversion. The filling however, is our responsibility. We have it only when, as believers, we are prepared to yield our life to God in self-judgment and surrender to His Word. By so doing, we allow the Spirit of God within us to 'fill' (control) every aspect of our lives.

What then are the signs of being filled by the Spirit of God? Speaking in tongues? Well, let us remember, among the carnal believers in Corinth some spoke in tongues. They were certainly not filled with the Spirit of God. They chose to use a spiritual gift in a manner under the control of the flesh, not the Holy Spirit. They had the Spirit indwelling and His gift of tongues, but they did not allow the Spirit to have control. Of all occasions where believers are recorded in Scripture as being filled with the Spirit, only one is associated with speaking in tongues - Acts 2:4, on that special day of Pentecost. This is not to say that the Gentiles in Acts 10 (or the Samaritans in Acts 8) were not so filled. However, the Spirit of God has sought to draw our attention to the occasions where those under the control (full) of the Spirit of God, are marked by attitudes and behaviour identified in the verses following Ephesians 5:18, not tongue-speaking, but rather speaking in psalms, giving thanks to God for all things, submitting to each other in Christ. *"Speaking to yourselves in psalms and hymns and spiritual songs, singing and making melody in your heart to the Lord; Giving thanks always for all things unto God and the Father in the name of our Lord Jesus Christ."* These were believers who, because of their wholesome spirituality, Paul could dwell upon their spiritual blessings in the risen Christ. There are no tongues or any other sensational exhibitions listed here, only reverent manifestations of praise to God, love of the flock and of the family - believers who yield to the control of the Spirit of God, honouring God in everyday life. And we note again, no praying to God in tongues (or any other tongue-speaking) is mentioned here at all in regard to being filled with the Spirit. Observe the solemn and incisive sermon by Peter in Acts 4:8-31, given while filled with the Spirit; the selection of Stephen and others as full of the Holy Ghost and with wisdom in Acts 6; Stephen's dignified and noble martyrdom in Acts 7 while filled with the Spirit of God; the wise ministry of Barnabas in Acts 11:24 while Spirit-filled; and finally, the sober, searching judgment of Paul in Acts 13:9 while filled with the Holy Ghost. Those under the control of God's Spirit are never seen to be 'out of control'. (It is nothing short of a gross abasement of the witness of Scripture and an affront to the reverent manner in which Christ and His disciples wrought miracles, to be told that diabolical obsessions of the flesh, such as the 'Toronto blessing', are the result of the filling of His Spirit).

Fruit of the Spirit

Finally, let us be guided by Paul when he speaks of the product of the Spirit-filled life to the Galatians. *"But the fruit of the Spirit is love, joy, peace, longsuffering, gentleness, goodness, faith, meekness, temperance* [enkrateia, which is more accurately translated as self control]: *against such there is no law. And they that are Christ's have crucified the flesh with the affections and lusts. If we live in the Spirit* [i.e. since we have the life of the Spirit within], *let us* [then] *also walk in the Spirit."* (Gal 5:22-25). We do well to note that as 'fruits', these manifestations are the *natural* produce of the indwelling and filling of the Spirit of God.

The Baptism by the Holy Spirit

We must first enquire what the word baptism means.[231] A most comprehensive definition is given by Wuest, who states baptism is:

"The introduction or placing of a person or thing into a new environment or into a union with something else so as to alter its condition or its relationship to its previous environment or condition".[232]

Put simply, baptism involves immersing someone (or some object) *into* something which changes their (it's) state. According to Rabbinical writings Jewish ceremonial bathing was immersion - *into* the water. Perhaps the best illustration of baptism and the definition above is in regard to dyeing material. The cloth would be thoroughly immersed under the dye in a basin - its altered colour reflecting a change in its state. Baptism, when it involves people, is often associated with a symbol to testify that it has taken place.

We can identify then four essential questions in regard to individual or corporate baptism.

1. Who is being 'placed into'? - the *subject.*
2. Who is doing the placing? - the *agent/baptiser.*
3. What is the evidence at the time? - the *symbol.*
4. What are they being placed into - the change in their situation (environment)? - their new *state.*

The fourth question identifies the purpose of the baptism (or *unto* what end?). It also implies emergence - a 'placing into' and a 'coming out of', as illustrated by the dyeing of cloth and believer's baptism (Matt 28:19; Gal 3:27; Rom 6:3-5).[233]

Let us be clear then, that 'baptism', or to 'baptise', from

---

[231] It is essentially a transliteration of the Greek *'baptizo'*.

[232] K. Wuest: "Word Studies" - Untranslatable Riches From the Greek New Testament, Volume 3 p. 85. Wm. B Eerdmans Publishing Company.

[233] Believer's water baptism and its identification with Christ: immersion (His death); submersion (His burial); emergence (His resurrection). How religious tradition has perverted the matter of water baptism for the Christian! The baptism of infants and 'infant sprinkling', for instance, is an invention of man which appeals to flesh and is nowhere enjoined in the Word of God!

grammatical principles and from illustrations in Scripture and secular life, means *'putting into'* - not receiving! The examples in the Table below illustrate this and address the four questions above.

Example/ Reference	The Subject	The Agent/ Baptizer	The Symbol	*Evidence* of what new state?
John's baptism *Gospels, Acts 1:5; 11:16; 19:4*	Jews	John the Baptist	Water	Jews entering into a new relationship with God through their repentance
The Son's baptism *Matthew 3:13-16*	Jesus of Nazareth	John the Baptist	Water	The anointed Son of God entering into His public ministry as the Son of God
Baptism of fire *Matthew 3:11; Luke 3:16*	Israel	Christ (Messiah)	Fire	Israel under the judgment of the Lord on His return (Second Advent)
The Saviour's baptism *Luke 12:50*	Jesus of Nazareth	Jesus of Nazareth (voluntary submission)	Fire, Cross	The Lord entering into His suffering as the Sacrifice for sin – as the Sin Bearer
Holy Spirit's baptism *Acts 2; 1 Corinthians 12:13*	Believers in Christ	The Holy Spirit/ (through the ascended Christ)	Cloven tongues as of fire, sound of wind	Believers put into one Body, creating a new relationship with Christ the Ascended Head
New Testament (believer's) baptism *Matthew 28:19; Acts 8; Romans 6*	Believers in Christ e.g. Ethiopian eunuch	Other believers e.g. Philip	Water	The believer having entered a new life in Christ as Lord when saved

The baptism by the Holy Spirit - What is it?

When we study this matter prayerfully within the whole sweep of God's Word, we find that the baptism by the Spirit refers to:

"Christ by the Holy Spirit *putting* those 120 believers gathered in Jerusalem at the time of Pentecost *into* a unified collective membership - the Body of Christ and uniting them to Christ, the Head of the Body. The baptism by the Spirit then, refers to the creation of the church, which is Christ's Body." [234]

We will take up the purpose and process of the baptism by the Spirit as it is given in 1 Corinthians 12:13 later. For the present, let us consider the promise of this baptism.

The Lord's promise of the Spirit's baptism - Acts 1:4-5

Having completed His work of redemption, the Lord must soon ascend to His rightful place at the right hand of God and there appear for us as our Great High Priest. But what will become of His disciples who remain? They are not to be left comfortless and He reminds them of the Father's promise - to send His Spirit (1:4). He centres on a particular aspect of this promise: *"ye shall be baptised with the Holy Ghost not many days hence"*(1:5).[235] Why does He not speak particularly of the Spirit's indwelling, sealing or filling (although these took place at that time)? It is because at this time of God's dealing with man, there is another needful work of the Holy Spirit that commands the stage. The Redeemer is about to depart. These 120 precious souls that belong to Him are not to be left comfortless or fragmented. They are to be recipients of a monumental act of grace and blessing. They will be welded *into* a blessed unity as members of

---

[234] *"He is the Head of the Body, the Church"*; Eph 1:23; Col 1:18

[235] The 'promise of the Father' speaks in general of the sending of the Holy Spirit which the Lord had referred to earlier (John 14:16-17; 15:26) - to indwell, seal, baptise and fill. The particular work of the Spirit referred to in verse 5 is baptism. In Acts 2:39 the promise is the gift of the Spirit as stated in verse 38 - the indwelling, sealing and filling.

Christ's Body, and united to a glorified Christ, the Head of the Body. How and when is this to happen? It is to be through the baptism by the Holy Ghost on the day of Pentecost. This is the baptismal blessing spoken of by Christ and John the Baptist. It is a divinely timed work of the Spirit through the ascended Christ. *All* 120 believers were commanded to gather in one place to be 'put into' the Body of Christ. (When looking at 1 Corinthians 12:13, we will see that this event included not just the 120, but in prospect all believers from that time to the coming of the Lord for His church.)

There are essential truths concerning Christ's victory and His relationship to us in all this. The 120 must wait together until the Lord ascends because His Body (His church) needs a Head, a risen and glorified (ascended) Head: a risen Head, because He speaks of life - victory over sin and death; an ascended glorified Head because the union between His body and Himself is in heaven. It is not an earthly union! It cannot be, for the Head is enthroned at the right hand of the Father (although the church has a visible presence on earth as evidenced through every living redeemed child of God).[236] We see in this promise a distinction once again between the OT dispensation and the NT in regard to the activity of the Holy Spirit. The OT saints were never united in such a Body. Where was the ascended Head in heaven *to* whom they could be united? Where was the Spirit of God *by* whom they must be united to the Head in heaven and to each other as members of His Body? The Spirit of God Himself had to be sent for this purpose once Christ had ascended to the father.[237] And, what of the time, Pentecost? Was it not the time of harvest, the Firstfruits having been presented in heaven?[238]

---

[236] How irrelevant then are man's vain attempts to create some earthly union! Christ's Body is not an aggregation of members, but a *unity* - the work of His Spirit, a unity to be kept not created (Eph 4:3).

[237] The very coming of the Spirit of God in this age and therefore all aspects of His mission had to await the glorification of Christ! See John 7:39 below.

[238] So we see the ascended, *"...Head of the Body, the church: who is the beginning, the firstborn from* [among] *the dead; that in all things he might have the preeminence"* (Col 1:18).

The promise then is not in regard to Israel, for they have been set aside in judgment, but in regard to the church, the heavenly spiritual Body of Christ comprising Jews and Gentiles unified as one in Him, "...*that the Gentiles should be fellowheirs, and of the same body* [the church], *and partakers of His promise in Christ by the gospel*" (Eph 3:3-6).

Now there is another reason why the Lord focuses on the baptism by the Spirit in Acts 1:4-5. His presence will no longer grace and temper the scene of time, carrying the Father's commission. Who is to do this when He is gone? Spirit-filled believers? We are told the believers will receive power after the Holy Ghost is come upon them (v.8) - that is, the filling of the Spirit. The Lord makes reference to the filling (clothed with power) in His closing words in Luke 24:49. He speaks of the need for Spirit-led witnessing (v.48). But here it is the church. Spirit-filled men were not something new, we hear of many so filled prior to Pentecost. It is the church which is now the object of promise, comprising the redeemed of Christ, indwelt and unified by the Spirit of God and gathered locally unto His name by His Spirit, which is to manifest Christ on earth.[239] But this is not its only calling, for it was conceived *"to the intent that now unto the principalities and powers in heavenly places might be known by the church the manifold wisdom of God".*[240] It is the presence and polity of His Body as 'members of Christ' and 'members of one another', that is to temper fallen Creation and reflect Christ's redemptive glory. And so the Spirit's baptism - the unifying of Christ's redeemed in Him and becoming united to Him, is brought into view. (When the church and the Spirit of God (in the sense that He now indwells) are taken out of this world at the

---

[239] In 1 Corinthians 12:13 Paul uses *"we"*, referring to the body of Christ as it includes every believer. In regard to this Body, he states we are all 'members'. (In v.27, he uses "ye", "ye are body of Christ" (no definite article), reminding the believers at Corinth of their holy local responsibility, for they are members of *the* Body of Christ.)

[240] Ephesians 3:10. Thus, a solemn responsibility devolves upon the local churches.

Rapture, a great tide of evil will roll over the earth.[241]) And, so, the Lord heralds the new dispensation which involves a particular work of His Spirit, with the specific promise - *"ye shall be baptised with the Holy Ghost not many days hence"* - symbolized by signs to the Jews: tongues as of fire and the sound of rushing mighty wind.

The purpose and process of the Spirit's baptism - 1 Corinthians 12:13

The only explicit teaching in Scripture concerning the purpose and process of the baptism by the Spirit, is given to us in 1 Corinthians 12:13: *"For by one Spirit are we all baptised into one body..."*. The action - baptising - in this verse, has as its clear object, to place believers into a new company - Christ's Body. The baptism by the Spirit cannot therefore refer to the Spirit being 'put into' or applied to an individual believer!

We see the process here also - *"For by* [in the power of] *one Spirit* [the Agent, through Christ] *are we all baptised into one body* [the new state]."[242] The blessed co-operation of the Holy Ghost with Christ is brought before us here.[243]

The second part of this verse is also instructive: *"...and have been all* [were all, every believer been] *made to drink*

---

[241] 2 Thessalonians 2: 6-7

[242] *"By means of the personal agency of one Spirit", we are placed in one body."* K. Wuest, "Word Studies - "Untranslatable Riches..." Volume 3 p. 86. We would understand this agency to be tantamount to 'in the power of' the Spirit through Christ.

[243] Debate exists over the use of 'by' or 'in' the Spirit in 1 Cor 12:13 (and over 'with' or 'in' the Spirit in regard to Acts 1:5). Some prefer to speak only of the 'baptism in the Spirit', 'baptism by the Spirit' or the 'Holy Spirit baptism', while others use the more common expression 'baptism of the Spirit'. The expression 'by the Spirit' is in keeping with the essential purpose and process of this baptism. The truth that is untouched by any debate, is that the baptism by the Spirit is the co-operative enterprise of the Father, the Son and the Holy Ghost; notwithstanding their distintive roles in relation to the body of Christ and the baptism that brought it into being - the *promise* of the Father, the *purchase* by the Son and the *presence* and *power* of the Spirit. An examination of the grammar is found in A. T Robertson "Word Pictures in the New Testament", Volume 111 p. 8. and K. Wuest, "Word Studies - "Untranslatable Riches..." Volume 3 p. 86-89. Also, *"In [or by] one Spirit"* is *"in the power of."* "The Collected Writings of J.N.Darby - Expository"; Vol. 26 p 275.

into one Spirit". We have here the Holy Spirit as the provider for and possessor of all in the Body. Paul, speaking against the divisions within the church at Corinth (vv.4-31), calls them to remember that *each* believer has been made (aorist tense) to partake of the life of the Spirit of God, i.e., all in the Body of Christ have been indwelt and unified by the *one* same Spirit - *"there is one Body, and One Spirit!"* [244] The Spirit of God Himself is thus the living power that unifies believers in the Body of Christ to each other and unites the Body to Christ - it is the unity of the *Spirit!*

In itself, 1 Corinthians 12:13 provides clear instruction concerning the baptism by the Spirit. However, we can gain a further appreciation of its teaching and relevance in the light of Acts 1:5, where we have the Lord's promise of the Spirit's baptism. In 1 Corinthians 12:13 we are given its purpose and the process by which it occurred. Both these verses speak of Pentecost. It is clear from the sequence of events - the Lord's death, resurrection and His impending ascension, that He is looking forward to Pentecost in Acts 1:5 and the coming unity in the Spirit for those who remain. His use of the words *'not many days hence'* has the day of Pentecost in view. It is equally clear, that Paul, speaking of the Spirit's baptism in 1 Corinthians 12:13, looks back to Pentecost with its essential unity through the Holy Spirit - racial, social, gender and gifts. Pentecost then is the common event, and the Body and its unity in the Spirit is the common subject referred to by Paul and the Lord. (For this reason also Peter looks back to the Spirit's baptism in Acts 11:16, as we see later).

A final remark may be made here regarding the change baptism brings to previous relationships, as noted in the definition of it earlier. Upon the Lord's ascension there was a Risen Head in heaven. But there was no Body on earth to whom He could be united. At the appointed time, the Spirit

---

[244] Ephesians 4:4

of God descended and placed individual believers into a corporate entity - His Body, through the baptism by the Spirit. At that moment, new blessed relationships came into effect - the vital relationship between the Body and the Head from whom it draws its character, and the relationship between members unified in Him as the Head. He is the *"...head over all things to the church, which is his body, the fulness of him that filleth all in all"* (Eph 1:22-23).

The past completion of the baptism by the Holy Spirit.

We now come upon a further truth concerning the baptism by the Holy Spirit - it was a once-only event. Scripture is very clear on this.

Firstly, in 1 Corinthians 12:13 Paul refers to a past and completed event, *"By one Spirit are* [were] *we all baptised into one body"*.[245] It is not that we *are* baptised as in the AV; neither is it that we are *being* baptized into one Body, implying this baptism is available today and repeatable. The tense of the verb 'baptised' (past - aorist) speaks of a single *event* - one completed *action* in the past. At Pentecost, the Holy Spirit baptised the 120 believers into the Body of Christ: the church, His Body was brought into existence. There can be no repeat of this baptism for the church can have only one beginning. Secondly, Paul associates every believer (*we all*) with this past completed action of the Spirit. All believers at the time of writing were seen by Paul as being involved in this single past event. If this was true for all believers at the time of Paul's writing, then it must be true for all believers at any point in time between Pentecost and the Rapture of the church. Every believer is thus included prospectively in the Spirit's baptism at Pentecost.

That the baptism of the Spirit is never to be repeated is supported by the biblical record. There was no baptism by

---

[245] A.T. Robertson "Word Pictures in the New Testament", Volume IV p. 171. *"..a reference to a definite act in the past......"*. Reference is to *a* past event not past events (plural) and is associated with the collective pronoun 'we'.

the Holy Spirit for those saved just after the events of Acts 2:4. In Acts 2:41 we see a multitude saved and baptised in water 'in the name of the Lord Jesus Christ' (vv.38-41). The promise stated in verses 38-39 refers to the indwelling - the gift *of* the Spirit - our receiving Him for *"He shall be in you"*. We hear of the Jews believing, being baptised in water, continuing steadfastly in the apostles' doctrine, but nothing of them being baptised with the Spirit. Neither do we hear of any Spirit baptism (or 'second blessing') in their activities in verses 44-46. Where, in these halcyon and fervent days of the Holy Spirit, is the tarrying for a second blessing by these converts? In the passionate teaching proclaimed by Peter during this critical inceptive time, there is no instruction to tarry and/or pray for a baptism by the Spirit. Being pricked in the heart, they actually asked, *"Men and brethren, what shall we do?"* (v.37). Peter then specifically implores the unsaved to repent and be baptised in water, but no expectation of, or praying for a Spirit baptism is mentioned. Why? It is because the baptism by the Spirit of God was the formation of the Body of Christ by the unifying work of His Spirit: it had already taken place and was a once-and-for-all event.[246]

A believer being baptized into the Body of Christ at conversion would contradict the teaching of 1 Corinthians 12:13 and require

---

[246] Some charismatics ask "Have you tarried for your Pentecost?" Well if a person is to tarry according to the command of the risen Christ (Acts 2), then it must be done according to His complete instruction, and they should repair to the city of David. Christ expressly enjoined the disciples to wait for (not pray for, for He was already promised) the promise of the Father *"at Jerusalem"*, not at Bethlehem, Damascus, Jericho or Nazareth. Further, not just to tarry at a certain place, but also at a time coincident with the Feast of Pentecost. When God determines to move among men, He always chooses an appointed time and place. The coming of the Holy Spirit had to be at Jerusalem and at the time of the Feast of Pentecost. Why? Refer again to Note 2, while considering the unique importance of Jerusalem, historically and prophetically. How apt a time and place for God to manifest his grace and judgment. These conditions can not now, or ever again be fulfilled, which confirms the teaching of Scripture that Pentecost was a once-and-for-all event. The Passover and Feast of Firstfruits were fulfilled by two once-and-for-all events - the death and resurrection of Christ respectively. So, too, the Feast of Weeks finds its fulfilment in the never-to-be-repeated day of Pentecost. We have no scriptural warrant to tarry for the Holy Spirit.

a 're-incorporation', a Pentecost every time a person is saved. The 'putting into' the Body of Christ took place 'potentially' for *all* believers at Pentecost! The moment we are saved we 'experimentally' (as a matter of experience) become part of the Body of Christ, i.e. by virtue of our salvation and the indwelling of the one Spirit, we become personally and practically associated with what took place at Pentecost through that same Spirit.

There are other occasions in Scripture showing we have been regarded by God as being part of a completed event before our time. Paul makes it abundantly clear we participated in Adam's act of sin. His declaration that *"death passed upon all men, for that all have sinned"* (Rom 5:12), means that we all in fact sinned when Adam sinned - 'sinned' (not 'have sinned' as in the AV) is in the aorist tense. The essence of this passage, indeed a major truth of Romans - the individual's ruin in Adam, rests on the same principle defining the baptism by the Spirit - a single completed event in the past in which *all* concerned have participated. We find the same truth in Romans 3:23 - *"For all have sinned,* [aorist - a single completed past event] *and come short* [because of it] *of the glory of God";* and in Romans 5:19, *"For by one man's disobedience* [Adam's sin, the Fall], [the] *many were made sinners.."*.[247] As further examples, we are told of the Israelites being baptised unto Moses in the cloud and in the sea: *"And were all baptised unto Moses in the cloud and in the sea."*[248] Again we have reference to a single event, completed in the past (aorist tense). The baptism into the cloud and the sea is said to have been partaken of by *all* the fathers - including those after the event - every Israelite is regarded as having participated in the deliverance through that crossing.

They were 'added'.

We read in Acts 2:41 of the three thousand converts being added. To what were they added? - to the 120 who comprised

---

[247] See Note 8 for a fuller presentation of this truth.
[248] 1 Corinthians 10:1-3

the church. In verse 47 the general principle is stated: *"...And the Lord added to the church daily such as should be saved* [i.e. added to the Lord]*"*.[249] There is a truth to be especially observed and cherished here, given the lifeless initiation rituals in Christendom. Membership in the Church of God is singularly conferred by Christ by virtue of one accepting Him as his/her personal Saviour. We note too, it is not the Holy Spirit adding (by baptism), but the Lord adding. The meaning here is 'kept on adding'.[250] This work is seen as the Lord's for He is the Lord of the Harvest - souls are brought to Him - sought, saved and sealed by His Spirit.[251] He (builds), adds to His church, viewed as a building - *"I will build my church"* (Matt 16:18). So Paul declares we *"...are built upon the foundation of the apostles and prophets, Jesus Christ himself being the chief corner stone; In whom all the building fitly framed together groweth unto an holy temple in the Lord: In whom ye also are builded together for an habitation of God through the Spirit"*(Eph 2:20-22). Believers are chosen in God, redeemed by the Son and sealed by the Spirit (Eph 1).

Finally, we remark that you cannot add to something if it does not exist! Therefore, the church [His Body], must have existed for such additions to take place and, to have existed, it must have had a defined beginning. The church's inception could not be left to the arrangements of man - for the church is not an organisation, but a organism. The church, any more than creation itself, could never come into being as a matter

---

[249] The 'Body of Christ' is viewed as complete at Pentcost, whereas the 'church' viewed as a building, is seen in progressive development with many being added to it from Pentecost to the Rapture. Ephesians 1:23 states "...the church which is his body", the figure views the church in its essential nature, its essential quality and life in Christ, its Head.

[250] *"The Lord added together such as would be saved"* is the correct reading. Imperfect active and the same as in verse 41 for the 3000 added i.e., kept on adding - together. A. T. Robertson "Word Pictures in the New Testament", Volume III p. 40.

[251] Beautifully prefigured in Genesis 24 - Abraham (the Father) sending his servant who was the custodian of all his possessions (the Spirit of God), to seek and secure a bride for his son Isaac (the Son of God). It was not for the son to seek and seal the bride, but the servant. So too the Holy Spirit, the vicar of Christ, in regard to the Body and Bride of Christ - the church.

of 'evolution' - a concept which is an anathema to a Creator-Redeemer. As was the case with the origin of the world and man, the church of God had to begin with a sovereign act of God and according to His divine timetable. What was the divine act that brought the church into existence? It is the act the Lord looked towards in Acts 1:5 and which Paul looked back to in 1 Corinthians 12:13. It is the act which follows the death, resurrection and ascension of Christ and which is timetabled typically with the Feasts - the Passover, Firstfruits and Pentecost. What divine act can it possibly be but the Spirit's baptism - the creation of the church which is His Body? Was it not the Spirit of God too that brooded over the world at its creation? The Spirit of God was sent by divine promise to baptise believers into the Body of Christ! If it was not the baptism by the Spirit that brought the church which is His Body into being, then what divine act did so and when did it occur? If the baptism by the Spirit of God is the divine act of bringing the Body of Christ into existence, then how can it be some infusion of the Spirit into an individual believer for 'power' and 'tongues'?

Charismatic error

The whole matter concerning the baptism by the Holy Spirit then, is not the charismatic notion of individual believers *receiving* the Holy Spirit and for 'power'.[252] It is rather that Christ through the power of the Spirit has put believers *into* the Body of Christ and united them to Him.

On this point alone, the charismatic notion of the Spirit's baptism fails absolutely. Why do many not see such a clear reason against their beliefs? We come back to the folly of interpreting Scripture by experiences - "My tongue-speaking proves I have been empowered by a baptism by the Holy

---

[252] Typified in the teaching of Torry, a prominent evangelist of the late nineteenth century and revered by charismatics : *"..the baptism with the Holy Spirit is a work of the Holy Spirit always connected with and primarily for the purpose of testimony and service."* R. A. Torry "The Holy Spirit"; Revell p. 117.

Spirit"! The divine evidence of the baptism by the Spirit however, was the tongues as of fire and the sound of a mighty rushing wind.[253] Satan has provided a cunning deception through an 'experience', which he knows is difficult to deny, though Scripture speaks against it!

There is an attack upon Christ here too. At the time of Pentecost, the believers were incorporated - baptised, put into one 'spiritual' Body by one Spirit. If Satan can persuade us to believe that the baptism by the Spirit is the placing of the Spirit into us, he directs our focus away from the blessed truth and unity of the Body of Christ, that which the Spirit through Christ has constituted (Eph 4:3), with its blessed relationship between the glorified Head and His Body. This in turn will lead to practical failing, as was the case with the Colossians who were not 'holding the Head'. This is a neglected relationship today. We hear much concerning the blessed relationship between God the Father and His children, but how often do we hear teaching on the Head and His Body; or, the Bride and the Bridegroom; Headship and Lordship; the responsibility of the local church to show forth the manifold wisdom of God? Moreover, to regard the baptism by the Holy Spirit as the Spirit being received, is a source of disunity, for it divides Christians into those who supposedly have and those who have not had such a so-called 'baptism by the Spirit (second blessing)'. And, further, in so doing Satan steals our attention from the distinguishing work of

[253] Both fire and wind (2 Sam 5:24; Psa 104:3; etc.) were used to signify divine presence. Of particular note here is the visual symbol of the cloven tongues as of fire. The grammar shows that the fire-like appearance came as 'one body' ('it' sat), which then parted so a portion of it rested on each person gathered. See A. T. Robertson, Word Pictures in the New Testament" Volume III p. 21. How figurative of the Body of Christ and its unity through the Spirit of God! The tongues spoken were also as sign of unity as we have seen, but they had a distinctive role for they also signalled the judgment of God upon Israel and given to continue until the completed canon of Scripture. The symbols (signs) indicating the baptism by the Spirit - the sound of a mighty rushing wing and cloven tongues of fire however, are never seen again, confirming this baptism was a once-only event. Further, tongue-speaking could never be a sign of the baptism of the Spirit, for Scripture teaches that the Spriit of God did not bestow this gift to all believers (Proposition 8).

the Spirit of God who accomplished the unity of the Body of Christ - yet another example of how a movement that appears so focused on the Holy Spirit actually denies Him. But there is a monstrous detraction here also of the work of Christ as Saviour, in that it is subordinated to the work of one who 'baptises individuals'. A 'baptism by the Spirit' is presented as the ultimate spiritual attainment for the individual; personal salvation is but one of many steps to it.[254] Such is the guile of Satan! So, we see how wrong it is to pray for the baptism by the Holy Spirit. Nowhere in Scripture are individuals told to pray for or seek a 'baptism by the Holy Spirit'.

Baptism of Fire - tongues of fire?

Many charismatics claim to have had, and exhort we should seek, a 'baptism of fire' - another case of error. The baptism of fire (Matt 3:11; Luke 3:16), does not refer to the 'tongues of fire' in Acts 2. The cloven tongues as of fire, signalled God's blessing and the presence of His Spirit. They were a once-only symbol of the Spirit's baptism at Pentecost showing He had come as promised, and to mark His indwelling and uniting of the believers on that occasion. Fire was used to signal the presence of God and His holiness to the Jews (Ex 3:2; 13:21; 19:18; 24:17; Deut 5:4.) The cloven tongues as of fire, that sat upon their heads were therefore an apt sign to the Jews of the presence of a holy God and His sanctifying Spirit. In contrast, the baptism of fire is associated with judgment! This is made clear by the passage following John the Baptist's mention of it: *"Whose fan* [used to separate the wheat from chaff] *is in His hand, and He will throughly purge His floor* [Israel, the corn of God's floor, Isa 21:10], *and gather His wheat into the garner* [Christ]*; but He* [Christ] *will burn up the chaff with unquenchable fire."* This baptism will occur after the church period at the Lord's second

---

[254] Torry's 'seven steps' to receive the baptism by the Holy Spirit (R. A. Torry "The Holy Spirit": Revell) is typical of the line taken by many contemporary charismatics.

coming - to the earth, and refers to Israel in its rejection of Him (Mal 3:2-3; 4:1; Isa 4:4 etc.). They will pass through His refining hand of judgment- a baptism of fire - the faithful saved as wheat, others burnt as chaff! The Lord's first advent and ascension were associated with blessing and thus the baptism of fire is, for this reason also, not mentioned in Acts by the Lord. His second advent and return to the earth will be to execute righteous judgment - the baptism of fire prior to His reign as King of kings and Lord of lords. We see here another example where charismatic doctrine supplants divine judgment with 'personal blessing'.

Unity of the Body

In an exhortation to unity among the saints at Ephesus (Eph 4:4-6), Paul reminds us of our position in one Body through one baptism. The expression 'one baptism' means a collective 'one placing into' - not 'individual placings into'.[255] We were all subjects of this one placing which occurred at Pentecost. Some suggest the reference here is to water baptism. However, water baptism, apart from being an individual baptism, is merely an expression of unity, not the substance of it, not a basis for it. What of those who are saved yet for whatever reason, have not undergone water baptism? Are they not part of the one Body of Christ? Are we to align ourselves with the error of Rome, that water baptism is a requirement for membership in the Body of Christ? Further, the seven-fold basis of unity identified in verses 4-6, comes under the province of the *"the unity of the Spirit"* (v.3), - that oneness which is wrought by the unifying work of the Holy Spirit - the baptism by the Spirit. Water baptism as an expression of unity is also seen in Galatians 3:27 based on the common public identification with Christ.

---

[255] *"hen baptisma"* - one common placing into the Body. K Wuest "Word Studies..." Ephesians, Volume 1 p. 96-97.

The Spirit of Adoption

As part of Adam's race we are inheritors of wrath. This truth touches upon another: the Spirit of God as the Spirit of Adoption and is integral to the 'new birth'. When we are saved we become children of God and inheritors in Christ. We are all placed in the family of God as *adopted sons* (*huiothesia*- placing as a son) a position of inheritance that was never our natural entitlement in Adam (Rom 8:15). Under Roman law a child not related by birth could be adopted and placed in its new family and given the status and rights of a son through natural birth. We had to be 'born again' into the family of God to receive such an inheritance. The Holy Spirit is the one who establishes us as adopted sons the moment we are saved.

'Baptism by the Holy Spirit' - the Gospels and Acts 1

This study has been reserved until now so we can more ably glean the truth concerning the promise of the Spirit's baptism recorded in these Scriptures.

· Matthew 3:11

"I indeed baptise you with water unto repentance but he that cometh after me [Christ] is mightier than I...he [Christ] shall baptise you with the Holy Ghost and with fire."

· Mark 1:8

"I indeed have baptised you with water but he [Christ] shall baptise you with the Holy Ghost."

· Luke 3:16

"I indeed baptise you with water; but one mightier than I cometh [Christ]......he [Christ] shall baptise you with the Holy Ghost and with fire..".

· John 1:33

"...the same is he [Christ] which baptiseth with the Holy Ghost".

In these Gospel passages, baptism means of course, 'immersion' or putting into. We see here the truth presented - the Holy Spirit's agency is cooperative with and through the will and supplication of Christ. All Gospels refer to Christ as the originator of the baptism by the Spirit. What then being said here is: He (Christ) will baptise (immerse) you with i.e., by the means or agency of, the Spirit of God.[256] Christ was in His rightful place, at the right hand of the Father, so His vicar, the Spirit of God, had to be sent to perform this task. Do not let this blessed truth be missed. We have here the perfect, harmonious operation of the Father, Son and Holy Spirit in regard to the church, His Body, over which Christ is the ascended Head.

As stated earlier, John the Baptist's reference to baptism with the Spirit and with fire represents two separate signal events - the first coming and the second coming of Christ - grace and blessing, compared with judgment respectively. In the Gospels, the baptism of fire is only mentioned by Matthew and Luke. Matthew mentions it because he presents Christ as the rejected Messiah-King, pertinent to the future judgment of Israel because of their rejection of Him. Luke speaks particularly of Christ as the Son of Man. It is as the Son of Man that Christ will come to take up His inheritance on earth with great power and glory (Dan 7), a time associated with judgment which will involve Israel.

· Acts 1:5

"For John truly baptised with water; but ye shall be baptised with the Holy Ghost not many days hence." The Lord asked them to wait for the promise of the Father (never

---

[256] This voids any notion that men can impart a 'baptism by the Spirit' or any other work of the Holy Spirit. Some disagree quoting Paul's desire to impart a spiritual gift to the Romans (Rom 1:11). The word impart however means to share. *metadidomi , "to give a share of, impart" (meta, "with"), as distinct from "giving." The apostle Paul speaks of "sharing" some spiritual gift with Christians at Rome, Rom 1:11, "that I may impart," and exhorts those who minister in things temporal, to do so as "sharing," and that generously, 12:8, "he that giveth"; so in Eph 4:28; Luke 3:11; in 1 Thess 2:8 he speaks of himself and his fellow missionaries as having been well pleased to impart to the converts both God's gospel and their own souls (i.e., so "sharing" those with them as to spend themselves and spend out their lives for them)."* W. E. Vine "<u>Expository Dictionary of New Testament Words</u>", p. 149.

to pray for it). Yes, they had to tarry. They had to wait together, in obedience to the Lord's command to be -

> permanently *indwelt* by the Holy Spirit as promised (John 14:17)[257]
> permanently *sealed* by the Holy Spirit (Eph 1:13-14)
> *baptised* by the Holy Spirit into the Body of Christ (Acts 1:5; Gospels; 1 Cor 12:13)
> *filled* with the Holy Spirit (Luke 24:49; Acts 1:8; Eph. 5:18).

The case of the 120 believers at Pentecost was *unique* in that they were the first subjects of the new dispensation upon whom the Spirit of God would undertake His ministry. This meant they were involved in all four works of the Spirit outlined above simultaneously - the permanent indwelling, sealing, filling and baptism. They were not to disperse or leave Jerusalem, because this Body had to be formed at Jerusalem, nowhere else would do. We do not wait today to be incorporated, this has already been done. Further, from our study of the Feasts of Jehovah (Note 2) we know that the coming of the Spirit of God at the time of Pentecost, after the Lord's ascension and at Jerusalem, was predetermined by the will God. The Holy Spirit at Pentecost (cf. pre-Pentecost) was not promised or given because of the prayers of believers. His coming at Pentecost was always the result of the expressed prayer of the Lord, and the will of God the Father.

· Luke 11:13

"If ye then, being evil, know how to give good gifts unto your children: how much more shall your heavenly Father give the Holy Spirit to them that ask him?" Is there support for a second blessing here? Now again, it is a matter of rightly dividing the Word of God. This was a time before Pentecost

---

[257] Being believers in Christ, prior to Pentecost, they would have been indwelt by the Spirit of God according to the manner of the OT. Now, this indwelling was of a permanent nature and inextricably associated with the Spirit's sealing.

characterized by the conditions under the Old Testament, when the Holy Spirit came upon individuals and also left them. We saw David testify that the Spirit of God could depart from him and prayed He would not do so. The Spirit of the Lord departed from Saul and, in the case of Samson, He came upon him when special works were needed.

· Luke 24:49

"And, behold, I send the promise of my Father upon you: but tarry ye in the city of Jerusalem, until ye be endued with power from on high." The Lord's words here speak generally of the need to wait at Jerusalem for the promise of the Father. There is no baptism by the Spirit mentioned here. The emphasis is regarding the call to preach the gospel to all nations (v.48), so He specifically refers to them being 'clothed with power from on high,' in order that this be accomplished. Again, the enabling (filling) of the Spirit dwelling within!

· John 7:37-39

"..If any man thirst, let him come unto me, and drink. He that believeth on me, as the scripture hath said, out of his belly shall flow rivers of living water. (But this spake he of the Spirit, which they that believe on him should receive: for the Holy Ghost was not yet given; because that Jesus was not yet glorified.)." The Lord speaks here of the promise of the Spirit who was to be given to those who *believe* in Him as Lord and Saviour! This was to happen after He was glorified - ascended into the presence of His Father. Note, the reference is to Pentecost and there is no instruction to pray for the Spirit - He was to be *given*, His coming predetermined according to the will of God, dependent upon the Lord being glorified! The Lord identifies Himself as the source of living water unto salvation - *"If any man thirst, let Him come unto Me, and drink."* How reminiscent of His offer to the Samaritan woman at Jacob's well (John 4:10). He then speaks of that wonderful portion of those who drink of His life-giving salvation - the believers, *"He that believeth on Me, as the*

153

Scripture hath said, out of his belly shall flow the rivers of living water." Now the focus here is not a portion received by a believer, but a portion flowing from the believer, which was to be the result of the indwelling of the Spirit of God, an indwelling never to be prayed for because it was promised by Christ, as we have seen! This indwelling (the message is to the individual here not the church) was to begin only after Christ was glorified! The Lord refers to the outflow of grace and truth to others who have drunk from Him who came with an infinite well of *"grace and truth"* (John 1:17).[258]

· John 20:22

"And when he had said this, he breathed on them, and saith unto them, Receive ye the Holy Ghost: Whose soever sins ye remit, they are remitted unto them; and whose soever sins ye retain, they are retained." It is not the person of the Holy Spirit being received here as occurred at Pentecost. The actual coming of the Spirit of God upon them collectively and His permanent indwelling of each had to await the Lord's ascension. The Lord breathed on them here to indicate that the Spirit within them (as he was upon others in the manner before Pentecost) is now associated with His resurrection glory.[259] It is in the power of the Spirit, now seen as co-operative in the resurrection of Christ, that they are now to go forth as disciples. The Lord's breathing here, indeed the whole scene, is symbolic and anticipatory. The occasion is wonderfully figurative and anticipates the church which was to begin at Pentecost. We see the saints gathered, the Lord as the risen Head in the midst, the Holy Spirit given, and all on resurrection ground![260]

---

[258] Some take the statement *"out of his belly"* to refer to Christ and not to the believer. The context furnished by 7:39 would put beyond doubt that the reference is to the believer and his receiving of the Spirit of God *through* which he would manifest the grace and truth of Christ.

[259] The same word is used as in the breathing of natural life into man in Genesis 2:7.

[260] The symbolism deepens when we consider the absence of Thomas on this first meeting. He symbolises the Jewish remnant by his absence and words, *"Except I shall see in his hands the print of the nails.....I will not believe".* In the next gathering he is present and views the imprint of the nails, figurative of that future day when the remnant shall see Him.

· Acts 1:8

We include this here as it is often misused - *"...ye shall receive power, after that the Holy Ghost is come upon you and ye shall be witnesses unto me..."*. Note here they 'shall' receive - it was divinely decreed and vouchsafed through grace, not to be prayed for. This power was to be the result of the Holy Spirit's indwelling and filling (not the baptism by the Spirit - the putting into).

The Gentile case

Acts 11:16 is often taken to prove that the conversion of the household of Cornelius (Acts 10) involved a 'baptism by the Holy Spirit'. We note here the reference to Jerusalem and Pentecost. Let us proceed by moving from what we know to be certain.

Firstly, the baptism by the Holy Spirit had to take place, as we saw earlier, according to God's timetable - at Jerusalem *and* during Pentecost. These conversions and manifestations of the Holy Spirit took place at Caesarea and not during Pentecost nor at Jerusalem. It thus fails this scriptural test. Secondly, the portion regarding the conversions and signs in Acts 10 does not mention any Spirit baptism taking place. Only in verses 47-48 do we find any reference to baptism, and it is water baptism! The third argument I wish to raise is in the form of a question. If, as supposed by some, the events documented in Acts 10:44-46 involve a baptism by the Holy Spirit, and this baptism, we are told is of a 'second blessing', then when was the praying and the tarrying to receive this second blessing? More strikingly, if this is their second blessing, when did these Gentiles receive their first blessing? There can be no 'second blessing' unless there is a 'first blessing'. We see nothing of it at all! There was no baptism by the Holy Spirit or second blessing here - no exhortation to seek it or any evidence of it.

Why then does Peter refer to the baptism by the Holy Spirit

155

in Acts 11:16? It is because he wants to focus on the unity of the Body of Christ. Up to this point in time, the Holy Spirit had only come upon Jews. What an extraordinary occasion it was for the Jews to witness the Spirit of God manifesting Himself through those whom they regarded as spiritually unclean! Peter remembers the Lord's words, having understood their deeper meaning (his vision in Acts 10:11-16); the church which was incorporated at Pentecost includes Jews and 'unclean' Gentiles, both saved and united in Christ! The sign-gift of tongues as the Spirit of God indwelt and sealed these Gentile believers (v.47) (they had received the 'gift of the Holy Ghost'), convinced him and his Jewish brethren, *"Then hath God also to the Gentiles granted repentance unto life"* (11:18). The manifestation of the Spirit's indwelling them is stated as He 'fell' upon them, not literally, but metaphorically.[261] The sign-gifts displayed by these Gentiles were those received at Pentecost by Peter and the other Jews. This likeness was demonstrated to Peter, enabling him to declare readily to his brethren that the baptism by the Spirit, the formation of the Body of Christ at Pentecost, was not just to include Jews but Gentiles also.[262]

---

[261] See footnote below on *Epipipto*.

[262] Why was there no reference to the baptism by the Spirit, i.e. to Acts 1 and Pentecost, in the case of the Samaritans? It is because from the moment God in His sovereignty chose Israel as His earthly people, all other nations (including Samaritans) were Gentiles, and more, they were 'aliens' from the commonwealth of Israel. Acts 10:45 is the case which represents all non-Jews. It was between *Jew* and *Gentile* that the 'middle wall of spiritual and physical partition' existed - (evidenced by the outer 'Gentile' court which was separated by a wall from the inner Jewish sanctum). It was Jew and Gentile that had to be 'reconciled into one Body'. So, when we come to Acts 10 -11 we are given much by way of evidence that the wall of enmity has been broken down. (1) The *cultivation* of the truth - the vision given to Peter - the great sheet with 'unclean' and 'common' food; the Lord's declaration, *"what God hath cleansed, that call not thou common"*; (2) The *climax*, the salvation of Gentiles - Cornelius and his house; followed by Peter's declaration before the Jews, *"Then I remembered the word of the Lord....ye shall be baptized with the Holy Ghost"*, referring to the Body formed at Pentecost by the Spirit of God. (3) The *consummation* of the truth in the words of the Jews, *"Then hath God also to the Gentiles granted repentance unto life"*.

Further, note that in the case of the Jews (Acts 2:17) and the Gentiles (Acts 10:45), the term 'poured-out' is used in connection with the coming of the Spirit of God upon them This was not so in the Samaritan (or Ephesian) case. In Acts 2:17 it is used to show the Jews that the coming of the Spirit of God at Pentecost was similar to the coming of the Spirit of God during the Millennium, as prophesied by Joel. By associating the Spirit's new coming at Pentecost with the words of their own prophet, the Jews would be inclined to accept the divine authenticity of the phenomenon at Pentecost (See Note 4). In Acts 10:45 the term 'poured out' links what happened at Caesarea with

Finally, we note that there was no laying-on of hands here (there was no need for ceremonial identification) and at the moment of belief, these Gentiles were simultaneously permanently indwelt, sealed and filled with the Holy Spirit! They were also added to the Body of Christ upon their belief.

Pentecost. The purpose here was to incline the Jews to accept the Gentiles as partakers of the pouring out of the Spirit at Pentecost. In Titus 3:6, Paul uses the term 'poured out' as well (translated 'shed' in the AV). He uses it to incline all believers ('shed on *us*' - Jews and Gentiles - Titus was a Gentile as noted in Galatians 2:3) to remember that because they are all partakers of the out-pouring of the Spirit at Pentecost, they should walk in the light of their new birth unto good works. Concerning Titus 3:6: *"the reference is to what took place at Pentecost. The aorist, or past definite tense points to the one act then fulfilled. All the work of the Holy Spirit in the renewing or filling of believers since, is consequent upon that initial pouring out. There never has been a second Pentecostal act such as recorded in Acts 2."* W. E. Vine: "The Collected Writings of W E Vine" Volume 3 p. 361). But why was there no mention of the pouring out in the case of the Samaritans or Ephesian disciples?

The term 'poured-out' then is used representatively and is employed to link the associated events with the Holy Spirit's coming at Pentecost. In Acts 2 it links the *Jews* with what happened on the Day of Pentecost itself (and to the words of their prophet Joel). In Acts 10:45 it links the conversion of Cornelius's household to the Spirit's out-pouring at Pentecost - representing the *Gentiles* and their link with Pentecost. In Titus 3:6 it links Jews and Gentiles representing all believers, linking them to Pentecost. A representative use of the term was not required in the case of the Samaritans, because they were Gentiles and thus represented by the declaration of the Spirit being 'poured-out' at Caesarea. (Their equality in Christ however was demonstrated prior to this by the Spirit's manifestation in deference to the divine order that the gospel was to begin at Jerusalem and then Samaria etc). The Ephesian disciples were Jews and they were represented by the case involving the Jews at Pentecost itself. The term 'poured out' in reference to the Spirit of God used by Paul to Titus (3:6) is also used representatively, here of both Jews and Gentiles.

Some suggest that the reference to the Spirit's out-pouring at Jerusalem and at Caesarea were 'two stages' or 'two parts' of the baptism by the Spirit. Because Pentecost involved Jews only, a second pouring-out, a Spirit baptism or "Gentile Pentecost", was needed to demonstrate unity in Christ. To the comment against such a view by W. E. Vine above we can add: (1) the Jews indeed required a *sign* of unity. They received this in the sign of tongues. We saw how this sign brought belief of equality in Christ. It was the Spirit's manifestation - the sign of tongues that gave Luke liberty to use the term 'poured-out', associating the Spirit's coming at Caesarea with that at Jerusalem. (2) The term 'poured-out' is a *general* term for the new way in which the Spirit of God exists among believers in this age, as it is used in a general sense by Joel ('pour out') to represent a similar coming of the Spirit in the Millennium. It cannot refer specifically to the baptism by the Spirit (Refer to Note 4). (3) In Acts 11:16 Peter quotes the promise of the Lord *"...ye shall be baptised with the Holy Ghost"*. His mention of the Lord's promise in association with the Gentiles at Caesarea, shows that he understood the Lord to have included the Gentiles when He first spoke of the promise in Acts 1:5 (as Paul expressly includes the Gentiles in Titus 3:6). Further, Peter omits *"not many days hence"*. This indicates Peter did not regard the events associated with the Gentiles at Caesarea as a 'follow-on' - a repeat of the baptism by the Spirit at Pentecost. The event promised by the Lord in Acts 2:5 which, by Peter's understanding (and as corroborated in 1 Cor 12:13; Eph 2:11-3:7) included Jews and Gentiles, verily took place a few days hence - never to be repeated! The Samaritans (Acts 8) and the Gentiles (Acts 10) were potentially part of the Body of Christ that was formed at Pentecost by the baptism by the Spirit. When they were saved they came into the Body experimentally - they partook of that which took place at Pentecost.

157

The Samaritan Case

But what about the Samaritans in Acts 8? There is a delay between their belief (v.12) and the 'receiving' of the Holy Spirit (v.15-17). Some regard the delay as teaching a 'second blessing', - the 'baptism by the Holy Spirit', which must be earnestly sought through prayer (v.15).

Now, we need to note that when the Samaritans were converted there were no outward manifestations of the Holy Spirit. We read only of their conversion and water baptism (v.12). How then do we account for the 'delay' in receiving the Holy Spirit in verse 17? The issue rests on what Scripture means here by 'receiving'. Receiving must be defined according to the context - opposite to 'not yet fallen' (v.16), i.e. to receive the Holy Spirit is to have Him fall upon them! Prudence demands we begin again with that which we know to be indisputable and allow Scripture to interpret itself. There are a number of certainties here.

Firstly, the falling upon (receiving) cannot be the indwelling or the sealing of the Spirit. The Samaritans believed the word concerning Christ (v.12) and at that moment they were indwelt and sealed by the Spirit of God. At conversion, they received the 'gift of the Holy Spirit'. We know this from John 14:17 and Romans 8:9. No mention is made of receiving the 'gift of the Holy Spirit' in verses 15-17 when they are said to have received 'Holy Spirit'.

Secondly, could the falling of the Spirit (receiving) be a baptism by the Holy Spirit? The 'subjects' here, each Samaritan, are said to 'receive', (have the Spirit fall upon them) not be 'put into', therefore neither can the receiving (or falling) of 'Holy Spirit' be any sort of baptism. Remember, to argue that this is a baptism contradicts the very meaning of the word - immersion, and the teaching of 1 Corinthians 12:13. Receiving (the Spirit falling upon) is not a case of the Samaritans being 'put into'! When the activity of the Spirit is mentioned in verses 15-17, no mention is made of Spirit 'baptism'; no reference is made to the baptism by the Spirit at Pentecost, the event prophesied by the Lord in Acts 1:5 (as was the case of the Gentiles, Acts 11:15).

The receiving of the Holy Spirit can then only be in regard to the manifestation of the Holy Spirit associated with the *gifts* of the Spirit - there is little doubt this was the sign of tongues. Peter and John prayed, not for the indwelling, sealing or 'Spirit baptism' of the Samaritan believers, but that the Spirit of God, who was already in them, might be made evident - that these Samaritans might show a sign that they had already received the *Gift* of the Spirit (v.12).

What reason can be given then for the 'delay' in the manifestation of the Spirit and the prayer associated with it? It is because the Jews would not believe that the Spirit was with or in any Samaritan unless such signs took place and, importantly, that it was all done under the prayerful and authoritative supervision of Jewish apostles.[263] We noted earlier, the Samaritans were a long-standing rival religious people, who had set up their own temple and worship of Jehovah.[264] The sectarian attitude is seen clearly in the declaration that *'Samaria'* had received the word of God'. Now, what does this situation require in order to convince both parties of their equal standing in Christ and overcome the deep mutual distrust? The Spirit of God sends two Jews of outstanding reputation, Peter and John, to confirm for the benefit of the Jewish believers, that the Samaritans' salvation and regeneration by the Spirit of God was authentic and not some rival imitation. If these Samaritans had really been saved, and therefore received the Spirit of God as the Jews had done, then let us have some evidence of it. A sign or manifestation was thus prayed for. On the other hand, to satisfy the Samaritans that there was no animosity from the Jews, the Holy Spirit

---

[263] Especially John, who was the one who wanted fire from heaven to rain down upon the Samaritans (Luke 9:54).
[264] Ezra 4:1-5. They wanted to help rebuild the temple in Jerusalem but were disallowed by Zerubbabel, even though they sought and sacrificed to Jehovah as did the Jews.

sent these two Jews to give the Samaritans a sign of unity - they must lay their hands upon them, the religious sign used by Jews to identify with others. We are left with the conclusion that receiving the 'Holy Ghost' refers to the aspect of His manifestation - associated with the gifts of the Spirit. The grammatical construction is helpful here in interpreting the sense of 'receive'.[265]

A *special case in circumstance but not an exceptional case in doctrine.*

The Samaritan case presents us with a unique set of circumstances. Yet these cannot overturn the teaching and example of Scripture, that the 'gift of the Holy Spirit' is received *at the moment of belief* in Christ. Consider the following occasions and the confirming doctrine - first the doctrine, Romans 8:9; John 14:17; then the examples: (1) *Acts 2:38* - individual Jews, the new converts, the gift of the Holy Ghost was received when they believed; (2) *Acts 10:43-45* - Gentiles, the gift of the Holy Ghost was at the time of belief [266]; (3) *Acts 19:4-6* - the Ephesian disciples believed on Christ (v.4-5) and upon this they

---

[265] *Epipipto* - to fall upon; used metaphorically of the Holy Spirit in Acts 8:16 (Samaritans); 10:44 (Gentiles) and 11:15 (Gentiles)". W. E. Vine "Expository Dictionary of New Testament Words", p. 74. A note of support from the grammar on this is found in "The Expositor's Greek Testament" Volume II; Wm B Eerdmans p. 216: Again, while such grammatical interpretation is helpful, we need to apply the events, context and axioms of Scripture to determine the sense in which a word is used. Note then, the Holy Spirit does not actually (literally) fall upon the believers. We have the metaphorical use of the word 'fall' in regards to fear, e.g., Acts 19:17, 'fear fell on them'. Fear did not literally fall on them. What is being stated here, is that their manner, expressions and actions showed that they were controlled by fear. That which was within (fear) showed itself outwardly. The outward manifestation, therefore, is the evidence that fear indwelt them. So too in regard to the Holy Spirit, In Acts 10, the Holy Ghost fell on them, i.e., they manifested the indwelling of the Holy Spirit which was given - their manner showed they were under His control (filled). Otherwise, how did they know that they had the gift of the Holy Spirit (v. 45)? Note in regard to the Gentiles, Acts 10:45, specific mention is made of the 'gift of the Holy Spirit', proving they were indwelt upon their belief - at that time (not so in Acts 8:15-17, mention is only made to the metaphorical falling of the Spirit, for they had received the 'gift of the Spirit' - indwelling - upon belief, v.12).

[266] Both sides of the debate will agree, the Spirit of God cannot be given *before* conversion (and neither can baptism be undertaken unless there is belief, Acts 8:37 etc)! Therefore, when Peter preached the necessity of belief for salvation (v.43), these godly people believed, whereupon the Holy Spirit was given (and water baptism permitted v.48). See also the order in Acts 11:17 - the like gift (Spirit of God) was given to them that believed!

received the Spirit of God. The manifestation is evidence that they received the 'gift of the Holy Spirit' - there can be no manifestation without having the Gift (but the Gift can be had without a manifestation, as in the situation when the Samaritans were converted). There are other instructive instances of the regenerating and renewing of the Spirit of God where no gifts of the Spirit were manifested - the Ethiopian eunuch (see below) and the Philippian jailer (Acts 16). In both these cases, God's servants were required to point the way of eternal life and light. No mention is made of a baptism by the Holy Spirit or tarrying for a 'second blessing'. When Paul and Silas are faced with the earnest plea of the jailer, *"Sirs, what must I do to be saved"*, they preach the 'full gospel' to him - *"Believe on the Lord Jesus Christ and thou shalt be saved"*[267]

Now some who deny the existence of a 'second blessing', regard the Samaritan case as an exception to Romans 8:9 - that the Holy Spirit indwells at conversion. They believe the reason for the 'delay' was the rivalry between Jews and Samaritans; that God 'withheld' the gift of the Spirit - His Spirit's indwelling, to allow time for the apostles to journey to Samaria and so publicly 'validate' the conversion of the Samaritans. They further argue that receiving means just that - receiving. However there are four reasons against this view.

1. Racial and religious rivalry can never be a reason to overturn the Lord's divine promise in John 14:17, that *"He...shall be in you"*. Neither can it provide any valid exception to the inviolable rule of Romans 8:9. Is God's assurance of salvation upon faith's moment, which is seized by faith and secured by His indwelling Spirit, to be excepted by racial difference? What gospel could Peter preach to these Samaritans, except that upon faith the

---

[267] Acts 16:31

indwelling of the one Spirit unites them in Christ and to Him?

2. There is no mention in Acts 8:15-23 at all of receiving the 'gift of *the* Spirit'. This is significant in view of the explicit mention of it in the cases in Acts 2 & 10, and implicitly in Acts 19 - there can be no manifestation of the Spirit's gifts without the gift of the Spirit being received; but there can be the receiving of the Spirit - the Gift, without a manifestation of His spiritual gifts.

3. The term 'gift of God' (Acts 8:20) is a general expression, its particular meaning determined by the context. What is it that Simon wanted? He saw the apostles lay hands on the Samaritans, after which they manifested the Spirit of God. As stated earlier, the laying on of hands itself carried no power to bestow spiritual gifts or the Holy Spirit Himself; it was purely a ceremonial identification. But it was associated with apostolic *authority* (not ability). Now this is an important distinction. The word Luke uses is not *dunamis* (ability or might), but *exousian*, meaning legal permission or the right to do something.[268] Simon wanted this authority (incorrectly translated 'power' in the AV). If he could gain this, it would indeed revive his diminished reputation as a sorcerer among the people of Samaria, who once believed *"from the least to the greatest...This man is the great power of God"* (vv.10-12). The 'gift of God' then, simply means the apostolic gift and its associated apostolic authority.[269]

4. Some say, 'received' simply means 'received'. However, the meaning of the word, indeed any word, is

---

[268] W.E.Vine. "Expository Dictionary of New Testament Words"; p. 89.

[269] Of particular interest here is the use of the expression 'gift of God' in 1 Cor 7:7. The word '*charisma*' refers, as in the case with spiritual gifts, to a gift of grace. Jewish extremists advocated celibacy as a means to greater spirituality. Paul says that whatever state, married or celibate, each believer has a gift from God, which can be exercised therein. He speaks here of his gift of apostleship and his own marital state. We cannot ignore the connection between the giving of spiritual gifts and God, as given in 1 Cor 12:28 - *"God hath set some in the church, first apostles etc."* The 'gift of God' is also used of salvation (John 4:10; Rom 6:23; Eph 2:8).

qualified by existing principles of truth (in this case Romans 8:9), associated expressions (here the expression 'not yet fallen') and by context. This last point is aptly illustrated many times in Scripture. For instance, Paul declares to Timothy, *"the woman...shall be saved in childbearing, if they continue in faith and charity etc"* (1 Tim 2:14-15). To be saved is to receive salvation, but what is being received here? Eternal salvation of the soul? Salvation of the body? We proceed from what we know - inviolable doctrinal truth - salvation of the soul is only through faith in Christ. The context determines it is the woman's good testimony and witness within the church that is being saved. By devotion to her family, she will be protected from the social evils of the day, which is consistent with the teaching of godliness in women through the whole passage.

A proper reading of Scripture, comparing doctrine with precept as we have seen, shows that the Samaritan case is not an exception to the permanent indwelling (and sealing) of the Spirit at the time of individual conversion. The exception, as we have seen, is a withholding of the Spirit's outward showing, associated with the gifts He gives. No violation of divine promise or principle exists here. Scripture never teaches the manifestation of the Spirit must take place at the time of conversion.[270] Only the manifestation (never the indwelling and sealing) was held over, to be a sign to the Jews that the Samaritans had been truly converted, having the Spirit of God indwelling - the gift of the Spirit.

---

[270] The case of the Ethiopian eunuch is of particular value here. We are told he believed and was baptised (water) and went away rejoicing (not speaking in tongues). Note also, it was Philip who had witnessed the eunuch's conversion, and this was just before his involvement in the conversion of the Samaritans. He was told by the Spirit of God to *'Go near, and join thyself to this* [the eunuch's] *chariot'* (Acts 8: 29) - the chariot of a man the Spirit of God had set apart for salvation. Yet, Philip spoke nothing of a 'second blessing' or 'baptism by the Holy Spirit' to the eunuch, when, under the control of the Spirit, he preached Christ to Him.

What better way to convince both groups of the oneness in Christ than to have two reliable prominent Jews - Peter and John, witness that the Spirit had indwelt Samaritans? What better public expression of acceptance and fellowship towards these Samaritans could these Jews perform than the laying-on-of their hands? A sceptical Jerusalem would accept no other proof of the Samaritan conversions, and the rival Samaritans accept no other expression of unity with Jerusalem, for the laying-on-of-hands was the Jewish expression of religious identification. (Also required in the case of the Ephesian disciples, another religious party, but not required in Acts 10, for these Gentiles were outright heathens, not a rival religious people). Can we not see God's order in all this?

Galatians 3:27 - "baptized into Christ"

Before concluding, we should address the view held by some that Galatians 3:27 refers to the baptism by the Spirit. There is no explicit mention of Spirit baptism here (or the collective term 'we all') to link to the aorist tense (which is also used in 1 Corinthians 12:13). We must therefore rely wholly upon the context. Paul speaks to the Jewish Christians who were being led astray by the Judaisers and their lust for the law. In verse 24, Paul declares the law was *our* (the Jews') schoolmaster and, in verse 25, he speaks of its extinct jurisdiction. In verse 26 he reminds them (the Jewish believers) how they became united to Christ - through faith in Him. Then in verse 27 he reminds them that their water baptism was an identification with Christ and thus an expression of the unity of all believers in Him. If Paul has any thought here of the baptism by the Spirit, it is in the sense that water baptism is an expression of that oneness in the Body of Christ, which was formed at Pentecost.

Conclusion

Rightly divided, Scripture unfolds four distinctive works of the Spirit of God. They may be summarized as follows (refer to the Table below for an overview):

· *Indwelling* (Anointing) - the Spirit's permanent *Presence (Purpose)* within (for) us;

· *Sealing* - the Spirit's principal *Pledge* to us of our eternal security;

· *Baptism* - the Spirit's past *Positioning* of us in the Body of Christ;

· *Filling* - the Spirit's prevailing *Presidency* within us.

The indwelling of the Holy Spirit speaks of our rebirth and renewal by the Spirit of God; the sealing pronounces our eternal security in regard to the new birth and renewal; the baptism presents the glorious truth of our position and union in the church which is His Body, over which Christ is the Head; the filling exhorts us to a life yielded to Christ, redolent of faith, hope and love. How Satan has tried to blur these distinctive works of God's Spirit, endeavouring to rob Him of His glory and trying to deprive us of feeding upon them so we may be built up in our holy faith. Failure to distinguish these works of the Spirit will mean failure to enjoy and, importantly, support other great NT truths such as the Body of Christ, the eternal security of the believer and Christ's Headship. Let us hold tenaciously to the precious truths attending all works of the Spirit of God. What terrible damage is being done by those who deny the Spirit of God His distinctive ministry.

Overview of the four works of the Spirit of God

	Indwelling (Anointing)	Sealing	Filling	Baptism
When received	At the moment of conversion	At the moment of conversion	Depends upon the believer's submission to the Holy Spirit	It took place at Pentecost for all believers (those present and future)
How received	Automatically - a matter of divine promise	Automatically - a matter of divine promise	Automatically - a matter of divine promise	Not applicable after Pentecost
Subjects	All believers	All believers	Available to all believers	All believers
Purpose	*Spirit's Presence:* Regeneration (rebirth) and renewing (renovation of the new life)	*Spirit's Pledge:* Eternal security of the believer	*Spirit's Presidency:* To enable a sanctified and Christ-like life	*Spirit's Positioning:* Formation of the Body of Christ
Duration	Permanent	Permanent	Depends upon submission to the Holy Spirit	Permanent place in the Body of all believers
Basis	Unconditional	Unconditional	Conditional - depends upon submission to the Holy Spirit	Unconditional for all believers
Key Scriptures	*John 14:17* *John 15:26* *Rom 8:9* *Titus 3:5* *1 John 2:27*	*Eph 1:13* *Eph 4:30*	*Eph 5:18* *Acts 2:4* *Acts 4:8-31* *Acts 11:18*	*Matt 3:11* *Mark 1:8* *Luke 3:16* *John 1:33* *Acts 1:5* *Acts 11:16* *1 Cor 12:13*

CHAPTER 9

'Miracle Healing'

There is much about 'faith-healing' and 'healing campaigns' that bring great sadness and distress among those who have been brought by the Holy Spirit to see God's sovereign grace in all aspects of life and the nobility with which the Great Physician performed miracles. We could speak at length of the mercenary methods that make merchandise of many and the questionable motives of 'faith-healers'. However we must focus on that which they claim as scriptural justification for their craft, for it is Scripture alone, not 'healing miracles' that will decide the matter.

One of the warrants alongside the promise of prosperity and wealth from the 'full gospel' pulpit, is the pledge of physical health. We are told that a life free from physical suffering is the bountiful prospect facing all believers in Christ. We noted earlier the error of the 'tongues universalists' who believe all Christians should speak in tongues. Well here we have the error of the 'healing universalists' - healing is readily available to all believers. Many preach that the believers are entitled to expect a life free of physical suffering. Should illness befall, there is the assurance that healing is available. If however healing fails to occur, then sin and unbelief dwells within. Does Scripture teach that we can live a life free from sickness and, if illness arises, is there a guarantee of healing?

The Lord's commission to His disciples
"These twelve Jesus sent forth, and commanded them, saying, Go not into the way of the Gentiles, and into any

city of the Samaritans enter ye not: But go rather to the lost sheep of the house of Israel. And as ye go, preach, saying, The kingdom of heaven is at hand. Heal the sick, cleanse the lepers, raise the dead, cast out devils: freely ye have received, freely give." (Matthew 10:5-8). Because the Lord gave power to His disciples over all manner of diseases, it is said we too can claim this power since we are His disciples.

As noted in our study of tongues and the Holy Spirit, the context and God's prophetic program is critical to the correct interpretation of Scripture. The claim of 'faith-healers' based on Matthew 10:5-6 ignores both. The commission given to the twelve was specific to the time and limited to the Jews - specifically prohibited to the Gentiles and Samaria. The power to heal was to be directed to the 'lost sheep of Israel'. Why? It is because the Lord was commissioning the twelve to announce the kingdom of heaven is at hand, to demonstrate its character through miracles and to draw the Jews to their Messiah-King, Jesus of Nazareth. It is not the church here at all, but the kingdom of heaven and the King Himself. The Jews would, however, have no king but Caesar and so at Pentecost, Israel, being set aside, the church begins and the commission to the twelve disciples ends. Then begins another commission which by the express command of the Lord, is to begin at Jerusalem, and then all Judea, and into Samaria and to the uttermost parts of the earth (Acts 1:8). The King is not on earth, but His Spirit descends to enable this new commission to the Jew first, accompanied by signs and wonders (until the cannon of Scripture is completed).

Scripture rightly divided shows clearly the commission to the disciples in Matthew 10 does not apply to us today. Let those who insist otherwise confine their ministry to the lost sheep of Israel and, moreover, show us the finger of God - the occasions where the dead have been raised.

Healing in the 'Atonement'
The argument here is that the sufferings of Christ and His

death (His 'atonement' of sin) provides for physical healing. Warrant for this view we are told is found in the words of Isaiah 53:4-5: *"Surely he hath borne our griefs, and carried our sorrows: yet we did esteem him stricken, smitten of God, and afflicted. But he was wounded for our transgressions, he was bruised for our iniquities: the chastisement of our peace was upon him; and with his stripes we are healed."*

When Isaiah pens these words, he never has the church period in view and, therefore he does not have believers in Christ in his eye at all! It is the nation Israel during the Millennial kingdom that is the focus of the prophet's vision. Israel crucified Christ, delivered Him up into the hands of cruel men and rejected Him as their Messiah, for they would have no king but Caesar. Now, having been delivered from the mouth of the Adversary during the Tribulation by that same Jesus, the Jews in the Millennial period realise that the One who reigns as King of kings and Lord of Lords, *"was [the One] wounded for our transgressions,....[the One] bruised for our iniquities: the chastisement of our peace was upon him; and with his stripes we are healed."* This is the nation's Millennial cry of recognition of the Messiah they delivered unto death.[271]

But what about Matthew 8:16-17 which speaks of the fulfilment of Isaiah's prophecy: *"When the even was come, they brought unto him many that were possessed with devils: and he cast out the spirits with his word, and healed all that were sick: That it might be fulfilled which was spoken by Esaias the prophet, saying, Himself took our infirmities, and bare our sicknesses."*? The first thing to note here is that if it is a 'fulfilment', then it takes place *before* the Atonement, the Lord's suffering and death at Calvary, denying the claim

---

[271] Isaiah spoke of a Deliverer (the Messiah) of the nation in a time to come. He, like all the OT prophets were not given to see the period between Daniel's 69th and 70th week - the Church period. Chapter 53 (and other Messianic passages) however, do pre-figure Calvary and foreshadow the suffering of Christ. As such it is fitting for us to use them in our worship of Him.

169

that healing is through the Atonement. The second matter to observe is that the fulfilment is not in regard to healing but in regard to *bearing*. The word here is *bastazo* which means "borne" on behalf of others. What they could not do and bear themselves, the Lord bore. Once again we have a partial quote of the prophets. It is quoted not to confirm a literal fulfilment of Isaiah 53:4-5, but cited to affirm that the One who is among them is the Messiah of the nation. This occasion falls within the time the kingdom was still being offered to Israel. The Lord had yet to withdraw His offer, which He does later (as seen in Matthew 12 and as noted above). The fulfilment here then is in the sense of defining the character and identity of Jesus of Nazareth as Messiah of Israel, One who is sympathetic to the spiritual and physical burdens of its people.[272]

So we see the matter is very clear indeed. Isaiah is not speaking about the believers during the Church period; neither is he speaking of any form of 'physical' healing of the individual, but of the *spiritual* healing of the nation of Israel, a nation which, as we have noted at length earlier, rejected Jesus of Nazareth in spiritual disbelief. Again we come upon a monumental error in biblical interpretation by the charismatics - substantiated this time by so-called 'miracle healings'. It seems that for every wrongful interpretation of the Word of God by the charismatics, Satan has some associated 'experience' to confirm it!

The gifts of healing given by the Spirit of God - a universal remedy?

The claim here is that healing is enabled and readily available through special gifts given to believers by the Spirit

---

[272] Matthew, unlike Mark, orders events topically rather than chronologically because it is Matthew's design through the Spirit of God, to bring to the fore the Messiah of Israel in the person of Jesus of Nazareth, their rejection of Him and the course of God's dealing with them because of it. (The 'fulfillment' is not included in the other synoptic gospels: Mark 1:29-34; Luke 4:38-41.)

of God (1 Cor 12 etc). Much the same can be said of the gifts of healing that was said concerning the gift of tongues: they were a sign gift to authenticate the oral doctrine of the apostles and manifest the Spirit's presence during the early church period; not everyone was given this gift (1 Cor 11; 12); and the gift petered out towards the end of the apostolic period. It was it not used by Paul (who had this gift) to heal three faithful servants of the Lord over whose physical health he expressed concern. The failure to employ this gift was not due to a lack of faith on their part. Paul explicitly testifies to the faith of Epaphroditus who became sick *"for the work of Christ"* (Phil 2:25-30).

The first observation concerning the character of the period in which the gifts operated is that believers were not to expect freedom from physical illness and suffering. This is plainly evident in the life of young Timothy (1 Tim 5:23), Trophimus (2 Tim 4:20), Epaphroditus (Phil 2:24) and Paul. It was Paul who thrice requested that the Lord remove the thorn in his flesh (2 Cor 12:7-8).[273]

Physical suffering is to be expected by the believer, not excepted. Although saved from the penalty of sin, we are not removed from its presence. We see here once more the failure of the charismatics to distinguish between the present day of suffering and the future day of glory. The whole creation groans under the weight and bondage of sin (Rom 8:22) and while we are in this earthly tabernacle we too partake of its pangs.

However, while physical suffering is common to saint and sinner, it has in the case of the former a particular threefold mission through the grace of God. We see this in the life of Paul, in whom the Lord saw fit to deny the removal of his thorn in the flesh, firstly so that he could be strengthened through weakness - lest he be exalted above measure.

---

[273] That this was some physical infirmity we can be fairly certain. Of its particular nature we have no idea.

Secondly, physical illness in the believer brings before us the special work of the Lord as our Great high Priest: *"For we have not an high priest which cannot be touched with the feeling of our infirmities; but was in all points tempted like as we are, yet without sin"* (Heb 4:15). Satan will have us turn to 'miracle' remedies in order to deflect us from the divinely appointed source of support: *"Let us therefore come boldly unto the throne of grace, that we may obtain mercy, and find grace to help in time of need"* (v.6). Such was the experience of Paul, who found the Lord's grace all-sufficient (2 Cor 12:9), and Epaphroditus who found mercy in God (Phil 2:27). Not only is the work of the Lord denied, but that of His Spirit, the Comforter and Teacher in the school of grace. The charismatic notion of healing sessions and gifts of healing rob us of that personal dependence upon God - which *is* universally available through Christ to every believer in Him.

Thirdly, physical illness cultivates that particular relationship between the Father and His children: *"Furthermore we have had fathers of our flesh which corrected us, and we gave them reverence: shall we not much rather be in subjection unto the Father of spirits, and live? For they verily for a few days chastened us after their own pleasure; but he for our profit, that we might be partakers of his holiness...it yieldeth the peaceable fruit of righteousness unto them which are exercised thereby"* (Heb 12:6-11). Cannot then physical illness be a chastening from the Father of lights (James 1:17-18)? And, if so, what purpose is served by the chastening of the Lord if a gift of the Spirit can be employed to remove it? What sanctifying effect can such chastening have if universal health is advertised for the believer through these gifts?

The Epistle of James

James pens his letter to the Christian Jews of the dispersion - those scattered throughout many nations (1:1). He is necessarily occupied with their trials, temptations, affections and relationships as they abide in a Gentile world. He prescribes precept and illuminates principle regarding many aspects of life, one of which relates to sickness among them. He asks if there are any sick, employing the word *asthenei* (essentially 'weary') which can refer to physical or spiritual illness. There are good reasons to conclude that he refers to the latter, that is, a low state of spiritual morale. Firstly, this question is the last of three he poses in this portion (vv.13-14). Because the first two questions relate to a state of spiritual morale, it is reasonable to conclude the third does as well, preserving consistency of thought and theme. Secondly, the 'sickness' James has in mind specifically involves the ministry of the spiritual overseers of the church, suggesting the malady is of a spiritual nature. He does not exhort summoning a physician; neither does he call upon 'faith healers' or those with gifts of healings which, given the early date of this epistle (prior to 50 AD) would exist at that time. These arguments taken with the broad context of the chapter which deals with sins, confession, forgiveness and spiritual regeneration, as well as the propensity for spiritual weariness among the Christian Jews by living in hostile nations, indicates that James is not referring to physical illness. What purpose then is served by the anointing with oil? It is not a ceremonial anointing (where *chrio* would be used) but a 'rubbing of oil' (*aleipsantes*). Believers who were in a low spiritual state could experience physical lethargy and the application of oil would revive their physical constitution. The prayer of faith will restore (heal) them spiritually and if they have faults (committed sins or transgressions) confession and disclosure is required (vv.15-16) as a step to spiritual health.[274]

What about the evidence of miracle 'healing"

We come again to the question, if all this is true, then how do you explain the healing miracles by faith-healers? Firstly,

---

[274] 'Healed' in verse 16 is *iaomai* which may be used in a physical or spiritual sense (e.g. 1 Pet 2:24; Heb 12:13).

many 'faith-healers' have been exposed for outright fraud and their campaigns nothing but a sham! The Lord will reward them according to their deeds. Many of their disciples claim to have seen the lame walk, but we ask, what was the real condition of the person prior to the healing? What clinical follow-up was undertaken? - many have professed to be healed only to have their illness reappear. Was there a bona-fide illness in the first instance or was the illness psychosomatic. But is not this condition a real illness? It may well be, but then no miracle is needed to cure it - one needs only to produce the required euphoric environment, for it can dispel a psychosomatic condition! Let us note further, there are many whom the 'faith-healers' fail to 'heal'. When this occurs they resort to the expedient assertion that such failure is because of unbelief and this unbelief is caused by sin. This only serves to cast many onto the tempestuous sea of uncertainty, dwelling on their sin and misery instead of counting their suffering as allowed by God to yield the peaceable fruit of righteousness in them.

CHAPTER 10

New Age Christianity

What is 'New Age Christianity'?
New Age Christianity embraces many of the beliefs and practices found in mystic Eastern religion, but its roots tap into deeper veins of evil, as we shall see. The Movement promotes self-awareness, finding our 'inner-selves', discovering the god within us all, the notion that the individual is 'one with the universe' and 'nature'. The techniques of the Movement include meditation, letting the mind roam in search of dreams and visions, yoga, reading of mystic literature, palmistry, astrology, crystals, hypnosis, and New Age (mystical and mind-absorbing) music. The Movement's vocabulary includes 'universal peace', 'inner harmony', 'god-consciousness', 'cosmic consciousness', 'children of the universe', 'Age of Aquarius', 'unity'.

In what follows, no attempt is made to present a detailed exposure of the Movement, only to outline the Movement's broad principles so that it can be identified, and place before believers some of the grave dangers inherent in it.

The dangers to Christianity of the New Age Movement
There is a smouldering desire in the heart of many to seek some new thing under the sun, something that presents a fresh swell of 'enlightenment'. Herein lies the fatal attraction causing many to forsake the 'old paths'. *"Thus saith the LORD, Stand ye in the ways, and see, and ask for the old paths, where is the good way, and walk therein, and ye*

shall find rest for your souls. But they said, We will not walk therein" (Jer 6:16). Note the following dangers.

1. *Its growing association with the Charismatic Movement.*
The teachings and practices of the New Age Movement are increasingly finding their way into many Christian gatherings. Why? Because resistance to these apostate principles and practices are in part being eroded by the Charismatic Movement. Its focus on 'experiences'- preoccupation with coming under a 'power' often manifested by tongues, being slain by the spirit, spiritual swooning and spiritual laughter, have made many vulnerable to the teachings and techniques of the New Age Movement. Far- fetched? Well, note the expressed teaching amongst some 'charismatic Christian clergy' and 'charismatic Christian churches', viz:

a) The Zodiac sign *'Aquarius'*, the water-bearer, is the astrological representation of Joel's prophecy of the Spirit of God who 'poured out His Spirit on all flesh' (falling into line with the charismatic doctrine concerning Joel's prophecy being fulfilled at Pentecost).

b) This sign of Aquarius represents the individual's responsibility and ability (as seen in a man shouldering a water pot) to take up his/her own burden, spiritual or physical - to look within, not just to God to find strength and direction in life.

c) Astrology as a guide to Christian faith has been permitted by Christ, being proved through 'visions and dreams' (in line with the charismatic view of Acts 2:17). These frocked felons of another faith even speak of their 'helpers', spirits of the dead (i.e. channelling or spiritism), perverting 1 John 4:1 as their liberty to contact the departed for extra revelations (as noted earlier).

d) The Bible contains 'hidden' or 'inner' meanings which are discovered through trances, meditations and channelling where the mind is allowed to yield to certain 'powers'.

Let there be no doubt, there is growing common ground between the charismatic and New Age movements, which is a portent of the coming world apostate church that unites all religions and creeds. It is not the biblical standard of 'having the same mind (understanding)' but having the 'same experiences' that forges the fraternity between charismatics and the New Age 'Christians'. Spiritualism which broods in the black heart of the New Age movement, is considered a religion among many religions. (Refer Deut 17:2-4; 18:9-13; 1 Tim 4:1. *"The entrance of Thy words giveth light"* (Psa 119:130).

2. Its denial of the essential truths of Christianity.
   Monism (all is one) and *pantheism* (all is God), both tenets of New Age doctrine, combine to create the idea that each person is God, denying the biblical doctrine of God as the Creator and man the created, a doctrine designed to blind man of his responsibility and conscience toward God as his Creator and Redeemer (cf. Gen 3:5). That God is a 'force' or some 'cosmic energy', not a person, stems from the pantheistic element of New Age philosophy. This denies the blessed relationship between God and the believer as revealed in Scripture - as children of God, as sons of God. The notion of 'a divine force' also shapes the New Age teaching concerning Christ - Jesus of Nazareth 'became' Christ. His eternal Sonship and Deity are denied. Because Jesus the man was endued with a divine force, he stands level with other men who have been so endued - e.g. Buddha and Krishna. *Mysticism* (inner 'divine' experiences), another source of 'inspiration' is said to reveal hidden meanings in the Bible, thus denying the truth was once for all delivered.

'New Age Christianity' is anything but new!
   "Vanity of vanities; all is vanity....there is no new thing under the sun" (Ecc 1:2,9).

177

Eden revisited

The essential error of the New Age Movement is rooted in the Fall, seen for all its evil attraction in the promise by Satan that *"ye shall be as gods"* (Gen 3:5)! The Movement is thus stamped with the diabolical design of the Adversary, evident in his temptation of Eve. The principal promise of New Age philosophy is self-deification attained through self-will! Once this is embraced, the moral responsibility of the individual to the only true and wise God is denied; and death ceases to be the consequence of sin against God. God's universal judgment upon man because of disobedience to Him is not conceded, so His love in providing salvation through Christ His Son is regarded as meaningless.

Gnosticism

'New Age Christianity' is seen masquerading during the early Church period under the guise of gnosticism, a manifestation of the error in Eden. Explicit condemnation of it is found in Paul's epistle to the Colossians. John, too, in his first Epistle, challenges it aggressively. We should therefore not be taken unawares by it or feel ill-equipped to deal with it. Satan has simply dressed it in contemporary clothing.

Gnosticism, comes from the Greek word for knowledge - *gnosis*. The Gnostics believed that knowledge nurtured in a composite cradle of astrology, asceticism, mythology and philosophy, was the key in finding union with God and salvation. God, they also believed, expressed Himself through spirits, emanations and angels. Some Gnostics believed Christ was an aeon that came and left the man Jesus at His baptism and crucifixion respectively. This very idea of Christ is taught today by many New Age votaries. There were other Gnostics who believed Christ had a 'phantom' body. The Christian doctrines brought into relief by Paul when writing to the Colossians were in answer to 'gnostic' thinking.

· Christ has the pre-eminence in creation - He is the Creator who is before all things and in whom all things consist (1:15–19). Christ is all or He is nothing at all!

· Christ is the One in whom all the fullness of the Godhead dwells (1:19; 2:9).

· Christ is the only source of veritable and pure knowledge (1:9) as opposed to vain philosophy (2.8).

· Christ is the only Mediator between God and man. The veneration of angels (2:18-19), an evolved Jewish predilection (given impetus by gnosticism), predisposed some to depreciate the mediatory work of Christ and their relationship to Him as the Head of the Body. It is through Christ, risen and glorified, that believers are knit together (2:19).

How must we guard against the New Age Movement?

Paul's clear message is that we must know more of the Christ of God - *"As ye have therefore received Christ Jesus the Lord, so walk ye in Him: rooted and built up in Him"* (Col 1:6)! It is the doctrine of Christ that affords the only safe anchorage for the soul in a restless world that through wisdom knows not God. When writing to the Corinthians (who were spoiled by philosophy), Paul forthrightly declares the folly and fatality of the wisdom of the world - for God has brought the worldly wise, the scribe and the disputer to naught (1 Cor 1:19-21)! What a fitting epitaph for all who seek light and life in philosophy, which can never explain man's ruin in sin or God's love to man because of it. Here all reason stumbles and faith is invited to act upon divine revelation once for all given - that Christ Jesus came into the world to save sinners! It is not Christ enthroned who is presented here victorious over earthly wisdom, but that doctrine which is particularly foolish to the natural man and forgotten by the carnal believer - the Christ of God, the despised and rejected Son of God who had to die on a felon's cross that man might have eternal life. We cannot see or keep before us the Lamb enthroned and exalted, if we fail to see or lose sight of Christ

179

who humbled Himself and died on the cross for us. Paul therefore professes to know only two things in the face of the failure at Corinth - Christ Jesus and Him crucified. This doctrine is the eternal spring from which the carnal Christian is to drink and be revived; it is also the life-giving stream from which the sinner must drink for salvation. Have you done so?

As believers in Christ, it is our preoccupation with Him as our Redeemer which is our safeguard, not just from New Age error, but from all apostate doctrine. To guard against our being led astray by the error of the wicked, may we seek to *"grow in grace and in the knowledge of our Lord and Saviour Jesus Christ. To Him be glory both now and forever. Amen"* (2 Pet 3:17-18).

> *Near the Cross! O Lamb of God,*
> *Bring its scenes before me;*
> *Help me walk from day to day,*
> *with its shadow o'er me.*
> (Fanny Crosbie)

Endnotes

1. Apostolic succession does not exist. The word apostle *'apostolos'* means one who has 'been sent forth'. It is used in Scripture of the Lord (Heb 3:1) who is the Apostle and High Priest of our profession (confession). It is used of the twelve chosen especially by the Lord (Luke 6:13; 9:19) and Paul (1 Cor 9:1; 15:8). The word is also used in a general sense to apply to others not of the twelve and Paul, who were sent forth on the Lord's business (Barnabas, Acts 14:4; Andronicus and Junias, Rom 16:7; Epaphroditus, Phil 2:23 (RV); Timothy and Silas, 1 Thess 2.6). In the case of Paul, the twelve and the others, the word apostle expressed their relationship to the Lord.

We may then identify three categories of apostles in the NT, viz:

· The Lord Himself as the Apostle - Exemplar, who was commissioned directly by the Father ("..wist ye not that I must be about my Father's business?" Luke 2:49).

· The twelve who were especially qualified (Acts 1:21-26). (i) They were directly chosen and commissioned by the Lord Himself (by His Spirit in the case of Matthias through the OT way of casting lots). (ii) They could bear testimony to the Lord from the time of His baptism by John to His ascension. (iii) They were witnesses to His resurrection. Paul is undoubtedly included in this category because of his special calling by the Lord, as one 'born out of due time' - the Damascus road revelation (1 Cor 9:1). Paul and these twelve are thus known as 'the apostles' and the 'apostolic period' ended when the last of this category died.

· All others who were called apostles in a general sense in

the NT - because of the work they did in co-operation with 'the apostles' and through delegation, as in the case of Timothy. Delegation is not succession.

a)   There *could not* be any 'apostolic succession' after the death of John the last apostle (circa 100 AD) because it is impossible for anyone else to meet the qualifications required to be apostles of the category of the twelve (and Paul).

(There being none else who can meet these qualifications, there can be none qualified to delegate others to do the work of an apostle).

b)   There was *no need* for any apostolic succession because:

· the apostles (and the prophets, see below) were commissioned to lay the foundation of the church. A foundation can only be laid once (Eph 2:20).

· With the completion of the Scriptures, there can be no 'additional' revelation - a particular work of 'the apostles'.

The foundation of the church was laid by the apostles *and* the prophets. They worked together in establishing through word and deed the footing of the church - the common base of truth that, as we have noted, was once in mystery, but then revealed to the 'holy apostles and prophets' by the Spirit (Eph 3:5).

2. Why did the coming of the Holy Spirit and tongue-speaking coincide with **Pentecost**? In answering this question we learn more of the historical context which gives us a better understanding of tongues as a sign to the Jews. Our interest here is with seven particular feasts of Jehovah to be observed by Israel (Lev 23 etc). These, along with other OT observances, were given to foreshadow that which was to come. They are not part of direct prophecy but prefigure by 'type' events and identities which were to come of which some are yet future.[275] The individual nature and order of

---

[275] In Heb 10:1 the OT Law is said to have a shadow of good things to come. In 1 Cor 10:6,10 we are taught that many experiences of Israel during their wilderness journey "happened unto them for examples (types)".

these seven feasts foreshadow God's redemptive program among men.

The Feast of Weeks (Pentecost), was one of three Feasts of Jehovah in the Jewish calendar that required pilgrimage to Jerusalem, the other two being the Passover (followed by the feast of Unleavened Bread and the feast of Firstfruits) and the Feast of Tabernacles. The Passover Feast celebrated Israel's deliverance from bondage in Egypt. The Passover lamb was slain and its blood applied on the doorposts and lintel for salvation from death (Ex 12:1-30). This Feast foreshadowed Christ and His death. The NT refers to Him as the *"Lamb of God"* (Jn 1:36), *"***Christ our Passover** *is sacrificed for us"* (1 Cor 5:7) and *"the lamb that was slain"* (Rev 5:12). God's plan was timed so that our Lord gave His life for sinners at the time of the Passover, a fact that would not be lost to the Jewish mind. The third feast was the Feast of Firstfruits which required the firstfruits of the (barley) harvest to be waved before God (wave offering, Lev 23:10-14). No Israelite was permitted to partake of the harvest before the firstfruits had been offered to Jehovah. This feast was celebrated on the third day after the slaying of the Passover lamb. It foreshadowed the resurrection of Christ, for on the third day after His death (Passover) He arose, and more, He arose as One *"risen from* [among] *the dead, and become the* **firstfruits** *of them that slept"* (1 Cor 15:20). We see Him as the authentic wave offering of firstfruits before God (Jn 20; Acts 1). The Feast of Pentecost (the fourth feast) was celebrated at Jerusalem fifty days after the Passover - the presentation of the wave sheaf before God (Lev 23:15).

This feast celebrated the (wheat) harvest (the in-gathering) with two loaves. First, we take particular note of the timing and nature of this feast. Christ was on earth forty days after His death prior to His ascension (Acts 1:3). The disciples waited ten days after His ascension until the coming of the promise of the Father (Acts 1:4). Fifty days then after the Passover (His death), the Holy Spirit descends, the day when the *"Feast of Pentecost was fully come"* [i.e. in the Antitype - this occasion was represented in the OT type] (Acts 2:1). Second, let us note the significance of there being two loaves waved before God. As we know, the day of Pentecost marks a new period, one of matchless grace, the beginning of the Church period when God brings the Gentiles into blessing. We noted earlier the two instances in the NT where reference is made to the Spirit of God being poured-out, Acts 2:17 and Acts 10:45. These two instances are representative, the former representing the Jews (one loaf), the latter representing the Gentiles (the other loaf), confirming "no difference" between Jew and Gentile in Christ. Concerning this new period and its unity between Jew and Gentile in the Body, tongues were a SIGN! These divinely timed events that coincide with the timetable of divinely ordained Jewish feasts prove the Jewish context, which is consistent with the use of a sign to a sign-seeking people - "this people" (1 Cor 14:21-22). They were a sign to God's chosen earthly people, the Jews, of the coming of the Holy Spirit upon both Jew and Gentile, harvested and incorporated by Him into the Church.

The Feasts may be summarised thus:

· The *Feast of Passover* (*& Unleavened Bread*) - His death (& perfect life)

· The *Feast of Firstfruits* - His resurrection.

· The *Feast of Pentecost* - His church, (which marked the setting aside of Israel and salvation offered to the individual Jew and Gentile.)

The next events foreshadowed are -

The regathering of Israel (after the church has ascended):

· The *Feast of Trumpets* - the regathering of the rejected nation of Israel - *"ye shall be gathered one by one, O ye children of Israel...in that day the great trumpet shall be blown."* (Isa 27:12-13).

The personal return of the Lord:

· The *Day of Atonement* - *"they* [Israel] *shall look on Him whom they pierced"* (Zech 12:10; John 19:37).

Then the Millennial period:
· The *Feast of Tabernacles* (the Millennial reign of Christ, Zech 14:16).

We should also note the terms *"fullness of the Gentiles"* and *"times of the Gentiles"* (Luke 21:24), which further substantiate Gentile inclusion and Israel's rejection. The former refers to the present Church period, which will end with the coming of the Lord for His saints. The latter includes the former and embraces the period of Israel's domination by Gentiles from the time of Nebuchadnezzar to the Millennium, when Israel will rule with Christ on earth (Dan 2, 7). When we observe God's dealings with Israel we will note that, when Israel was obedient to God, Gentiles were either subjugated by Israel or at peace with Israel. When Israel was disobedient, the Gentiles were used by God to chasten Israel. Is this not so, even today?

3. Fruit of the Spirit, the gifts of the Spirit and the Gift of the Spirit. It is beneficial here to distinguish between the *fruit* of the Spirit, the *gifts* of the Spirit and the difference between the *gifts* of the Spirit and the *gift* of the Spirit. In Galatians 5 Paul enumerates nine facets of the fruit of the Spirit. These facets are evidenced through the working of the Spirit of God *in* us, according to our will in subjection and obedience to God. In 1 Corinthians 12 and Romans 12, Paul deals with gifts of the Spirit, bestowed by the Spirit of God *to* us, to every man severally, as He will, to profit withal.[276] There does appear to be an unfortunate tendency for some in evangelical circles to conduct themselves in a manner which ignores such distinction, for they often mistake spiritual gifts for the fruit of the Spirit. This has led to the failure to rightly discern the purpose of tongues.

The gift of the Spirit (the Person Himself) is bestowed on

---

[276] 1 Corinthians 12:7&11. Note, the gifts in Eph 4:11 are given by the Lord to the church in its universal aspect (Body) and refer to the persons themselves as the gift - apostles, prophets, teachers.

all who believe that Christ Jesus died and rose again for their justification. Every child of God receives this gift when they are born again! *"That which is born of the flesh is flesh; and that which is born of the Spirit is spirit."*[277] *"If any man have not the Spirit of Christ, he is none of His."*[278] At the moment of salvation the Holy Spirit indwells; there is no warrant for so-called "tarrying" to receive the gift of the Spirit of God.

4. Why, on this occasion, does the Spirit of God inspire Peter to quote this passage from **Joel**? Some believe it is because the events contained in the prophecy have their fulfilment at this time - partially or completely. However, upon careful examination of Scripture, we will see this can never be the case. Joel 2:28 is a prophecy concerning Israel, not the church. It speaks of a new order on earth - the Millennium, a particular feature of which is the pouring out of the Spirit, which is merely a foreshadowing of the essential character of Pentecost. Consider the following reasons:

a) If we were to interpret Joel's prophecy as relating to the Church age, then we make the Church period a prediction of the OT. The Church period is never the subject of OT prophecy, although it is seen in parenthesis (e.g. Gen 49; Isa 9:6; 61:2; Dan 9), and in shadow and type (e.g. the Feasts of Jehovah). The church was in 'mystery' in the OT. The mystery of Christ (His church, His Body united in Him) *"...How that by revelation* [not prophecy] *he made known unto me the MYSTERY;...which in other ages* [OT] *was not made known unto the sons of men, as it is now revealed* [again, not prophesied] *unto his holy apostles and prophets by the Spirit; that the Gentiles should be fellowheirs and of the same body* [the church], *and partakers of his promise in Christ by the gospel"* (Eph 3:3-6). This is the first proof (and it is a sufficient one) that Peter is not identifying the times

---

[277] John 3:6
[278] John 14:16; Rom 5:5, 8:9

prophesied by Joel as being fulfilled partially or totally at Pentecost. We will make little progress in dispensational truth if we fail to apply the rule that the church is never the subject of OT *prophecy* but of NT *revelation*. The student of Scripture must lay hold on the truth, that where prophecy is concerned, there will always be a distinction between the Jew and Gentile. However, in all that is revealed in regard to the church, this distinction does not exist.

b) The direction and entire context of the Book of Joel concerns *Israel* - (he was a prophet to the Southern Kingdom). His appeal in chapters 1 and 2 is to the *'inhabitants of the land'* (1:1; 2:1) and to the *"children of Zion"* (2:23) - God's earthly people. He refers to their priests, drink offerings and meal offerings throughout. He speaks to 'Israel', using its theocratic name (2:27) and mentions the holy city Jerusalem on mount Zion, the site of deliverance of God's earthly people (2:32). He speaks of Israel's departure and devastation in his day; their future national repentance; then divine Millennial blessings within the restored land - first the physical blessings (2:21-27), and 'afterwards' the spiritual blessings (2:28-29); as well as the preceding judgment of nations who have troubled Israel - the Great and Terrible Day of the Lord (v.31).

c) Peter's words, chosen under the Spirit's guidance, confirm Joel's prophecy is of a period not relating to the church. Joel refers to a time identified as a period that *"shall come to pass afterwards"* (Joel 2:28). Peter refers to this period as the *"last days"* (Acts 2:17). Now the term 'last days' in the OT refers to the Millennium, the time of Israel's earthly blessings - *"in the last days...the Lord's house shall be established ...and shall be exalted above the hills...and all nations shall flow unto it."* (Isa 2:2-4; Micah 4:1-7). These are the days before the 'eternal state'. This is quite distinct to the use of *'Latter Days'* in the OT which is the time of Tribulation. Joel 2:30-32 speaks of the latter days - Israel's salvation (the faithful remnant) during the Tribulation (see

Deuteronomy 4:30 etc.). In all this, the Church period is never in view.[279]

d) Why then, if the prophecy of Joel refers to Israel and not the church, does the Spirit of God inspire Peter to quote it at the beginning of the Church period? There was a need to convince the Jews of the *character* of the new age, its *place* in God's program for man and, most importantly, to provoke their *responsibility* in regard to it. Specifically, to convince them that:

i. God's grace was now to be made known to every nation and tongue.

ii. The Spirit had now come to be with and in them as promised by the Lord.

iii. The phenomenon they are witnessing - the outpouring of the Spirit on all flesh - is nothing 'unusual', it is of God, and will occur again when God blesses Israel in a future day.

iv. Christ was greater than David and is the Messiah who will bring such blessings to pass.

v. They must repent and be baptised in the name of Him whom they crucified, for the remission of sins.

To convince them of all this, the Spirit of God does two things:

· He provides the Jews (a sign-seeking people) with a miraculous sign of foreign (Gentile) tongues, so they may believe the Spirit of God had indeed come, and the grace of God is unto all flesh.

· He inspires Peter to quote from a sacred prophet of Israel

---

[279] As remarked earlier, the truth concerning the Church was in *mystery*, i.e., hidden in the OT. If we believe the church is coincident with and the recipient of the blessings promised to Israel in the OT, then we fall into the error of Amillennialism. When the OT prophets speak of the latter days or last days, they do not have the Church period in view. We note however, the 'last days' is used in the NT to refer to a time within the Church period (2 Tim 3:1-5), but it is a time associated with the closing of that period, its apostasy and evil, not (Pentecostal or Millennial) blessing. Further, Paul enumerated the moral and ecclesiastical decline expected at the close of the Church age - the 'latter times' (1 Tim 4:1). In Hebrews 1:1, we have mentioned the 'last days', but the correct rendering here is - *"at the end of these days"* - the close of the former periods (W.E. Vine, "The Collected Writings of W E Vine" Volume 3 p. 369).

- Joel, whose prophecy best reflects the character of the new age. A new era has dawned, marked by the outpouring of the Spirit of God on all flesh. In the past, the children of Israel had been selectively indwelt and filled by the Spirit of God, but never an outpouring. This was difficult for them to grasp and to accept because it was unparalleled in their history. The church too was not the subject of their prophets, thus creating a natural ignorance and disbelief among them, especially in requiring them to accept Gentiles as spiritual equals. By quoting the words of their *own* prophet, which identifies a similar divine phenomenon in a day to come, Peter attempts to dispel this ignorance and scepticism. The Jews should not regard the Spirit's outpouring, and His outpouring upon all flesh, as something strange, for their prophets spoke of a similar phenomenon - *"this is that* [phenomenon] *which was spoken by the prophet Joel"*. The Jews wanted an explanation of the sign they had witnessed - the *miraculous* speaking of *foreign languages* by Galilaeans, which signalled the presence of this new phenomenon, the Spirit of God coming on all flesh. It is this sign which provokes their question, *"what meaneth this?"*. This phenomenon then, the presence of the Spirit - outpouring on all flesh (not foreign tongues spoken miraculously) - is also a characteristic of the blessed age to come for Israel, the Millennium. An outpouring of the Holy Spirit is common to both periods - the Church Age (*"...He dwelleth with you, and shall be in you"*) and during the last days concerning Israel of which the prophets speak (Isa 32:15 - *"until the Spirit be poured upon us from on high, And the wilderness be a fruitful field...."*; Ezek 36:24-26; 37:14; 39:29 - *"for I have poured out my Spirit upon the house of Israel"*; Joel 2:28-29[280]). Of all the OT prophets, Joel is the only one who informs us that the Spirit's pouring is upon all flesh during the Millennium -

---

[280] Joel 2:30-32 speaks of the latter days - Israel's salvation (the faithful remnant) during the Tribulation, (the work of the Spirit of God).

this is why the Spirit of God inspires him to quote Joel and not the other prophets. When Peter seeks to dispel their scepticism and ignorance of this miraculous tongue-speaking phenomenon, he informs them that what they are now seeing, the outpouring of the Holy Spirit, is that same *phenomenon* - the outpouring - of which Joel spoke concerning Israel in the last days - the Millennium. Therefore accept it as from God. So, when Peter declares, *"this is that which was spoken by the prophet Joel"*, he is drawing attention to the *phenomenon* - the coming of the Holy Spirit and His distinctive ministry on earth - of which tongues was a sign. Peter is not identifying the present period with the period prophesied by Joel - the Millennium.

But there is another area of Jewish disbelief that must be addressed by Peter - that God's salvation is granted to Gentiles. And here, we note, the complete prophecy of Joel is excluded by Peter. He deliberately stops halfway through verse 32 of chapter 2, omitting *"..for in mount Zion and in Jerusalem shall be deliverance, as the Lord hath said, And the remnant whom the Lord shall call."* Deliverance here refers to salvation for those who, during the Tribulation period, call upon the name of the Lord and are saved by His direct intervention when He returns to earth to deliver the faithful remnant. We know that Jews and Gentiles will be saved during Jacob's Trouble through the preaching of the Gospel of the Kingdom.[281] Christ will then establish Jerusalem as the centre of His reign on earth. This portion proves clearly that the Church is never in view in Joel's prophecy and that Peter's quote from Joel is selective and used purely to dispel scepticism and ignorance. He omits it because it is not relevant to this age - the church. Instead he uses the abridged portion of verse 32 to focus on another characteristic of this

---

[281] Isaiah 2:4, 14:1-2, 49:22-23, 60: 1-5, 61:5; Jer 3:17; Ezek 38:23 etc show that Gentiles will enter and exist in the Millennium because of their salvation and survival during the Tribulation. In Rev 7:9 those from all nations come with the Lord into the Millennium.

new age which is also a feature of another age, the Tribulation period - that salvation is to 'whosever will' - Jew and Gentiles.[282] Salvation to all races and tongues was also unparalleled in the history and heart of the Jews. However, they need not be sceptical about this either, for it too is mentioned by their own prophet Joel. We see here why the Spirit of God inspired Peter to quote from Joel and not Ezekiel or Isaiah, all of whom speak of the Millennial outpouring of the Spirit of God. It is Joel who mentions the full extent of the Millennial outpouring - upon *"all flesh"* [283] and who expresses the breadth of salvation - to *whosoever will* (which is also the message signalled by the miraculously spoken foreign tongues).

Up to this point (v.22), Peter has sought to satisfy and appeal to the national conscience of the Jews. After using prophecy to counter disbelief and ignorance by the Jews in regard to the new phenomena, he arrests their individual consciences, focusing on the Psalms. It is here that he lays the ground for their individual need to repent and be baptised in the name of the Lord, showing that Christ, whom they crucified, was the One who is greater than their patriarch David. Indeed, the words of David foreshadowed His resurrection (vv.25-34).

The use of Joel's prophecy and the teaching from the

---

[282] Isaiah 61:1-2 speaks of the Millennial blessing to Israel through their Messiah King (the acceptable year of the Lord) and the coming of the Messiah to deliver Israel just prior to it (day of vengeance of our God). The Lord Himself employs prophecy to dispel disbelief from the Jews in Himself as being their Messiah, and to illustrate the character of the time in which He was speaking. He quotes from Isa 61:1-2 (Luke 4:17-21) where the prophet tells of the acceptable year of the Lord and the day of vengeance of God. The Lord stops short, omitting half of verse 2, "the day of vengeance of our God"! His object is to focus on the character of the immediate day - the acceptable day - His offer of grace to *Israel* as their Messiah. It is in regard to this offer to Israel as their Messiah then, not the Church, that the Lord declares, *"This day is this scripture fulfilled before you"* (Luke 4:21). They reject Him (Matt 12:14; Luke 6:11) and He then sets them aside (Matt 12:46-50) and turns to 'all men' by revealing the progress and conditions within the Church age that is to come in the seven parables of Matt 13 i.e. the kingdom programme due to Israel's rejection.

[283] The Gentiles will be the servants of Israel during the Millennial period (Isa.14:1-2; 60:14 etc.)

Psalms were then used to convict and provoke the desired question from the Jews. It is not now *"what meaneth this?"*, but, *"Men and brethren, what shall we do?"* That same prophecy and ministry has also laid the foundation for Peter's answer - *"Repent, and be baptised everyone of you in the name of Jesus Christ for the remission of sins, and ye shall receive the gift of the Holy Ghost. For the promise* [the giving of the Holy Ghost] *is unto you, and to your children* [the Jews], *and to all that are afar off* [Gentiles], *even as many as the Lord our God shall call...."*(vv.38-39).

e) We can add further argument here to show that Joel's prophecy is not a prediction of the *event* of Pentecost. It is only a foreshadowing of its character, quoted by Peter under the eye of the Spirit of God, to facilitate repentance by the Jews. First, Peter nowhere states the events at Pentecost are a 'fulfilment' of Joel's prophecy. Indeed, we noted the Millennial Kingdom will be characterized by the outpouring of the Spirit of God - the actual fulfilment of Joel's prophecy. This will follow the events of the Great and Terrible Day of the Lord, which occurs just prior to the Millennium. Second, the events quoted in Acts 2:19-20 described by Joel - the celestial portents - relate to a period just *before* the 'Great and Terrible Day of the Lord' - the day of the Son of Man's sudden personal intervention in world affairs. This Great and Terrible Day of the Lord is future, as proved by the fact that such events (signs) have not yet occurred. That Day lies beyond the Church period, preceded by the Great Tribulation - 'Jacob's Trouble' (Jer 30:7), throughout which the church is in heaven. Reference to its advent in Scripture after Pentecost clearly distinguishes it from the events of Acts 2. We noted earlier, that the Day of the Lord refers to the time after the Church has been 'Raptured' (the day of Christ), refer to Chart B.

Some erroneously interpret Joel's reference to the *"former rain"* as the event of Pentecost itself and the *"latter rain"* as a period of Pentecostal revival in the last days, - i.e. today

(Joel 2:23). This assertion is untenable, since, as stated above, the Church period is never the subject of OT prophecy. Joel's prophecy focuses on Israel as a nation, *"ye children of Zion"* (v.23), their receipt of past divine blessings (former rain moderately, the rain which moistens the earth to receive the seed). The divine bestowals to come, the former rain and the latter rain in the first month, (latter rain - the rain that grows and ripens the harvest) refer to the Millennial earthly Kingdom, a time of national blessing, for the Lord will restore so that they will eat in plenty and be satisfied. Earlier in chapter 2 Joel speaks of the time of the Great Tribulation (Joel 2:1-11). Further, the convergence of prophecy and history mark the last days of the present age not with a ground-swelling revival, but by a falling away, many *"giving heed to seducing spirits, and doctrines of devils"* (1 Tim 4:1). The closing days of the Church age, are characterized by widespread apostasy - denials concerning Christ's return, 2 Pet 3: 3-4; liberty, 1 Tim 4:3-4; the faith, 1 Tim 4:1-2, Jude 3; sound doctrine, 2 Tim 4:3-4. etc.

5. Unintelligible Tongues. Mormonism, the "Church of Jesus Christ Latter Day Saints", was founded by a man, one Joseph Smith, who was given to necromania, visions of "bleeding ghosts" and unintelligible tongues. He claimed these tongues were evidence of the Spirit of God being received. Edward Irving founded the "Catholic and Apostolic Church", a movement which took his name (Irvingism). His followers, who believe in apostolic succession, claim powers of prophecy and unintelligible tongues. Their meetings are characterized by "revelations" and "strange utterances". Buddhists, Moslems, Quakers, Spiritists, Shintoists also speak in unintelligible tongues.

I include here the telling personal testimony of Robert Baxter, a Christian and prominent London barrister and once staunch Irvingite. He admitted to a power coming upon him. He wrote, *"God has shown us the rule of Trial by Doctrine, and had I been jealous for the Holy name of my God and enquired into the doctrines, I might have been kept from the power, as afterwards, when I did enquire, the Lord opened my eyes and delivered me. Looking back on all that is past, whenever the power rested upon me leading me up to prayer or testimony or thanksgiving, I seemed to have joy and peace in the Holy Ghost, and I cannot even now, by feeling only, discern that it was not truly such."* Feelings aside and applying the test of Scripture, he wrote, *"Indeed the whole work is a mimicry of the gift of tongues....It is Satan as an angel of light, imitating as far as permitted, the Spirit of God.."* (page 135 "Narrative of Facts" by Robert Baxter). We rejoice in every believer who by the grace of God, is brought to a similar confession.

Ecstatic tongues among heathen peoples have also been well documented by missionaries. Observe the ranting of the "whirling dervishes" who claim power to speak in unintelligible languages. We only need refer to our encyclopaedias and anthropological writings to become aware that many primitive tribes speak in ecstatic tongues.

6. How else are we to explain the large scale acceptance by many sincere people of doctrines such as purgatory, transubstantiation (conversion of the Eucharist elements into the body and blood of Christ), the heresy of the progenitors of Unitarianism, JWism, Mormonism, and Christadelphianism (which denied the existence of the Trinity and salvation through the grace of God), except that they were **beguiled by Satan** and his spirits?

7. Empirical evidence exists to suggest some proportion of present-day tongue-speaking (and other 'charismata') may be the product of **psychological conditioning** rather than demonic influence - working through the body and soul. (In what can only be described as gross carnality, some charismatics actually have programmes through which people are induced to speak in tongues.) We must say, the psychological conditioning is often the avenue for demonic influence. Meetings are designed (innocently in some cases), to elevate the (involuntary) emotional state over the voluntary nervous state. This is achieved by creating an hypnotic environment through emotionally charged sermons often presenting health and wealth as the rewards for conversion to Christianity; focus on experiences; up-beat gospel-rock music, so much of which is produced by the charismatics; handclapping, body swaying and dancing; continual pleas to 'let go', 'be filled', 'fall', 'submit to the power' etc.; demonstrations of so-called 'miracles' - healings, tongues and people being 'slain in the spirit'. Invariably, the 'miracles', together with the emotion and euphoria generated, are taken as evidence of the Holy Spirit. Regular exposure to these meetings builds a repertoire of experience, which is then sadly used to (mis)interpret Scripture. Let us be aware too, that all this is not far removed from spiritualism and occultism, which also have as their stock-in-trade yielding to 'powers', inner visions, dancing to rock music, etc. It is no coincidence that charismatic following has been rampant within Third-World countries known for their cultism and occultism. Neo-Pentecostalism (and the charismatic phenomenon) has had its greatest successes in the Caribbean, sub-Saharan Africa, and Latin America.

8. In Adam or in Christ: This truth is reinforced in Romans 5:13-14. Between Adam and Moses, men were regarded as sinners and bore the penalty of sin (death) even though during this period there was no direct or written law from God for man to sin against. (During their life they did not sin as Adam did i.e. disobey a direct divine commandment. God's will is seen through His commandments.) Yet, they were regarded as sinners and death reigned over them. Why? Because all persons, past, present and future had actually sinned when Adam sinned. We must be clear on this point - we are sinners and have the penalty of death upon us not because of the sins we commit during our life (these are the result of inheriting Adam's sinful nature), but because God regards us as having sinned when Adam sinned. We are, by nature, children of wrath (Eph 2:3). Confirmation of this truth is seen in Romans 5:19, *"For by one man's disobedience* [Adam's sin, the Fall], [the] *many were made sinners....."*. The grammatical structure is most interesting here.[284] Note also 'the many' (who are made sinners), is a representative expression which refers to all mankind. So, through the obedience of One (Christ), (the) many shall become righteous. All mankind shall become righteous - if of course all believe. This truth, as always, braids with others. The Psalmist declares. *"None...can by any means redeem his brother"* (Psa 49:7). Job laments, *"Neither is there any daysman betwixt us, that might lay his hand upon us both"* (Job 9:33). A man cannot redeem his brother because he is himself under Adam's condemnation and separated from God. Who is the Daysman then? It must be one who does not partake of Adam's sin and bear his condemnation - one who was not of Adam's race. It must be one born of a virgin, who knew no sin (Paul's testimony), who did no sin (Peter's testimony) and in whom there is no sin (John's testimony). It must be one who is the Creator, not the created. It must be God manifest in flesh - His only Begotten Son. And so we read that Christ is the last Adam (the last federal representative Head) and the second Man (1 Cor 15:45-47).

This truth is brought to us by Paul when he states that all in Adam die.[285] This Scripture (indeed the whole passage) states that we are *all* under God's condemnation because of

---

[284] There is a striking grammatical correspondence here between 1 Cor 12:13 (*were all baptised*); 1 Cor 12:13 (*were all made to drink*) and Rom 5:19 (*were made sinners*). All are in the first aorist passive indicative. (The first aorist passive indicative refers to a definite past event or a definite act in the past. A. T. Robertson, <u>Word Pictures in the New Testament</u>" Volume IV p. 171; p. 360. On Rom 5:12, *"The transmission from Adam became facts of experience"* p. 358).
[285] 1 Corinthians 15:22

what *Adam did*. Paul deliberately and clearly makes the link between Adam's sin and our condemnation. This is because he wants us to understand what is available to *all* because of what *Christ did* - the removal of that condemnation - he establishes the link between Christ's work and our salvation, and, at the same time, contrasts the different *positions* under two representative heads - the fallen head, Adam, and the risen Head, Christ! Paul's complete statement is *"For as in Adam all die, even so in Christ shall all be made alive"*[286] (Who are those in Christ? All who accept Him as Lord and Saviour, 1 Cor 15:22.) It is our fallen judicial *position* in Adam, our fallen head, that condemns us all. When we are born we become part of Adam's race (in Adam) and God's judgment of eternal death rests on us all. This is recognized in the OT when David declared in Psalm 51:5, *"in sin did my mother conceive me"*. Is this not why the Lord Himself commanded all to be "born again", to become, through faith in Him, part of His redeemed race (i.e. in Christ)? - ruin through Adam, remedy through Christ. The Lord declared, *"he that believeth not is condemned already.."* (Jn 3:18). Why? Because those who believe not are already condemned in Adam. Finally, we see this yet again in Romans 5:18. *"Therefore as by the offence* [one offence] *of one* [Adam] *judgment came upon* **all** *men unto condemnation"; even so by the righteousness* [one accomplished righteousness - Calvary] *of one* [Christ] *the free gift came unto* **all** *men unto justification of life."* (This free gift, of course, has to be accepted for us to be justified). Where then do our individual sins fit in as believers? Are they irrelevant? Certainly not, for we shall all be judged according to our deeds. As far as believers are concerned, all our sins were laid on Jesus Christ our Lord - past, present and future sins - all blotted out for eternity. Although our

---

[286] Note here the contrast is between spiritual and eternal death in Adam and spiritual and eternal life in Christ. It cannot be anything else, for the promise of life in Christ is abundant life, eternal life, not the removal of physical death!

salvation is secure through that grace which abounds more than sin abounds, our works and words, however will be judged; judged at the Judgment Seat of Christ (2 Cor 5:10), to determine our *rewards*.

We are not sinners because we began to commit sins. Rather, we commit sins because we began as sinners.

An Overview of 1 Corinthians 14

It is important we review the error at Corinth concerning tongues (and indeed other spiritual gifts). The Corinthian believers who had this gift were proud of it and sought to display and elevate it every time they came together, without regard to order and the presence of unbelievers (14:23). In their carnality (3:1-3), they coveted this more "spectacular" gift above others (12:31; ch. 13). They regarded speaking in tongues as something every believer should do (12:30). They tried to out-do each other when speaking in tongues (14:23-32). If we were to observe a typical meeting of theirs, we would witness a situation of disorder and confusion, a gabble, believers simultaneously speaking different languages, causing the unlearned to declare justifiably, 'ye are mad.'[287] Paul declared this situation as dishonouring to the Lord and set out procedures to follow regarding tongues spoken within the church.

These were

· They were to be spoken by two or three at the most (v.27).

· They were to be spoken in order, one at a time (v.27).

· Tongues, if unknown, were not to be spoken unless interpreted (vv. 27-28).

---

[287] 1 Corinthians 14:23

· The exercise of tongues was to be under self-control as indicated in these verses.

· Those who had the gift were able to determine *when* and *where* they would exercise it.[288]

The chapter can be divided into three sections Paul's *catalogue* of the error at Corinth in respect of tongues (vv.1-11), his *censure* because of their error (vv.12-20), and subsequently, his directions for *control* over the use of tongues in order to avoid error.

Verse 1: Continues the teaching of chapter 13, that tongues (spiritual gifts) are not greater than love. It is valid to desire spiritual gifts (i.e. desire to be so blessed by the Spirit of God), but have as your greater desire prophecy (forthtelling, not foretelling).

Verse 2: Presents a consequence of the error of speaking an unknown foreign language in the church without an interpreter. If a man speaks within the *church* in such a tongue and those listening do not understand that foreign tongue, his speech is only understood by God and not men. *"No man in the church* [those present, not the whole world] *understandeth him howbeit in the spirit* [his spirit guided by the Holy Spirit communicates with God who understands, but no man there at that time understands him] *he speaketh mysteries."* If an unknown tongue is not interpreted the mysteries remain within the spirit of the speaker (v.14 *'my spirit prayeth'*). The use of 'mystery' here, as noted earlier, does not refer to that which is incomprehensible but to truths previously not revealed. He speaks of those hidden wonderful truths of God, now revealed by His Spirit (e.g. as in Acts 2), that had to be

---

[288] The question of whether or not women are permitted to speak in tongues in the church does not arise, since women are not permitted to speak within the church (vv.34-35)! There are no recorded instances of women speaking in tongues anywhere in Scripture. The fact that we see women speaking in tongues today within some churches, is an example of how one false practice gives liberty to another!

made known through interpretation where the foreign tongue was unknown. The Body of Christ was one such mystery (Eph 3:3-5). Tongue here is singular in keeping with the fact that the personal pronoun is singular, i.e. a man can only speak one particular language (tongue) at any one time.[289]

Verse 3: Prophecy needs no interpretation for it is spoken in the native tongue and it edifies, exhorts and comforts all. The contrast here (and throughout the chapter) is between speaking and coveting an unknown tongue in the *absence* of interpretation, and prophecy. Tongues were a mere sign and were to be used as such. Tongues were not intended for building up the church. If a man spoke an unknown foreign tongue and others were to benefit there must be an interpretation if the wonderful works of God were to be revealed. Not so with prophecy. It was not, in the first instance, a sign, but an essential gift to feed the church of God, therefore covet (value) it (v.1).

Verse 4: Re-affirms and broadens the contrast. He that speaks a Gentile language that is not known to others builds up himself only, for only he knows what the speaker says. Paul speaks here of the case where the speaker also had the gift of interpretation. (Although not all were given every gift, some were given more than one gift). Prophecy, however, builds up the church because it is spoken in the local known tongue. The exercise of any spiritual gift will edify the individual who possesses it. A person who had the gift of healing would have been spiritually uplifted to see others healed through him. However in this case, and in that of tongues, the benefit to the individual was not the purpose of

---

[289] Obviously, this imperative raises the possibility of those who had the gift of tongues not speaking them - i.e. there would be no tongues spoken at all - when none was able to interpret. These situations, the absence of tongue-speaking, are not spoken of by Paul as those which are spiritually damaging to the church or to the individual! Why? Tongues were not given for edification or comfort - they were a sign.

the gift. The individual may benefit from tongues (v.4), but the purpose of tongues was to be a sign to them that believe not (vv.21-22) [290].

Verse 5: Confirms that not all were given the gift of tongues, nor was it desirable that all should have it. If all believers in Corinth could speak in tongues, then there would be no room for childish boasting! *"I would that ye all spake with tongues"* is an argumentative statement - directed to the problem at Corinth. It is not prescriptive, since the Holy Spirit bestows according to His will! Above this, he would have it that they all had the gift of prophecy, also argumentative! Again Paul uses the collective pronoun 'ye', - the believers at Corinth, not 'we' - all believers. Also the plural (tongues) is in keeping with the collective personal pronoun (ye - all). Paul presents a hypothetical case where speaking an unknown tongue would be of equal value to prophecy - where the speaker himself at the same time interprets it to the church! This is an impossibility! Therefore if there be no other interpreter, let him keep silent in the church. Thus, prophecy is superior!

Verses 6 -9: Paul speaks of the confusion and lack of profit in their wrongful use of tongues - indistinct sounds, uncertain sounds, misunderstanding sounds - where there is no interpretation. Hearing an unknown foreign language, as we can attest, is like listening to mere sounds. These verses contain figurative examples and are illustrative. A single case is used in verse 8, the 'uncertain trumpet note' which is employed to reinforce the argument - the uncertain bugle call cannot rally the soldiers! 'Tongue' in verse 9 is the organ or instrument of

---

[290] Two recent publications in support of modern-day tongues, both of which were written by prominent international charismatic leaders, each state that verse 4 proves that Paul had times of *private* tongue-speaking. Such a statement is an appalling error, given the context is plainly stated by the last word of the verse itself: the contrast is between speaking an unknown tongue in the church which does not edify the *church*, only the speaker, - who has the gift of interpretation, and prophecy, which edifies the *church*! See comment on verses 15&20.

speech (not the gift) in context with the other instruments of sound in this section - trumpet, pipe, harp!

Verse 10: There are many kinds of voices (foreign languages) - the figurative method is continued (languages). Where? In the "world"; not in heaven or some ecstatic domain, but in the world. None of these is without meaning i.e. they are capable of interpretation.

Verse 11: If a believer speaks in one of these voices (foreign languages) and the hearer cannot understand him (it is unknown to him), the speaker may as well be a barbarian to the hearer - literally a foreigner or Gentile.

Verse 12: Exhortation to edify the church through spiritual gifts. A principle based on preceding illustration and argument. Note again the context is within the church!

Verses 13 & 14: The church context continues, evident by the passage and the use of 'wherefore', (on account of the need to edify the church) - and since you are zealous of pursuing and displaying spiritual gifts in the church, (you are keen to speak in tongues), then go further, and pray for the gift of interpretation. Paul speaks here of the situation where the person does not possess the gift of interpretation, lacks the ability to interpret their tongue - obviously the prevalent condition in Corinth. This case follows naturally from the emphatic illustration and consequence of the uncertain sounds in the preceding verses. By having this gift, the speaker can also use it to build up the church when others speak in tongues - collective benefit (reflex to v.12). Verse 14 deals with the personal benefit to the tongue-speaker of having the gift of interpretation. He was to pray for this gift - to meet the case at Corinth. This does not mean he was going to get it, for bestowing of these gifts is the prerogative of the Holy Spirit! If his prayer was not granted, he must stop speaking in his foreign/unknown tongue for it will not be fruitful to him. There was no spiritual loss to the individual (or to the church) in refraining from speaking in a tongue!

After all, as Paul is about to remind them, tongues are but a sign to unbelievers!

Verses 15 - 20: The two gifts (tongues & interpretation) possessed by the individual complement each other. We should pray with the spirit (our spirit, the inner part of us that is conscious of God) and with the mind (our understanding and reason as determined by knowledge of the Word of God). This speaks against the emptying of the mind required in charismatic circles! The complementary benefit of the two gifts move to the general - within the church, verses 16-19. There is reinforcement of that which was stated before, that all be done for building up the church through understanding. Paul excelled in tongue-speaking (v.18), and uses himself as an example. Even with his greater endowment, he would seek to edify the church by speaking in a known tongue. His speaking in tongues more than the Corinthians, as is suggested by the use of the plural - *glossais*, refers predominantly to a variety of tongues, rather than their frequency of use. Verse 19 suggests Paul spoke in tongues outside the church (...yet in the church'...). However, this can never be taken to say he must then have used them to speak to God in private (i.e. between the individual and God). We know that tongues were for a sign. Throughout Acts, all tongue-speaking was in public outside the church!

It is important to note, that the verses in this chapter thus far and indeed those preceding them in 1 Corinthians, do not by themselves resolve whether or not tongues are foreign languages or ecstatic languages. Paul's purpose was never to resolve such an issue. He knew what tongues were and he is to this point building a case against the error among the Corinthians in regard to their use of unknown tongues. This case is underwritten with a statement on the purpose of tongues in the next two verses.

Verses 21 & 22: Now Paul begins to present the meaning of tongues and their purpose. Having catalogued the error in their use of tongues and censured them as children, he seeks to instruct the Corinthians on doctrine, to provide the basis for his regulation of speaking in tongues in the church. Suppose Paul was referring to 'ecstatic tongues' in the earlier verses. It would be very odd and utterly confusing if he suddenly turns his attention to tongues that are clearly Gentile languages as a sign to 'this people' - the Jews! These verses really deflate the flesh of the Corinthian tongue-speakers. Keep tongues in their proper place - they are given for a sign to unbelievers, says Paul using a lesson from the OT. If you wish to use them in the church then make sure your tongue is known to all. If not, then keep it to yourself and God - use it silently.

Verses 23-26: Two groups here - "unbelievers" (those who knew and disbelieved) and "unlearned" (those who did not know) who would come as visitors to the church. Unknown tongues were not the only problem at Corinth, speaking many tongues at the same time was also causing strife within the church. This could have given a visitor (v.23) the impression that they were 'mad'! Prophecy would, however, instruct and speak to the unbeliever or unlearned. The modern-day tongues prayer meetings where many speak in 'tongues' at the same time are a flagrant violation of Paul's directions (see also v.27). They, indeed, appear as 'madness'! In verse 26 the expression 'every one of you', must be interpreted in the light of the diversity of gifts given by the Sovereign Spirit of God (12:4-31), i.e., every one of you has some spiritual gift that enables a psalm, the speaking of a tongue, a revelation etc.

Verse 27: A limit is placed on the number of persons who may speak in tongues, and the command to interpret is repeated. "By course" (*ana meros*) means in turn - one after the other, and the one interpreter interprets for all. If one person is to do the interpretation, then two people cannot speak in tongues at the same time.

Verse 28: Paul repeats, that if there is no one else to interpret within the church, there must be no speaking in

205

tongues where the tongue is unknown. He must refrain from public and audible speaking of the tongue. If one desires to speak in a tongue unknown to the church he may speak inaudibly, to himself (the case where he also has the gift of interpretation) and to God, for God can understand him (i.e. *"let him speak to himself and to God"*). In this way he brings no condemnation upon the church and edifies himself (v.4). Note again, this injunction is prescribed as one of a list of apostolic regulations concerning unknown tongues within the *church*.

Verses 32-33: The importance of order within the church is again raised. The spirits of the prophets are not loose cannons, uncontrollable, their bodies seized and contorted by some 'power'! Self control under the guidance of the Spirit is the essential characteristic in the exercise of a spiritual gift (see v.40)![291] After addressing issues relating to prophecy and forbidding women to speak within the church (also violated by many 'tongue-speaking' churches today), Paul takes up the matter of tongues again.

Verse 39: Tongues are not to be coveted. Their inferiority is again stated. Yet, their use in the church is legitimate, provided it is consistent with the regulations Paul has stated under the Spirit's guidance. Tongues then were merely a sign - a Gentile language supernaturally spoken. Tongues were never intended for building up the church or the individual - not for edification, comfort or consolation, there were other gifts for these purposes. If unknown, foreign languages must be interpreted so that some benefit will be derived. It is not wrong to exercise any spiritual gift within the church, providing it edifies. The speaking of an unknown foreign language will not edify those who cannot understand what is being said concerning the wonderful works of God. It is proper

---

[291] See Note 4. Read the numerous contemporary accounts of tongue-speaking and 'spiritual laughter' and note that those involved speak of a "power" coming upon them and taking control!

then, that another interpret so that benefit will be derived.

Verse 40: The principal aim in this passage is given in verse 26, *"let all things be done unto edifying"* and in verse 40, *"let all things be done decently and in order"* - within the church! Those Corinthian believers who spoke foreign languages and could not understand them (i.e. unknown to them), if they were to be zealous of spiritual gifts, they should desire the gift of interpretation above speaking in tongues. Consequently, they could understand what they themselves said, and use it to edify the church (when another spoke in an unknown foreign tongue - v.27). Coveting (desiring) the gift of prophecy (or any gift), as stated earlier, is not in the sense of receiving it, but of valuing it for its benefit to the church!

APPENDIX 2:

An Overview of the gifts in the New Testament

	1 Corinthians 12:8-10	1 Corinthians 12:28-39	Romans 12:6-8	Ephesians 4:11
Date	c.57 AD	c.57 AD	c.57 AD	c.60 AD
Occasion	Paul's third Missionary journey	Paul's third Missionary journey	Paul's third Missionary journey	Prison Epistle
Giver	Holy Spirit	Holy Spirit	God	Ascended Lord
Gifts	Word of wisdom Word of knowledge Faith *(the faith associated with the sign gifts of the Spirit)* Healings Miracles Prophecy Discerning of Spirits Tongues Interpretation of tongues	Apostles* Prophets* Teachers* *(associated with the gift of teaching - along with the gifts of prophecy and knowledge)* Miracles Healings Helps Governments Tongues	Prophecy Ministry *(i.e. service)* Teaching Exhortation Giving Ruling *(i.e. leading)* Mercy	Apostles* Prophets* Evangelists* Pastors* *(i.e. Shepherds)* Teachers*
Greek Word	*Charismata*	*Charismata*	*Charismata*	*(edoken)* He 'gave'
Context	Unity in diversity	Unity in diversity *The gifts are listed according to their value during the early Church period*	Responsibility in diversity	Unity and building up of the Body
Those that exist scripturally today	None	Helps Governments	Ministry Teaching Exhortation Giving Ruling Mercy	Evangelists Pastors Teachers

* Persons given: Note the primacy of the apostles in 1 Corinthians 12 and Ephesians 4.

CHART A: Early Church Period (Dates vary between 2-3 years. Time lines not to scale)

Gospel of Christ: Increasing Jewish opposition and rejection; increasing Gentile acceptance - *Tongues waning*

Tongues Ceased
Completed
Scriptures ↑

Mark 16 Tongues foretold by the Lord - "these SIGNS shall follow them."

Acts 1-8:4	Acts 8:4-12	Acts 13-14	Acts 15:1-35	Acts 15:36-18:22	Acts 18:23-21:16	Paul in Captivity
1. Pentecost - ch.2 Tongues Spoken	1. Jews-dispersion—ch.8 2. Samaritan conversion—ch.8 3. Damascus Paul's conversion-ch.9 4. Cornelius conversion -ch.10 Tongues Spoken	1. Barnabas & S(P)aul-Antioch 2. Acts 13:51. The Jews in Pisidia reject the Gospel. Paul etc. reject the Jews!			1. Paul rejects Jews (Acts 18:6) 2. Ephesian disciples (Acts 19) Tongues spoken 3. Paul writes 1 Corinthians Tongues spoken Tongues shall cease! Tongues are a sign!	His epistles to: Philippians, Philemon, Colossians, Ephesians, 1 Timothy, Titus, 2 Timothy No Tongues!
Jew first	**Jew and Gentile** (Transition period) 5. Peter's sermon to the Jews at Jerusalem- "Gentiles (also) granted repentance unto life."	**To the Gentiles**				
		Paul's 1st Missionary Journey	Jerusalem Conference	*Paul's 2nd Missionary Journey*	*Paul's 3rd Missionary Journey*	Hebrews Epistle (64-69AD - No Tongues! Epistles of Jude, Peter, John - No Tongues!
		Epistle of James No Tongues!		1 & 2 Thessalonians No Tongues!	4. 2 Corinthians No Tongues! 5. Paul writes the Galatian and Roman Epistles No Tongues! 57-59AD	Jews at Rome reject the Gospel (Acts 28:16-29) Jerusalem sacked - Jews dispersed by Titus 70AD

G O S P E L

30AD — 37 — 47 — 49 — 50 — 54 — 58 — 63AD
7 yrs / 10 yrs / 2 yrs / 1 yr / 4 yrs / 4 yrs / 5 yrs close
17 yrs / 16 yrs
33 yrs
close of Acts circa 90-95AD

209

CHART B: Overview of various Dispensations (as they relate to the subject of the study)

(Christ's coming for His Church - Pretribulation: Christ coming to the earth - Premillennial)

Transitions (left to right):

- Descent of the Holy Spirit (Pentecost) / Formation of the Body of Christ / (Baptism of the Holy Spirit)
- Tongues a sign of judgment and grace in the early Church period
- Church taken up to meet the Lord in the air, His coming return to the earth. His coming *with* His saints. *for* His church (Rapture)
- The great & terrible Day of the Lord preceded by signs and wonders (Joel 2:30-32)
- The Lord's personal return to the earth. His coming *to* the earth. His coming *with* His saints.
- The Great White Throne Judgment

OT PERIOD (Ended with Daniel's 69th Week)	CHURCH PERIOD in 'mystery' during the OT (Unspecified duration)	*Latter Days* TRIBULATION PERIOD 7 Years (Daniel's 70th Week)		*Last Days* MILLENNIAL PERIOD (1,000 Years)
Israel chosen by God to be His earthly people. Through certain gracious unconditional covenants - Abrahamic (Gen 12:1-3); Palestinian; Davidic and New covenant. God promised Israel earthly blessings - their own land, to become the great international power and through them all nations will be blessed. These await literal fulfilment at a later time - the Millennium. Because of Israel's rebellion against their God. They are placed under judgment!	Israel is set aside because of unbelief. God brings all men into blessing through His redeeming work of His Son on the cross. All persons who accept Christ as Lord and Saviour are added to the Body of Christ which was formed at Pentecost. They constitute ONE NEW MAN in Christ (Eph 2). Upon belief, each is indwelt and sealed by the Holy Spirit, and is called upon to be filled by the Spirit through surrendered life to Him. This period is the subject of NT revelation not OT prophecy and closes with the coming of the Lord for the church, His Bride.	The Beast covenants with Israel ($3\frac{1}{2}$ years)	Jacob's Trouble ($3\frac{1}{2}$ years)	The Lord returns to the earth with His armies to defeat and destroy the enemies of God and Israel, after which He will rule over the earth (Joel 3). The blessings promised to Israel in the OT covenants will be literally fulfilled. Israel will be restored to God and united, unchallenged, in the promised land as subjects of the Prince of Peace, marking the end of Gentile domination of Israel. Peace and prosperity will reign over the world. The Spirit of God is poured out on all flesh (Joel 2:28-29; 3:17-21) and Jerusalem becomes the world's religious centre. The latter rain and the former rain; Satan is bound and shut up over this period (Rev 20).
		With the church taken up to be with Christ, God resumes His program for Israel. The Day of the Lord begins as a 'thief in the night' (2 Pet 3:10). This period is divided into two halves. During the first half, Israel is chastened by God and covenants with the Beast (world ruler), and a false peace exists. Half way through the 7 years the Beast breaks this covenant and terrible persecution begins - the time of Jacob's Trouble (Jer 30; Matt 24).		

Timeline (bottom):

- Nebuchadnezzar's reign. Israel under Babylonian captivity.
- THE DAY OF CHRIST
- THE DAY OF THE LORD
- Fullness of the Gentiles
- Times of the Gentiles
- ETERNITY